CIVIC INTIMACIES

In the series *Insubordinate Spaces,* edited by George Lipsitz

ALSO IN THIS SERIES:

Barbara Tomlinson and George Lipsitz, *Insubordinate Spaces: Improvisation and Accompaniment for Social Justice*

Greg Burris, *The Palestinian Idea: Film, Media, and the Radical Imagination*

Rachel Ida Buff, *Against the Deportation Terror: Organizing for Immigrant Rights in the Twentieth Century*

NIELS VAN DOORN

CIVIC INTIMACIES

Black Queer Improvisations on Citizenship

TEMPLE UNIVERSITY PRESS
Philadelphia • Rome • Tokyo

TEMPLE UNIVERSITY PRESS
Philadelphia, Pennsylvania 19122
tupress.temple.edu

Copyright © 2019 by Temple University—Of The Commonwealth System of Higher Education
All rights reserved
Published 2019

Cover photo: "Birdhouse Bath House Frat House." (Photo and artwork by Daniel Wickerham and Malcolm Lomax of Wickerham and Lomax.)

Library of Congress Cataloging-in-Publication Data

Names: van Doorn, Niels, 1981– author.
Title: Civic intimacies : black queer improvisations on citizenship / Niels van Doorn.
Description: Philadelphia : Temple University Press, [2019] | Series: Insubordinate spaces | Includes bibliographical references and index. |
Identifiers: LCCN 2018044535 (print) | LCCN 2018046477 (ebook) | ISBN 9781439918449 (E-book) | ISBN 9781439918425 (cloth) | ISBN 9781439918432 (pbk.)
Subjects: LCSH: African American gays—Maryland—Baltimore—Social conditions. | Citizenship—Maryland—Baltimore. | Social networks—Maryland—Baltimore. | Community development—Maryland—Baltimore. | Baltimore (Md.) —Social conditions—21st century.
Classification: LCC HQ76.27.A37 (ebook) | LCC HQ76.27.A37 D66 2019 (print) | DDC 306.76/608996073–dc23
LC record available at https://lccn.loc.gov/2018044535

Contents

Acknowledgments · vii
List of Abbreviations · xi

1 Citizenship and Its Outside · 1
2 Ambiguity City · 27
3 Capture, Containment, Composition · 67
4 Forces of Faith · 95
5 Pleasure, Violence, and the Past's Presence · 123
6 Support Structures: On Negativity and Reparativity · 151

Notes · 189
References · 221
Index · 239

Acknowledgments

To be perfectly honest, I have been dreading the moment I would have to start writing these acknowledgments. This book took eight years to complete, and along the way countless people directly and indirectly affected its content, shape, look, and feel. While I realize the folly of the sentiment, I worry that I won't be able to recall a share of them to mention here. At the same time, I have frequently felt isolated during the process of writing, especially after leaving Johns Hopkins University in September 2012 and returning to Amsterdam to start my new position, which also returned me to a field of research and teaching that had little connection to the book I was working on. If the Acknowledgments section is where one is expected to represent and thank one's expansive academic community, I fear that I may come up short here. To be sure, this sense of isolation was largely self-inflicted, to the extent that I compartmentalized the book project as "my own" ongoing endeavor that often had to take a back seat to new teaching responsibilities. I could have reached out, but never really did, to the many wonderful new colleagues in other departments at the University of Amsterdam, whose expertise surely would have provided an at times much-needed impulse to my thinking and writing. This is neither the place nor the time for laments, however, so I now get on with the task and responsibility I have so far been deferring.

First and foremost, I express my deep gratitude and indebtedness to all the people in Baltimore who generously allowed me into their lives, their communities, their homes, and their venues. Without their openness, their patience, their boundless positive spirit, and their willingness to help out whenever they could, this book could never have been written. Baltimore's amazing LGBTQ/SGL communities have disclosed the city to me in ways I never could have imagined when I arrived, and they made my stay at once tremendously challenging and thoroughly rewarding. The knowledge and experiences shared with me during two years of fieldwork indelibly changed my sense of self and of the world I co-inhabit.

Second, I thank Jane Bennett, who from the very start showed an interest in my project—which at the time was merely a proposal—and remained invested even as it continued to move in different directions, away from the original proposal, taking up new issues and research interest over time. I am incredibly grateful for how she welcomed me to Johns Hopkins University and its Department of Political Science, for all of her guidance and feedback, and for how she went out of her way to make sure I felt at home. Many thanks also go to the members of our interdepartmental reading group, for feedback on early paper drafts and ideas I was working on: Jennifer Culbert, Drew Daniel, Veena Das, Clara Han, Naveeda Kahn, Katrin Pahl, Anand Pandian, and, again, Jane Bennett. Likewise, I received valuable input from audiences at the conferences and workshops where I presented my work in progress. This input consistently challenged and refined my thinking, for which I am very thankful. Meanwhile, back at Johns Hopkins University, Alex Livingston was always a smart and savvy interlocutor within the department, one whose company I greatly enjoyed.

The research conducted for this book was made possible by a Rubicon grant (#446-09-021), awarded by the Netherlands Organization for Scientific Research. The writing of the book itself would not have been possible without the sustained support I received from my colleagues in the Department of Media Studies at the University of Amsterdam. Most directly, I thank Richard Rogers for giving me the time and space to bring this project to fruition. Yet I am equally indebted to everyone who helped make my transition as smooth as possible, all of whom have since then consistently offered not only their wonderful company but also their invaluable practical advice and much-needed intellectual stimulation. I am very lucky to be surrounded by such amazing colleagues. Beyond my department, I owe so much to Sally Wyatt, who has been my mentor for nearly twenty years. Her presence has always been an anchor and a compass in my professional life, and I deeply cherish our friendship.

As mentioned, this book took eight years to complete. There were many times, in fact, when I thought it would never see the light of day. Things took a radically different turn when Sara Cohen at Temple University Press expressed interest in my manuscript. From that moment onward things felt different—indeed, *were* different—because here was someone who believed in the project and wanted to work with me to complete it successfully. I cannot thank Sara enough for her faith, her editorial and moral support, and her expert guidance during this entire process. A special thank-you also goes to George Lipsitz, who has likewise been committed to the publication of this book since I first sent him a prospectus and sample chapters. His generous and insightful feedback has greatly benefited the book's arguments, and I am so happy to see my work included in the *Insubordinate Spaces* series. Furthermore, I am grateful to the two anonymous reviewers of the manuscript, whose critical comments and questions pushed me to get more out of my research than I had previously thought possible. Joan Vidal and Susan Deeks did an excellent job copyediting the manuscript, for which I am also extremely thankful. Daniel Wickerham and Malcolm Lomax of Wickerham and Lomax created the powerful image that graces the front cover. They were a pleasure to work with, and I am so delighted with the end result.

Finally, none of this would have been possible or meaningful without the knowledge that I can always rely on the unrelenting support structure composed of my family and friends. I thank my parents, Nelly and Ruud van Doorn, for simply always being there for me and caring about what I do. I thank my sister, Caroline, and her husband, Luís, for keeping me grounded. I thank all my Amsterdam friends, especially the members of "Re: Afleiding," as well as my friends in Baltimore and New York (Kieran, Janet, and Adam, in particular), for all the good times and for never growing apart, despite the large distances that often separate us. This leaves me with one person to thank, even though words really fall short here. For the past twelve years Melanie Bühler has been my everything, and I cannot begin to express how grateful I am for her presence in my life. May it always be.

Prior versions of some of the material included in Chapters 3 and 4 appeared in some of my previously published articles:

Chapter 3: "Treatment Is Prevention: HIV, Emergency and the Biopolitics of Viral Containment," *Cultural Studies* 27, no. 6 (2012): 901–932, © 2012, doi: https://doi.org/10.1080/09502386.2012.727010; "Between Hope and Abandonment: Black Queer Collectivity and the Affective Labour of Biomedicalised HIV Prevention," *Culture, Health and Sexuality* 14, no. 7 (2012): 827–840, © 2012, doi: https://doi.org/10.1080/13691058.2012.700325.

Chapter 4: "Forces of Faith: Endurance, Flourishing, and the Queer Religious Subject," *GLQ* 21, no. 4 (October 1, 2015): 635–666, © 2015, doi: https://doi.org/10.1215/10642684-3123725. Reprinted by permission of Duke University Press.

List of Abbreviations

BCHD	Baltimore City Health Department
BDSM	bondage and discipline/dominance and submission/sadism and masochism
BEAP	Black Educational AIDS Project
Black BEAT	Black Expression Alternative Tastes
BESURE	Behavioral Surveillance Research
BGA	Baltimore Gay Alliance
BHT	Brother Help Thyself
BMX	Black Men's Xchange
BUGLE	Blacks United for Gay and Lesbian Equality
C2P	Connect to Protect
CBE	Center for Black Equity
CDC	Centers for Disease Control and Prevention
CDCs	community development corporations
CTCA	Critical Thinking and Cultural Affirmation
EBDI	East Baltimore Development Inc.
ECHPP	Enhanced Comprehensive HIV Prevention Plan
FIST	Females Investigating Sexual Terrain
GCCB	Gay Community Center of Baltimore
GLCCB	Gay, Lesbian, Bisexual, and Transgender Community Center of Baltimore and Central Maryland

HERO	Health Education Resource Organization
HIV	human immunodeficiency virus
HSWM	HIV Stops with Me
IDEHA	Infectious Disease and Environmental Health Administration
IRB	Institutional Review Board
JHMI	Johns Hopkins Medical Institutions
JHSPH	Johns Hopkins Bloomberg School of Public Health
LGBT	Lesbian, Gay, Bisexual, Transgender
MCC	Metropolitan Community Church
MLK	Martin Luther King
MOCAA	Men of Color against AIDS
MOCAPP	Men of Color AIDS Prevention Project
MOCHA	Men of Color Health Awareness
MSM	men who have sex with men
MTA	Maryland Transit Administration
MVBA	Mount Vernon–Belvedere Association
NCBG	National Coalition of Black Gays
NCBLG	National Coalition of Black Lesbians and Gays
NHAS	National HIV/AIDS Strategy
NIH	National Institutes of Health
PrEP	pre-exposure prophylaxis
SGL	same-gender-loving
SMEAC	Save Middle East Action Committee
TIF	tax increment financing
TLC+	Testing and Linkage to Care Plus
UFCB	Unity Fellowship Church of Baltimore

CIVIC INTIMACIES

1

Citizenship and Its Outside

How can citizenship be rethought from the perspective of its outside, or that which is superfluous, excessive, or unintelligible to modern citizenship regimes? And why should it be? In this book, I advance the notion of "civic intimacies" in an effort to answer these questions, examining how and to what extent different forms of intimacy catalyze the cultivation of collective belonging, care, and support among Black queer folks—quintessential outsiders who are systematically marginalized, not just by society at large but also within Black and LGBT communities. On the basis of my ethnography of Black queer world-making practices in Baltimore, Maryland, I argue that civic intimacies perform the everyday reparative work of building support structures that draw on carefully cultivated intimacies, thereby enabling Black queer Baltimoreans not just to survive but also to thrive, despite the proliferation of violence and insecurity in their lives. Thus, civic intimacies are not just a matter of speaking publicly about private intimacies or making rights claims in defense of intimacy to protect it from state interference, as much of the scholarship on sexual citizenship would have it.[1] Rather, they point to the queer relational forces that constitute the intimate as itself an underappreciated mode of articulating citizenship, one of its "regimes of enunciation" (Latour 2011) that is folded into many others—political, economic, moral, and aesthetic, to name a few. In other words, this project aims to rethink citizenship through Black queer intimacies. Rather than conceiving of citizenship as a practice that predominantly consists of claims making or other types of acts in the official public sphere, I urge an analytical shift, based on my experiences in Baltimore, that treats citizenship as a practice of composition. As such, it forges affective attachments in and across a variety of public and private spaces in which Black queer Baltimoreans collectively seek to sustain the things that imbue their lives with meaning, worth, and joy in order to expand their agency and to stake out their place in a hostile polity. From this perspective, then, citizenship and intimacy are formally similar in that they are both saturated with the optimism of building worlds. However, this obviously does not mean that the terms "citizenship" and "intimacy" are identical or that their optimistic investments are always warranted.

As psychoanalysis and psychoanalytically inspired queer theory have insisted, intimacy and its accompanying affects are not the most dependable resources for building a cohesive life, whether individual or collective.[2] For example, Lauren Berlant (2000: 2) has noted how intimacy's "potential failure to stabilize closeness always haunts its persistent activity, making the very attachments deemed to buttress 'a life' seem in a state of constant if latent vulnerability." Intimacy is a volatile adhesive, so to speak. It comes loaded with expectations and demands. It is sought out for its promise to deliver all those things we (are supposed to or think we) want and need in life: comfort, trust, safety, stability, recognition, understanding, and reciprocity. It can also offer a break from ourselves, or the chance that something amazing might happen, a fortunate event or connection that would sweep us off our feet, away from the drudgery of reproducing ordinary life. But whenever intimate connections do take shape, there is always the concomitant risk of rupture, detachment, excess, incoherence, cruelty, obsession, and, yes, trauma.[3] Indeed, many of my interlocutors in Baltimore suffered various forms of violence and carried with them the scars, visible and invisible, of being disappointed by the very intimacies in which they had invested. Yet they still managed to carry on and allow themselves to be affected by new impulses, daring to be vulnerable with others in the hope of generating intimate episodes that, this time, will be rewarding. While such episodes frequently assumed the couple form, their aspirations and practices also stretched far beyond the boundaries of coupled domesticity, assembling and maintaining much more expansive kinship networks that were vital to the survival of Black queer life in the city. Despite the opacity and negativity inherent to intimacy, then, the stories collected in this book attest to the political value of intimate moments, gestures, and connections that mediate the composition of Black queer forms of life, whose social and cultural expressions are structurally depreciated, marginalized, appropriated, and depleted.

Meanwhile, critics have been less than sanguine about the category of citizenship and have questioned its relevance for analyses that aim to interrogate both the violence perpetrated against sexual and racial minorities and the ways these groups cultivate their own forms of community in response to such violence. For many scholars in the fields of queer theory, queer of color critique, and critical race studies, the "legitimate violence" enacted by citizenship as at once a biopolitical and a disciplinary institution perpetuates the structural subordinations and exclusions it should ostensibly protect against (Agathangelou, Bassichis, and Spira 2008; Brandzel 2016; Reddy 2011: 17). While, in principle, I concur with such assertions, and even though the argument I develop in this book is indebted to the abovementioned fields of scholarship, I nevertheless make a case for retaining a (thoroughly revised) notion of citizenship when studying how Black queer outsiders manage to sustain themselves and others in the city of Baltimore. As my study shows, the frequently precarious settings that Black queer Baltimoreans have to navigate on a daily basis also harbor alternative infrastructures and imaginaries of the good life, despite their recurrent lack of resources. Instead of rejecting citizenship wholesale as a critical term for the analysis of minoritarian worldmaking practices, I believe it is more fruitful to inquire how we can harness the potential of this overdetermined concept. As Linda Bosniak (2006: 12) has argued, "Describing aspects of the world in the language of citizenship is a legitimizing political act," and given that this language is highly contested, efforts to reorganize it and take it beyond itself can become a mode of "political innovation." This innovation is necessary if the notion of citizenship is to mean anything at all to the communities I have studied, which articulate modes of collectivity, care, repair, and belonging that persist under the radar of conventional citizenship imaginaries.

Citizenship, to borrow the words of Étienne Balibar (2010: 2), should be conceived of as "a problem, a stake, an enigma, an invention, a lost object or treasure to be sought and conquered again." This enigmatic character of citizenship as a partly withdrawn or obfuscated object-to-think-with, which we should continue to probe and experiment with even though it can be approached only obliquely, highlights the political nature of its constitution—both in conceptual work and in everyday struggles. Rather than as a given or as an institution or practice with clearly defined attributes, citizenship is more productively conceived of as something that has to be *taken* or made anew by actors whose commitments arise from concrete political stakes, even when these stakes are poorly articulated or fail to be identified as properly political. In fact, the question of how, when, and where the political can be articulated—and, indeed, what counts as political practice in the first place—forms an important thread running through this book. One of the central arguments developed in the following chapters is that appreciating the civic intimacies of Black queer life is crucial to the task of rethinking citizenship, which requires critical scrutiny of the immunitary (bio)political logic that lies at the heart of modern citizenship regimes. Here I follow Roberto Esposito, for whom the paradigm of immunization—in which the "self-preservation of life" in the face of continual threat becomes central to all logics of governing self and others—is not a symptom of modernity but, rather, "invents modernity as a historical and categorical apparatus able to cope with it" (Esposito 2008: 55). In other words, the development of Western (i.e., white supremacist and heteropatriarchal) modernity forms an ongoing response to, and marks an intensified preoccupation with, a defensive imperative that mandates the protection of proper/propertied life from outside (i.e., foreign, alien, nonwhite) forces that threaten to negate it.[4] Accordingly, I argue that to break away from this immunitary model of citizenship we have to look for alternatives at—and beyond—the margins of civic intelligibility, taking cues from Black queer outsiders who problematize the very boundaries between inside and outside, self and other, through the exuberant and improperly political world-making practices I call civic intimacies.

As Engin Isin has convincingly argued, the category of citizenship has always been shaped by its outside. Thus, its meanings and values have been negatively defined throughout its history. Indeed, one of the most pertinent conclusions of Isin's study is that the boundaries of citizenship have been significantly more permeable and dynamic than many had hitherto believed to be the case. In his important work, Isin shows how "strangers," "outsiders," and "aliens" have historically constituted themselves as political beings, whose "becoming political" is enacted through various practices that strategically question and destabilize existing technologies of citizenship. In this way, his concept of "citizenship as alterity" not only points to the fact that categories such as woman, slave, and immigrant exist in mutually constitutive tension with the category of the citizen (in the sense that each category becomes legible only in relation to its others) but also elucidates the extent to which citizenship is a radically discontinuous and antinomic phenomenon whose transhistorical unity has been retrospectively constructed (Isin 2002: 3). Yet as important as Isin's contribution to the study of citizenship is, especially in its effort to assert the immanent nature of the alterity that shapes citizenship's constitution and texture, he tends to underestimate the racist immunitary violence exerted on strangers, outsiders, and aliens within the (bio)political architecture of modern citizenship. As Esposito's work (2008, 2011) teaches us, immunization operates through the partial integration of the negative force that threatens proper life, which allows the body politic to suppress this force that is no longer excluded by but, rather, safely contained within its boundaries. So while it is true that citizenship has never been an autonomous, impermeable category and requires outsiders to achieve its shape and consistency, it is exactly this plasticity that allows immunitary citizenship regimes to constantly experiment with new ways to govern and violently neutralize difference (cf. Cervenak and Carter 2017).

In Baltimore, as I discuss in Chapter 2, such experimentation is mobilized to discipline, contain, and ultimately ruin Black lives, which historically have figured as the alien yet constitutive outside of American modernity. This means that without the institution of chattel slavery and its systematic proliferation of anti-Black terror, modern notions such as liberal humanism, market capitalism, citizenship, and personhood could not have emerged in the United States (Baptist 2014; Best 2004; Jung, Vargas, and Bonilla-Silva 2011). Even though Black Americans have been nominally included as full citizens of the U.S. body politic in the wake of the Civil Rights Movement, Black life and wealth continues to be devalued, expropriated, and rendered superfluous to the entangled imperatives of state and market (Barrett 1999; Sharpe 2016; Wilderson 2010). This duplicitous violence underwrites the logic of our immunitary citizenship regime. While, until the advent of the Trump era, the outsider's entry into the fold of liberal citizenship was generally hailed as an occasion for celebration, this admission has by and large been formal and symbolic: racial outsiders are allowed to roam inside the parameters of civic recognition without ever being fully legible or legitimate as humans (Wynter 1994). We should thus be careful not to praise the insurrectional potential of the "xenos," as the figure of political alterity, without attending to how some outsiders' claims can be acknowledged while others cannot due to the sheer negativity of the claimants' existence.[5]

Making Something from Nothing

For Cleo, a radical Black community organizer who had recently relocated to Baltimore from Atlanta, such negativity was always acutely at the forefront of his thinking and activism.[6] Perhaps the primary object of his anger and frustration at the time was the city's HIV-prevention system and its outreach programs, which he deemed entirely ineffective without a broad and concerted effort to face up to what he termed "the perpetual tax on Black men in this country." As he told me in an interview, "The things that harm, hurt, or compromise the lives of Black people are dimensional; they're not just one thing. They have to do with living in a white-biased society, a history of slavery in this country, and not having been encouraged to heal, only to pray." In response, Cleo has been developing his own programs and strategies since the late 1980s, when he founded two organizations that provide (mental) health services and promote cultural affirmation by teaching African Americans to value, love, and take care of themselves and their communities. One of his organizations, Black Men's Xchange (BMX), focuses specifically on Black queer men, although he refrains from using the words "queer" or "gay" because he believes that these historically white terms "have no relevance for the Black experience." Instead, to explicitly distinguish his projects from the white gay community he deems "racist and self-serving based on its own agenda," he coined the term "same-gender-loving (SGL)" in the early 1990s to reclaim and affirm a specifically Black experience of homosexuality and bisexuality. I noticed a resurgence of this term in Baltimore as I was conducting my fieldwork, among not only young people but also an older generation of Black men who previously identified as gay. This increasing popular appeal, which followed Cleo's arrival in the city, seemed to index a need among Baltimore's Black queer community to articulate a sense of collective identity and experience that clearly distinguished itself from the white gay culture dominating the city's visual and discursive representations of homosexuality. As I discuss in the next chapter, this need had been articulated in various forms for a much longer time—most notably, through the annual Black Pride festivities—but I believe that the defiant antagonism introduced by Cleo's presence on the scene intensified the racial tensions that circulated throughout Baltimore's LGBT community. Through his scathing condemnations of the structural violence against Black people in general, and against Black SGL people in particular, together with his affirmation of Blackness against its continuing pathologization by white hetero- and homonormative institutions, he fueled a climate in which Black queer Baltimoreans could carve out their own sense of space and time in a more conscious, articulate, and determined manner.

Cleo did not like to talk about his background or private life with me, unless the subject matter directly related to his message or his accomplishments as a community organizer and "health strategist." He had been involved in social services ever since he was a teenager growing up in South Central Los Angeles in the 1970s. After finishing high school, he continued his education at various institutions, specializing in public health, education, religion, and cultural anthropology. In the late 1980s, the death of his partner due to AIDS pushed him to dedicate himself more completely to the Afrocentric cultural affirmation of Black homosexual and bisexual men, leading to the foundation of BMX in 1989. By the time he was invited to give a presentation at Baltimore's Metropolitan Community Church in 2008, BMX had become a national organization, with other chapters operating out of Detroit, Atlanta, New York, Chicago, and Kansas City. After his presentation, he was asked to open a Baltimore chapter, and even though he lived in Atlanta at the time, he agreed to create and remotely coordinate a BMX program at the Portal, a fledgling African American LGBT community center that opened in 2002 but had been experiencing recurrent problems trying to maintain a regular program and attracting young community members. "We began training and preparation early the following year, focusing on leadership training, because BMX is a leadership-development organization," he said. "We teach Black men how to be leaders, how to be self-sufficient, self-determined, and constructive. We teach them to have an analysis." This was Cleo's idiom of choice. To "have an analysis" means to practice rational, critical thinking that promotes Black affirmation in an effort to counter and subvert anti-Black discourses that induce self-hate among SGL men.[7]

However, as he was organizing leadership training he quickly found out that the Portal was in much bigger trouble than he had anticipated. After its director asked him for help, he decided to move to Baltimore. A couple of months later, the Portal and BMX merged, and the new entity assumed the latter's nationally established name. Since the merger Cleo has been trying to get more involved in the city's HIV-prevention system, because he feels that his affirmative message and training and most sorely needed among the young Black men this system is consistently failing. I first met Cleo at a meeting convened by and at Maryland's Infectious Disease and Environmental Health Administration (IDEHA), which I attended regularly.[8] These monthly meetings provided a space where organizations engaged in HIV care and prevention work targeting Black "men who have sex with men" (MSM) could come together to coordinate and plan their projects pertaining to Baltimore City and its surrounding counties—at least on paper. As an unfunded and discretionary entity, the working group remained relatively powerless in terms of decision-making or project-initiating capacities, which was a source of frustration for many who attended its meetings. It was not uncommon for members to be absent for longer periods of time, and some stopped coming altogether. Those who did show up regularly worked on prevention projects in three subgroups, yet these projects never seemed to materialize, which added to a general sense of discontent. Cleo, for whom this was only his third meeting, was most vocal about his dissatisfaction with the group's inefficiency, and his caustic performance caught my attention as much as it seemed to annoy and embarrass the others in the room. I later learned that Cleo had quickly gained a reputation as an antiwhite troublemaker, and several individuals and groups had apparently made attempts to discredit or shun him. He did not seem to mind and even appeared to relish the hostility, knowing that his notoriety would get him more attention from the people he was looking to reach: Baltimore's Black community. Cleo aired his grievances with respect to IDEHA's working group to me, saying:

> Frankly, I can't stand those meetings. They are potential resources but have very little value in changing the epidemic. Because people around the table . . . I'm just telling you this because you asked me: . . . all the data presented there was the logical outcome of the fact that there's no interventions truly catering to Black men. The whole culture of it is just so dysfunctional. What has happened all over this country is funders have put an HIV carrot job in these people's faces, and it's, like, "A job! I need to fucking eat!" And they take these jobs, [and] they have no skills, no clue, and the whole system is dysfunctional. . . . [*I ask him about the problem of poverty in the community.*] This poverty thing is bullshit as far as I'm concerned. It's race and it's self-concept. Otherwise you'd see a[n] HIV epidemic among poor white people, and there's none. You can be poor and still be functional; Black women do it all the time. They learn how to become more actively involved in self-preservation when they have the skills to do so and when they feel valuable enough to implement those skills. You got to realize you have value; it's Black self-hate that kills.

In Chapter 3 I examine how race, self-preservation, and "self-concept" are co-articulated in Baltimore's HIV epidemic, but here I want to make a different observation. I believe that what many of Cleo's white peers found most threatening about his positioning (some called it posturing) within the city's LGBT community and HIV-prevention system was his grassroots mobilization of a particular notion of racial negativity that in recent years has become a much debated issue in the field of Black studies, where it has gained traction under the moniker of "Afro-pessimism." Although Cleo never used this precise terminology, his analysis of Blackness in the U.S. context is inextricably tied to and shaped by the afterlife of slavery. To reproduce Saidiya Hartman's (2007: 6) well-known formulation: "If slavery persists as an issue in the political life of Black America, it is not because of an antiquarian obsession with bygone days or the burden of a too-long memory, but because Black lives are still imperiled and devalued by a racial calculus and a political arithmetic that were entrenched centuries ago. This is the afterlife of slavery—skewed life chances, limited access to health and education, premature death, incarceration, and impoverishment." Such an anti-Black climate produces Blackness as a negative space associated with disease, decay, and death, which forms the very condition of possibility for non-Black life to thrive in the national body politic.[9] However, this space also harbors a negative remainder, a nothing that is also something that cannot be fully assimilated or accounted for. Hartman again notes: "On the one hand, the slave is the foundation of the national order, and on the other, the slave occupies the position of the unthought. So what does it mean to try to bring that position into view without making it a locus of positive value, or without trying to fill the void?" (Hartman and Wilderson 2003: 184–185). In this book I aim to sit with this question, to critically interrogate it in order to formulate a provisional answer that is informed by my interaction with Cleo and other interlocutors who have so generously shared their time and knowledge.

While Cleo's analysis converges with Hartman's in its identification of the paradoxical position occupied by the slave, whose captive body metonymically stands in for the persistent captivity of Black people and of Blackness as a structural (ap)position, their respective responses to this diagnosis differ significantly. For Cleo, as for other community organizers in Baltimore, to try to bring this negative position into view without rendering it amenable to affirmation or the attribution of "positive value" would be deeply counterproductive insofar as, in their daily practices, affirmation as revaluation is an indispensable tool that enables Black queer (trans) men and women to resist death and survive this anti-Black/queer world.[10] Cleo's life is dedicated to the arduous work of "filling the void," which emphatically does *not* equal the pursuit of citizenship as "an integration into the national project" (Hartman and Wilderson 2003: 185). He abhors this national project for the systematic way it kills so many Black people and lets so many more of them die, but this is precisely what drives him to teach his community to—as he says—"become more actively involved in self-preservation, making sure they have the skills to do it when they feel valuable enough to implement those skills."

Now, of course, this difference in response may be rather obvious, given that both thinkers/teachers have their own personal and professional commitments with respect to the afterlife of slavery in the United States, but I nevertheless want to highlight the conceptual and political space that mediates their diverging positions because it points to a tension between critical and reparative approaches to anti-Black/queer violence that I address in Chapter 6. Cleo's work poses a pressing question to Afro-pessimist scholarship: if Black queers survive in and through "social death,"[11] then what about belonging, kinship, intimacy, or collective flourishing? What capacity for common world making and political agency can Black queerness embody, and how could this capacity be nourished? Should it be nourished at all? I address these questions most explicitly in Chapter 6, where I discuss my ambivalence with respect to negative ontological theorizations of Blackness and queerness, but each of the chapters that follow contributes to the elaboration of a response that is rooted in the experiences and perspectives of Black queer Baltimoreans.

My project thus exists in close proximity to recent scholarship in the field of Black studies that broaches Blackness as something that is more than nothing, or a queer nothing constituted by anti-Black forces but not exhaustively so, not fully exhausted and void due to the lifegiving forms of care and celebration that persist despite and *because of* the violence that never ceases to inform them. Christina Sharpe's *In the Wake* (2016) and Ashon Crawley's *BlackPentecostal Breath* (2017) are two poetically incisive contributions to this thought of the otherwise as immanent to the given, which I see as being in generative conversation. Both works reimagine the space of Black (queer) possibility by attending to cultural practices and resources that are mobilized "to produce a break with the known, the normative, the violent world of western thought and material condition" (Crawley 2017: 5).[12] For Sharpe (2016: 18), such practices and resources constitute "wake work," an ethical project that insists on imagining "new ways to live in the wake of slavery" by inventing "a mode of inhabiting *and* rupturing this episteme with our known lived and un/imaginable lives." Without seeking to somehow remedy or resolve the systematic negation of Black life, wake work strives for the cultivation of a "Blackened" ethics of care and consciousness as material and epistemological iterations of the "enfleshed" labor of imagining otherwise (ibid.: 21–22). One modality of this ethical project comes in the form of "aspiration," the word Sharpe uses to describe the activity of "keeping and putting breath back in the Black body in hostile weather" (ibid.: 113). It is here, in her emphasis on the necessity of breath and breathing (space), that Sharpe's analytical framework most explicitly touches Crawley's, in which breath features as the central concept with which to think through the "otherwise possibilities" immanent to "Blackqueer aesthesia" (Crawley 2017: 238). Starting from the premise that "I can't breathe"—Eric Garner's repeated exclamation as he was being choked to death by New York City police officers in 2014—does not just form "raw material for theorizing" but also is a call to action (ibid.: 1), Crawley offers a lyrical meditation on Black Pentecostalism as an alternative mode of social organization deeply rooted in performative and visceral forms of knowledge production whose queerness destabilizes white epistemologies and theologies that continue to produce a world "wherein Black flesh cannot easily breathe" (ibid.: 3).[13] Like Sharpe's wake work, and like my notion of civic intimacies, Crawley's celebration of Blackpentecostal breath is invested in the survival and thriving of Black flesh, that queer nothing or "non/being" (Sharpe 2016: 20), which, as both theorists know, is also "a multitude, a plenitude, a social world of exploration" (Crawley 2017: 267). Yet whereas neither author seems interested in theorizing the relationship between such survival/thriving and citizenship as anything other than mutually exclusive, I posit the concept of civic intimacies to problematize this dichotomy and to rethink what being a citizen—and being political—can encompass when approached from the outside.[14]

The Political Stakes of Civic Intimacies

What *does* it mean to be political? And what does it *take* to be political? To answer these questions in a way that is responsive to what my interlocutors in Baltimore have told and shown me requires that I distance myself from a strand of radical democratic theory that underscores the a(nta)gonistic processes constitutive of the political realm. But let me first explain what I find valuable about this school of thought, which includes scholars such as Wendy Brown, William Connolly, Ernesto Laclau, Chantal Mouffe, and Jacques Rancière. Despite their considerable differences, these scholars have been persistent in their efforts to imagine modes of *becoming political* that resist the all-too-present tendency to withdraw into the safety of the known and the similar, favoring instead a more courageous engagement with difference that cannot be neutralized or assimilated. To put it in terms closer to my project, radical democratic theory offers models of political citizenship that deviate from the modern immunitary tradition to the extent that they break with its privatizing logics of self-defense and boundary policing, instead promoting a different orientation that associates citizenship with collective struggle. Take, for example, Brown's (1995: 25) argument for conceiving of freedom as "a project suffused not just with ambivalence but with anxiety." True political freedom, in Brown's influential account, is ambivalent because "it is at odds with security, stability, protection, and irresponsibility" and requires that we give up "familiarity, insularity, and routine for investment in a more open horizon of possibility" (ibid.). It is anxiety inducing because, far from dispensing with power, political freedom is faced with the problem of power everywhere, necessitating "a permanent struggle against what will otherwise be done to and for us" (ibid.).

Brown's ambitious and courageous vision resonates with Isin's work, which likewise identifies political conduct with ongoing struggles and takes "acts" as the constitutive unit of citizenship, positing the city as the transhistorical arena formative to both. As he writes: "The city is neither a background to . . . struggles *against which* groups wager, nor is it a foreground *for which* groups struggle for hegemony. Rather, the city is the battleground *through which* groups define their identity, stake their claims, wage their battles, and articulate citizenship rights, obligations, and principles" (Isin 2002: 283–284). Despite its conceptual appeal, I find this abstract image of the city much too restricted and preoccupied with incessant contestation to account adequately for daily life in specific cities such as Baltimore, which have experienced decades of stagnation and depletion. To many Baltimoreans, their city feels less like an open and dynamic force field than an enclosed neighborhood whose sedimented physical and social boundaries keep insiders and outsiders neatly separated. As I discuss in Chapter 2, everyday life in Baltimore is often marked by inertia and immobility, which contrasts the image of action and mobility conjured up by Isin's imaginary. Moreover, the kinds of action that Isin prioritizes as central to citizenship—staking claims, waging battles—do not speak to how many of my interlocutors negotiated a sense of collectivity and belonging. For them, the city is not so much—or, at least, not predominantly—a political battleground, as it is for Isin. Instead, it forms an ambiguous environment in which care, coasting, and daily improvisations are frequently more vital to "being of the city" (or the neighborhood) than are antagonistic orientations.

Yet does this mean that these practices, insofar as they do not articulate rights claims or stage a scene of conflict in the public sphere, fail to live up to the criteria of "proper" citizenship? And does this, in turn, entail that those who engage in such practices fall short of becoming political (Isin 2002: 275)? As much as I appreciate the radical democratic vision of political life proposed by Brown, Isin, and others, and despite the fact that I normatively subscribe to many of its arguments and objectives, my experiences in Baltimore have pushed me to recognize the limits of identifying political citizenship solely with scenes of conflict and "permanent struggle." Ultimately, even though such a vision breaks with the paradigm of immunization that structures our modern citizenship regime, it nevertheless retains a strong investment in the sovereign acts of claim- and decision-making citizens who can afford to relinquish their security and routines in favor of disruptive and anxiety-inducing modes of political conduct. For many Black queer Baltimoreans, in contrast, the intensity of living with recurrent psychic, physical, and socioeconomic pressures generates a precarious situation in which rupture is not a deliberate strategy but a frequently overwhelming state of affairs that needs to be navigated and can only intermittently be circumvented. Their tenuous acts of citizenship are more about developing and maintaining infrastructures of care and support than the breaking up of existing structures, however ambivalent their nature.[15] If we accept that Black queers are positioned "outside the structures of human filiation, hegemonic consent, and the social contract through which civil society is composed" (Woods 2013: 439), and as such occupy a world that is located at once inside and outside the world inhabited by non-Black citizens and strangers, their only viable claim to the city is articulated through fugitive experimentations with civic intimacies.

But how, then, do civic intimacies diverge from the modern immunitary citizenship regime that conditions their existence? Surely the persistent pressure on Black queer support structures generates a desire for, and the necessity of, protective measures that provide a degree of immunity from the various forms of violence that threaten the world-making practices that depend on these structures. However, as I show in the following chapters, the kind of immunity that civic intimacies help to cultivate is rooted less in an individual will to power and self-protection, modeled on and appealing to the political sovereignty of the state, than in a political ethics of maintenance and repair that tentatively accomplishes what one might call, following Esposito (2011: 177), a "common immunity." Having essentially been abandoned by market and state institutions, many Black queer folks look for alternative anchors to secure their turbulent existence and experiment with new ways not just to endure their predicaments, or to bear them more gracefully, but also to thrive. These experiments take place at parties, fundraisers, workshops, support groups, leather BDSM classes, HIV outreach facilities, church services, and many other spaces where Black queer life proliferates. In these spaces, the old guard often teaches younger generations how to conduct themselves in relation to others, informing them about the gestures, rituals, and values passed on as a common inheritance, as well as opening up newcomers to a shared sense of what Elizabeth Povinelli (2011a) has called "immanent obligation."[16] Central to civic intimacies, immanent obligation emerges from a deep ethical attunement and commitment to the lives and life stories that accrue as a collective history of love, loss, hope, defeat, and transformation. This transformation does not have to entail radical change or rupture, and it much more often emerges from ongoing and patient work on self and others. Once again, the civic intimacies presented in this book are *political* because they embody the flourishing of Black queer culture through a range of practices that express its variegated modes of existence. Refusing their imposed disposability, my interlocutors translate their intimate encounters and relationships into collective articulations of support, maintenance, and care that not only distribute the necessary resources for survival—such as food and medication—but also preserve and promote the rich, dynamic vernacular cultures that form an enduring testament to the incalculable value and vitality of Black queer life. Thus, to paraphrase Bonnie Honig (2009: 10), who in turn follows Jacques Derrida, civic intimacies are political to the extent that they surpass the *mere* life of survival and strive for the *more* life that is also part of survival, as disclosed in its etymological roots: to live beyond, to outlive or "overlive" the historical present of racist immunitary violence. Civic intimacies generate "the surplus that exceeds causality" (ibid.).

Still, civic intimacies clearly do not represent some kind of panacea, and neither do they exist in a vacuum. I instead develop this concept to describe and appreciate a range of world-making practices and support structures that persist at the margins of possibility. In this space, they are at least partly *embedded in, dependent on, subordinated by,* and *resistant to* larger institutions, such as Baltimore's HIV-prevention system (Chapter 3), the Black Church (Chapter 4), and the city's majority-white gay leather/BDSM community (Chapter 5). Accordingly, in Chapters 3–5 I attend to the struggles that take place at this threshold, focusing primarily on the Black queer "mediators" who move between margin and center in an effort to safeguard the well-being of their communities. Furthermore, the scenes and stories relayed in these chapters are deeply informed by Baltimore's vexed history of racial segregation and economic depression, which have created the setting for its contemporary struggles with poverty, drug-related crime, property vacancy, and alarmingly high rates of new HIV and hepatitis C infections (see, e.g., Bor 2007; German and Latkin 2012; Pietila 2010). As I detail in Chapter 2, the city's LGBT community historically has borne the brunt of these problems, although since the late 1990s white, middle-class gays and lesbians have increasingly unburdened themselves as they have found a place at the table of civil society's governing institutions, subsequently relinquishing their political obligations to communities of color that saw many of their problems intensify. The scenes of care, support, creativity, pleasure, love, and activism that I encountered across the city form necessary responses to this abandonment, which is exacerbated by the increasing withdrawal of federal and state-organized safety nets. These developments have placed the burden of responsibility in the hands of nonprofit community-based organizations and other networks of frequently underpaid staff and unpaid volunteers who attempt to keep their communities healthy and vibrant. In other words, it is in this climate of social and economic precarity that Black queer Baltimoreans see themselves forced to draw on their kin to invent and reproduce forms of coping and thriving that allow them to maintain their nonjuridical right to the city they cannot give up on—even if it has frequently given up on them.

Inside Out/Outside In: Reflections on Positionality and Method

It took me a while to get a grip on all of this, as my initial research plan had a different focus. This plan was part of a postdoctoral research grant application I submitted in the summer of 2009 while putting the final touches on my dissertation. At the time I was a doctoral candidate at the Amsterdam School of Communication Research and a lecturer in the Department of Communication Science, both at the University of Amsterdam. My doctoral work examined online identity formation, with a specific focus on the digital performance of gender, sexuality, and embodiment, but as my trajectory developed I became increasingly motivated to expand my research beyond the parameters of digital culture and representation. Inspired by the so-called affective turn in social and queer theory, as well as by "nonrepresentational" approaches in human geography and urban studies, I wanted my next project to examine how queer communities mobilize networked digital technologies to form affective support networks that traverse physical and virtual environments. This literature was pushing me to consider the role of material as well as intimate infrastructures in the creation of spaces for and by sexual minorities, rather than just studying how these social formations are represented in online settings. Moreover, it suggested that such infrastructures were *political* matters whose pertinence exceeded the field of representational politics, which gave me a different perspective on the notions of sexual and intimate citizenship I had been thinking through within the context of my doctoral work. Ultimately, the concept of citizenship grew increasingly enigmatic and compelling as it became more detached from legalist and identity-based frames of reference, and while I was no longer able to integrate my ideas into my soon-to-be-finished dissertation, I decided to pursue this problematic in the research project, whose proposal I was drafting that summer.

When I received notice in February 2010 that I had been awarded the research grant, I knew I was moving to Baltimore in the summer. The grant stipulated that recipients were expected to conduct their research at an acclaimed foreign host institution, and I had chosen Johns Hopkins University because I admired the work being done in its Political Science and Anthropology departments. Other than this, however, I had no previous connection to, or much knowledge of, Baltimore—I hadn't even seen *The Wire* at that point. Moreover, I had never lived or worked outside the Netherlands before, so this opportunity was quickly starting to feel like an overwhelming endeavor. To prepare the best I could, I decided to survey the web and make a provisional inventory of Baltimore's LGBT organizations and resources, which turned out to be more difficult than I expected, given that only a few organizations had a solid Internet presence, and, as I would later find out, the city's LGBT community was generally rather "low-tech" at that time. After compiling a short list of resources and sending out introductory emails that explained my research and inquired into fieldwork opportunities, I ended up with two responses. The most promising one came from the executive director of the Gay, Lesbian, Bisexual, and Transgender Community Center of Baltimore and Central Maryland (GLCCB). His email was welcoming, and so was the center's website, so it seemed like a good place to start my project. This *was*, after all, the city's official LGBT community center. I was bound to meet a lot of people there.

After my arrival in blazing hot Baltimore at the end of August 2010, the first thing I did after finding a place to live and settling into my new academic environment on Johns Hopkins's Homewood campus was pay a visit to the GLCCB, which was only a five-minute walk from my new apartment in the center of Mount Vernon. I remember thinking that the center was probably on some kind of summer break, because there was so little activity. I didn't run into anyone on the first two floors, and the computer lab was empty, so I kept wandering around, knocking on doors and peering through windows until somebody greeted me, somewhat hesitantly and surprised. "Perhaps I should have called in advance?" I thought, suddenly worrying that this might not have been the best decision and searching for the proper words to put the man in front of me at ease. After I introduced myself, I learned that the man was the center's program coordinator and that the executive director wasn't in that day. He told me a bit about his job and gave me a tour of the entire building, which was quite spacious, and finally we discussed volunteer opportunities I could take up while conducting my research there. I left the center that day feeling mildly anxious yet hopeful about the time to come and was eager to start my fieldwork, which, unfortunately, was delayed pending the official approval from Johns Hopkins's Institutional Review Board (IRB). However, as I was awaiting the approval and spending a large chunk of my time in the campus library over the following weeks, my anxiety increased considerably when, after more informal visits and a volunteer shift sealing envelopes, it started to dawn on me that nothing substantial was happening at the GLCCB. There were no running community projects or upcoming events to speak of, and I met only a handful of people—some assistants, a couple of volunteers—other than the program coordinator. Where was the rest of the community? Around this time, I also met the executive director, who seemed rather standoffish and perhaps had second thoughts about my conducting fieldwork at the center, which made me feel even more insecure about my position and the future of my project. Nevertheless, I decided to hang in and make a renewed effort once I received the IRB approval that would allow me officially to begin conducting interviews and participant observation, and when I got the green light in early October, my plan was to focus on the peer support groups that met on the second floor of the community center during weeknights.

Sitting in on a number of these groups, which ranged from gay-oriented Alcoholics Anonymous meetings to lesbian spiritual healing classes and transgender support networks, gave me my first opportunity to meet and get to know some community members beyond the GLCCB's staff. It also allowed me to get an initial sense of the importance of material and psychic support structures as technologies of care and belonging. But since most groups met rather sporadically and didn't draw many people, I felt the need to further expand my network, also because I was now learning about different kinds of initiatives happening around town. In addition, I found out that a lot of these initiatives and programs were health-related and focused especially on HIV prevention, given the city's exorbitant rates of new HIV infections among its African American population and particularly among young Black queer men. Not only because Baltimore's LGBT community has a long history of fighting HIV/AIDS and has spawned important grassroots organizations such as AIDS Action Baltimore and HERO (the Health Education Resource Organization) in response to the crisis during the 1980s and 1990s but also because HIV prevention was one of the few activities that could still attract funding for community-based organizations, quite a few LGBT groups and individuals were teaming up with the city's Health Department and its two partner research universities—Johns Hopkins and the University of Maryland—to develop new programs and projects that could stem the tide of infection.[17] Although the GLCCB had made little effort to seriously engage with the issue of HIV/AIDS in the community over the past two decades, it was still interested in the possibility of securing funds for prevention initiatives that would improve the relevance of the center and provide a modest revenue stream, which is why its program coordinator had recently started attending meetings of a collective named Connect to Protect (C2P), which convened at the University of Maryland's Baltimore City campus.

After some negotiations and checkups with the other members I managed to convince the center's program coordinator to let me join the next meeting, which really formed a "watershed" moment in my research to the extent that it opened me up to the existence of many different people and organizations in the city—a great number of them not present during that particular meeting—as well as their ongoing struggles and tensions with city officials, funding agencies, and other community-based organizations. Moreover, it highlighted the pertinence of race, racism, and racialized poverty to whatever I was hoping to study in Baltimore—I wasn't so sure anymore at that point. Even though I was obviously aware of the entanglements of gender, sexuality, race, and class in the city, the latter two notions did not yet figure explicitly as focal points in my research project. Now, however, it was becoming painfully obvious that I had been relying on a color-blind and therefore inadequate understanding of queerness, unable or unwilling to see how it was articulated within an urban climate of anti-Blackness. I had to seriously rethink what I was doing and try to attune myself more carefully to how this climate was affecting so much of what I wanted to learn more about. I needed new conceptual tools, as well as practical guidance. I was also feeling increasingly overwhelmed by the sheer number and complexity of issues, interests, group dynamics, networks, funding schemes, and power relations. What was I to make of all this? How did it connect to the initial aims of my research project? To make matters worse, the first C2P meeting I attended also turned out to be the last because the collective's funding had been abruptly discontinued, leaving several members suddenly at risk of unemployment and threatening partnered projects. Baltimore's HIV-prevention network and its many allied LGBT-oriented initiatives were obviously experiencing tumultuous times, and I wanted to understand what had led to this situation and how it affected the Black queer youth this network was supposed to serve and protect.

In the meantime, helped by my new contacts at the community-based organizations involved in HIV prevention, I also began to establish connections to a host of other groups operating in various realms of LGBT culture and politics, including artists, (mental) health and wellness programs, civil rights advocacy groups, the city's gay leather and BDSM scene, and faith-based organizations. Probably due to a backlash of sorts in the wake of my period of relative inactivity at the GLCCB, I decided that I should attempt to get a grasp of Baltimore's LGBT communities that was as comprehensive as possible. Over the next several months I tried to attend as many events and meetings as I could and speak to as many people as I could manage to sit down with. I found myself on buses and light rails traveling between different parts of the city, from Towson to Dundalk and from Upton to Middle East, all in an optimistic and ultimately vain, yet not unproductive, effort to achieve a sense of the "totality" or "ecosystem" of LGBT life in Baltimore. A lot of the time I was in a state of controlled mania, in transit and in between destinations and ideas about which leads to follow up on, which direction to take my research, and how to translate the different threads I was trying to weave together into a coherent narrative argument.

One device that played an increasingly crucial role in ordering my thoughts and research activities was my smartphone, which I bought when I arrived in Baltimore. Whether I was making phone calls; sending and receiving text messages; conducting interviews; or producing notes, pictures, and videos, it assisted me with aligning the different rhythms, trajectories, and worlds of (potential) participants as they intersected with my project's own shifting coordinates. When conducting what is traditionally called participant observation, one usually has to negotiate a variety of actors and environments that each has its own characteristics in terms of habits and routines, history, scale, pace, accessibility, and atmosphere, to name but a few attributes. This results in a great amount of logistical and affective labor that takes up most of one's research time, to such an extent that "observation" often seems like a minor activity on the daily to-do list—if it adequately represents the process of ethnographic knowledge production at all. Rather, the practice of alignment, or calibration, is a much more crucial and omnipresent aspect of ethnographic fieldwork when it is understood as the gradual and tentative movement toward the translation of intimate interactions and embodied knowledge into a sustained account of a particular social scene. For such an account to obtain a sense of consistency and coherence, much of the logistical and affective labor of fieldwork must be geared toward an alignment of the multiple currents and cadences that constitute the research field, which effectively means learning to maneuver, order, and respond to the diverse challenges that come up along the way. In my project, these challenges came from various angles and assumed different shapes, ranging from limited mobility and having to navigate flirtation during an interview to dealing with racial, gender, class, and sexual difference.[18]

Looking back, I realize that my urge to keep spreading out also made me spread myself too thin, and my holistic intentions inevitably detracted from the thickness my ethnographic account could have achieved if I had started out with a focus on the Black queer contingent of Baltimore's LGBT community rather than trying to map all of its complex iterations. What makes this especially regrettable is the fact that so much of my fieldwork—all of the mapping, tracing, and recording I was doing for months—eventually hasn't made it into the book. This omission can be partly explained by the sheer unwieldiness of the data I amassed, which made it increasingly difficult to translate my findings into a narratively coherent and conceptually/politically relevant argument. But, more important, I also became less interested in the very idea of creating a holistic account of the "totality" of Baltimore's LGBT community as the months passed, instead developing a more sustained focus on the resources that enable Black queer collectivities to survive and flourish in the city. During my fieldwork in the HIV-prevention community, I had already become acquainted with several members of Baltimore's Ballroom scene—an alternative kinship system organized around competitive dance and gender performance that formed a crucial support structure for Black queer youth who find themselves "at risk" of much more than HIV infection. About halfway into my research I was also spending an increasing portion of my time studying two other key—and, as I was to find out, interrelated—resources for Black queer world making: religious faith and kinky (leather) sex/BDSM. More specifically, I started attending services and classes at a Black Pentecostal congregation with a gay and SGL clergy, which I had heard about through my engagement with the Interfaith Fairness Coalition of Maryland, while also spending more time in the gay leather and BDSM scenes to get a better understanding of how Black practitioners negotiate their position in a community that is overwhelmingly white.

It was during this part of my fieldwork that I was most deeply confronted with the ethical, political, and epistemological difficulties—if not outright impossibilities—of attempting to navigate stark sexual, racial, and gender differences and translate them into an ethnographic account. In the most practical sense, there were physical limits to what and who I could include in my "field" of study. While I was welcome at various public events and people were usually very hospitable, patient, and generous, some sites and occasions remained inaccessible to me as a male-identified researcher—most notably, the private lesbian play parties that were organized at Baltimore's premier BDSM venue, the Playhouse, and in the homes of practitioners.[19] Next to such gendered spatial boundaries, I also frequently had to negotiate and come to terms with a more intimately felt limit that marked an epistemological incommensurability between embodied forms of knowing. How could I ever hope, let alone claim, to bridge the extensive gap between my white, Dutch, middle-class, heterosexual sense of the world and the sense of what, for all intents and purposes, is another world inhabited by my Black queer American interlocutors, many of whom were working class and poor? Could ethnography, this exemplary method of embodied knowledge production that ostensibly is well equipped to tease out and interpret the most obscure sociocultural idiosyncrasies, really allow me to "understand" what they had been through, how they sensed and made sense of their daily environments, how they struggled to survive and to flourish, or what it is like to be Black and queer in the United States? Obviously, the answer in each case was and remains a resounding "no."

Yet if this is so, then how do I account for the possible misalignment between my conceptual and political commitments and the concerns and aspirations of those who have participated in my research? Quite a few interlocutors felt confused or weary about my intention to rethink citizenship by studying the intimate ties that hold together Baltimore's LGBT communities. Juxtaposing these terms, let alone reading one through the other, did not make sense to a lot of people I spoke with insofar as civic institutions were mostly irrelevant—if not antagonistic—to the intimate relationships and practices that held up their worlds. Citizenship simply had very little to do with their immediate needs and desires other than, for some, speaking to a rather abstract aspiration to achieve full legal inclusion in the unforeseeable future. Yet despite this terminological incongruity, I repeatedly encountered collective efforts to build and maintain support structures for belonging, survival, and flourishing, which I understood as deviant/defiant and invaluable improvisations on citizenship and have chosen to call "civic intimacies." I have ventured to expand and revise the language of citizenship not just as a "legitimizing political act" (Bosniak 2006: 11) but also in an attempt, as Didier Fassin (2014: 46) writes, to "render visible and intelligible what may not [have] been seen or grasped by the agents" in my study, given that it is not always easy or possible to think "beyond one's biography and experience" or to account for "the social structures and political events that frame them."[20]

This rendering visible and intelligible was done in collaboration with my research participants as much as possible. Through participant observation, formal interviews, and informal conversations, I have sought to make sense of their sense making by linking their biographical narratives and personal experiences to the impersonal forces—"social structures"—that inform their texture. This allowed me to dialogically explore what motivated my interlocutors to create alternative ways of being in and *of* the city with others and to examine how or to what extent these practices could meaningfully be associated with the notion of citizenship. These conversations, which were often difficult and certainly hesitant at first, not only provided much needed contextual information that could augment my field notes but also opened up a mediating environment that enabled me to interpret participants' vernacular language, theorizing, and sense-making styles in light of my own conceptual framework—and vice versa. This turned out to be a space of insurmountable gaps as well as evocative resonances: sometimes it felt senseless to translate among the different languages, concerns, and explanations I was assembling from a variety of different sources, while at other times a theoretical argument I had been mulling over made an illuminating surprise appearance in or between the words a participant used to narrate an event, describe an institution, or justify a decision. Words and things seemed to suddenly fall into place, at least for a while. And then there were times when the words directed at me seemed inscrutable or nonsensical, forcing me to dig deeper, talk to other community members, and look for additional conceptual (re)sources that could help me reduce the distance between my sense of their world and their own (cf. Stack 1974). Reducing this distance was the most I could hope for, given that a full "understanding"—a complete closure of the gap—was and remains impossible, given the aforementioned epistemological incommensurability of our differently embodied and inhabited worlds. While I cannot claim that I really got to *know* the world of my interlocutors, I can say that I have *learned* a lot in the relatively brief time they shared some of it with me. And as I demonstrate in the following chapters and return to near the end of this book, one of the most important things I have learned during this necessarily partial and incomplete process of sense making is that citizenship, if it means anything at all to Black queer Baltimoreans, is about making space for new forms of kinship and solidarity, about sharing memories and faith, about caring for others' health and well-being, about getting each other off and lifting each other up. Proliferating against and besides dominant immunitary citizenship regimes, civic intimacies pervert citizenship by rendering it ecstatic, turning it inside out.

Outline of the Book

In Chapter 2, which sets the scene for the analyses presented in the subsequent three chapters, I take the reader on a historical journey through Baltimore. Drawing on my fieldwork, as well as on literature and archival research, my account is guided by three central features that shape the city's urban fabric: superfluity, immunity, and ambiguity. I start by examining the long and profitable relationship between the City of Baltimore and its largest employer, Johns Hopkins University, whose extensive history of displacement and exploitation of African American residents has received remarkably little attention. I then move to a discussion of Baltimore's public transit system as a way to analyze the city's long history of racial segregation, accomplished by legal and extralegal means. This leads to a consideration of the Black Church's ambiguous role in this history, deepening my historical account of segregation in Baltimore while addressing how certain prestigious middle-class Black churches have become tied up in activities that exclude and damage poor Black communities. Moving on to more recent ways the city's successive administrations have attempted to extract value from racialized urban (re)development projects, I show how the efforts of Martin O'Malley, Baltimore's former mayor, to cultivate a "creative class" in designated areas of Baltimore builds on earlier endeavors to govern and revitalize the city by managing its immunitary geographies of cultural production and consumption in the wake of deindustrialization. These efforts have also implicated Baltimore's LGBT community, whose own racially tense historical present I survey before focusing on the history of Black queer Baltimore.

Chapters 3–5 present three case studies, each of which examines one intimate matter of concern that is central to Black queer life in Baltimore: HIV/AIDS (Chapter 3), religious faith (Chapter 4), and kinky pleasure (Chapter 5). Focusing on the biopolitical capture and containment of Black queer youth, Chapter 3 assesses federally orchestrated HIV-prevention initiatives dedicated to a scaling up and integration of testing, treatment, and linkage to clinical care in select cities such as Baltimore. I pay particular attention to the fundamental incongruity between a biomedically defined notion of life that informs immunitary prevention strategies and the carefully cultivated yet precarious form of life articulated in Baltimore's Ballroom community, which serves as a vital support structure for Black queer adolescents and young adults. On the basis of my engagements with Ballroom community members who work as peer outreach specialists and are thus responsible for mediating between their community and Baltimore's HIV-prevention system, I suggest a different take on prevention strategy that is inspired by Ball culture's vernacular intimacies, imaginaries, and capacities. I continue my reflection on the conditions of Black queer endurance in Chapter 4, where I look at how religious faith informs Black queer practices of self-formation and world making at a Black Pentecostal church with an LGBT/SGL clergy. Both chapters show how day-to-day survival is never "merely" anything, given that it requires collective effort and is suffused with aspirations to flourish and build more accommodating good life architectures that draw their energy from a variety of sacred and worldly sources. This focus on religious spirituality as a vital resource for Black queer flourishing returns in Chapter 5, where I examine how the ethics of sexual pleasure and violence shape the life-making practices of Black queer women in Baltimore's predominantly white gay leather and BDSM community. I argue that, as a minority presence whose sexualized racial alterity forms an object of both denial and fetishism, Black queer women disrupt the purported unity and universality of the gay leather and BDSM lifestyle. The chapter's central protagonist is Monica, who continually negotiates her ambivalent investment in an intimate support structure that offers her valuable resources for experimenting with pain, pleasure, and power, despite this structure's historical marginalization of Black (women's) sexuality and its reluctance to critically scrutinize BDSM's fraught relationship to the history and afterlife of slavery.

Finally, following from my discussion of the racially charged tension between pleasure and violence in Baltimore's leather/BDSM scene, Chapter 6 offers an extended reflection on the valences of negativity and reparativity as forces that inform and propel the civic intimacies I describe in this book. I start with a comparative assessment of the death-driven (a)political nihilism that connects the otherwise disparate work of Frank Wilderson and Lee Edelman, providing a critical reading of what I call Edelman's "digital metaphysics" and its problematic understanding of survival and relationality. After developing a different, more ambiguous perspective on these notions, I consider the intellectual exchange between Fred Moten and Afro-pessimist scholars such as Wilderson and Jared Sexton in light of the persistent negativity that marks Black queer world-making practices in the past, present, and future tense. Drawing on the ethnographic narratives presented in the preceding chapters,

I argue that the reparative value of ethnography is to affirm and revalue the often tentative ways people give form to their lives and to the political as the empowering potential for things to be otherwise. While Blackness and queerness may be ontologically defined by dereliction and nothingness, this is never the entire story. The mode of existence that is Black queerness is also the unstable outcome of ongoing efforts to work with/through/against the force of the negative and collectively compose an aberrantly joyous life that is worth living—that indeed *claims its worth through the obstinate practice of living*. This is the wager of *Civic Intimacies*.

2

Ambiguity City

David Harvey's view from Federal Hill afforded him an "impressive introduction" to the "great book of time and history" that is Baltimore's city center (Harvey 2001: 128). From this vantage point he could discern the architectural vestiges of power that reveal how Baltimore in a few decades had transformed from a manufacturing industry hub, benefiting from its location on the Chesapeake Bay, into a node within a global network of finance capital flows channeled through the city by tax breaks and other public instruments mobilized for the development of private property. Using his view as a stepping stone for an investigation that attempts to "read all the signs of the landscape" (ibid.), Harvey tells a story of a once thriving port city whose path of steady decline pushed local officials to adopt an entrepreneurial approach to government and initiate an ever increasing number of public-private ventures that resulted in a plethora of urban renewal projects, heralding Baltimore's much lauded "urban renaissance" in the mid-1980s. Yet Baltimore's spectacular rebirth, fueled and represented by the unlikely makeover of its Inner Harbor area as a place for tourism and other forms of leisurely consumption, hid and continues to hide two important realities. First, it obfuscates how the Inner Harbor functions as "an island of affluence and power in the midst of a sea of impoverishment, disempowerment, and decay" (ibid.: 143)—one navigated primarily by Baltimore's African American population. Most Black residents you see on this island do not spend their money there but are working one of the many low-wage service jobs that keep businesses running along the shoreline. Second, it distracts from the way the City of Baltimore increasingly relinquished its sovereignty in its ongoing fight against the perils of becoming superfluous within a highly competitive global economy, having opened up its markets to international finance in the 1980s. Of course, Baltimore, as a port city, had always been susceptible to international forces of capital and commerce, and Harvey reminds us that "historically, the governance of Baltimore has been heavily influenced by a small group of local banks" (ibid.: 148). Moreover, as the largest independent city in the United States, Baltimore is cut off from the tax base of its surrounding county—Baltimore County, one of the main destinations of middle-class white and (later) Black residents leaving the city since the 1950s—which fostered its dependence on federal funding schemes (Berger 2007). Nevertheless, City Hall's entrepreneurial desire to turn the city around by way of extensive (re)development schemes, together with severe cutbacks in federal funding, has increased its reliance on global finance capital over the past four decades and eroded its capacity to govern the city without some form of dependence on the many national and international private organizations—both nonprofit and for-profit—that participate in and manage urban "revitalization" across town.

Harvey, from his Federal Hill location, could see only the beginnings of Baltimore's massive governmental transformation—from liberal managerialism to neoliberal entrepreneurship—when he wrote his piece in the very early 1990s (cf. Harvey 1989). Although he picked up on a number of important trends and problems that have continued to mark the city, particularly with respect to its progressive integration into a web of speculators and developers whose blatant disregard for the public good has extracted enormous private profits from the creation of a highly differentiated urban landscape where flourishing pockets of wealth contrast starkly with their contiguous zones of survival and attrition, his story leaves a number of themes underexplored. In this chapter I provide another take on Baltimore, one that is deeply indebted to Harvey's historical account, as well as to a number of other authors who have examined the city from a variety of perspectives, but that also stems from my experiences with its environments and inhabitants. Drawing on my fieldwork, I specifically focus on three important features that, in my view, have shaped—and continue to shape—the city's urban fabric: superfluity, immunity, and ambiguity. Next to Baltimore's aforementioned battle against superfluity within a global network of supply chains and capital flows, it has a long legacy of rendering its Black (queer) population superfluous to its vision of the good city and its attendant entrepreneurial pursuits. One of the spatio- and biopolitical strategies it has honed over centuries is (partial and uneven) immunization, creating pockets of white wealth (such as the "island" of the Inner Harbor), which are relatively protected from the decay and deprivation surrounding them, and granting only temporary access to Black residents to extract value from their labor power before sending them back to their pockets of captivity. Paradoxically, as I have noted, these strategies are increasingly the result of the city's own lack of immunity vis-à-vis outside influences on various scales of government. This paradox also prompts its share of ambiguities, the sources and manifestations of which, however, exceed the realm of government proper.

Baltimore, despite its continual transformation, is characterized by a widespread experience of inertia and immobility, which many of my interlocutors referred to in conversations. Once you end up in Baltimore, it's often hard to leave, they would tell me, because the city tends to grow on you and you learn to love it, but also because it is easy to get stuck in its groove. The tension between transformation and inertia is just one of the many contradictions that shape the particular feeling of Baltimore life and contribute to its penchant to both absorb and propel ambiguity, which is something I tried to wrap my head around during my fieldwork. A friend who is a Baltimore native likes to call it "Ambiguity City" because of all the strange, sometimes subtle and at other times baffling, juxtapositions and incongruities it manages to reconcile for varying periods of time, which makes it an impossible place to pin down permanently or with great accuracy.[1] I think one source of the city's ambiguity is its geo-historical location right below the Mason-Dixon Line, which still signifies the cultural distinctions associated with the split heritage of the North and South. As Harold A. McDougall (1993: 1) has noted, "Baltimore is the southernmost city of the North, and the northernmost city of the South, its population and physical structure marked by the slave plantation, the merchant ship, and the factory." Although city officials do their best to compete with other metropolitan areas in the Northeast, most residents will agree that the pace, customs, and sentiments of the South run deep in their town. Long before it rebranded itself "Charm City," Baltimore acquired the name "Mob City" due to the riotous nature of its population, and it cemented this epithet into the then fragile national consciousness after crowds had violently turned against "invading" Union troops that marched through the city on their way to Washington, DC, as part of the Union's mobilization efforts at the start of the Civil War in April 1861 (Puhak 2015). Yet this, of course, is only one possible explanation for Baltimore's foundational ambiguity. There are other sources and manifestations, which surface below.

The following section starts with an examination of the relationship between the City of Baltimore and Johns Hopkins University. I then turn to Baltimore's public transit system as a way to analyze the city's history of racial segregation, followed by a section focusing on the Black Church's role with respect to such policies. The subsequent section examines more recent attempts by city administrations to extract value from racialized urban development projects, which build on earlier endeavors to govern and revitalize the city by managing its cultural production and consumption in the wake of deindustrialization. In the final section, I look at the emergence of the gay and lesbian community (now commonly represented by the LGBT abbreviation), focusing particularly on the city's Black queer history and the community's response to the HIV/AIDS epidemic.

A View from the Johns Hopkins Medical Campus

About halfway into my fieldwork I had my own, instructive view of the City of Baltimore, this time from the seventh floor of one of the buildings that make up Johns Hopkins's East Baltimore Medical Campus, that quintessential "island of affluence and power in the midst of a sea of impoverishment, disempowerment, and decay." It conveyed a certain truth about Baltimore, whose symptoms I had already encountered many times before, both in writing and in person, yet it would take me months more to process the gravity of its repercussions. Actually, I had two views of two distinct Baltimore realities that day, which nevertheless shared a single truth: both the composition and the prosperity of the city, since its inception, have been contingent on the systematic subordination and dispossession of Black people. As Achille Mbembe (2004: 382–383) has argued with respect to Johannesburg, "Racism became a constitutive dimension of the city's modernity. . . . The geography of the city; its cardinal orientation; its planning, zoning, and codes; its infrastructure, streets, and utilities; and its residential patterns and distribution of wealth and income all told a larger story of conquest and the divisive power of race and capital." This is also the story of Baltimore, whose modern fate has been intimately tied to that of one of its main protagonists: Johns Hopkins University. I got to appreciate the first view after my interview with one of the doctors involved with the Lighthouse, a community-based research center that is part of the Department of Health, Behavior, and Society at the Johns Hopkins Bloomberg School of Public

Health (JHSPH). We had just finished our conversation about the various HIV-prevention initiatives she was conducting with her team and the many challenges they faced in the communities they were attempting to serve and improve. As I stood up to say goodbye, I noticed the expansive view her office window afforded for the first time.[2] Apologizing for my impertinent curiosity, I walked over to the window behind her desk and, to my delight, could see the tip of the Washington Monument in the Mount Vernon neighborhood where I had rented an apartment shortly after I arrived in the city. From this seventh-floor office I could see a lot more of the city than I had anticipated, the clear, crisp morning sky stretching my view all the way to the downtown area and including even some of the taller buildings that mark West Baltimore. But what really caught my eye was right below my feet: a large outdoor pool, glistening in the sun, in which a small number of students or staff were enjoying themselves and swimming laps. It looked instantly appealing but also felt acutely out of place in its surrounding environment, from which it was fenced off. This environment, the neighborhood of Middle East Baltimore, for the past four-and-a-half decades has been one of the most impoverished, drug-ridden, and abandoned areas in the city, and its endemic problems—which include myriad public-health concerns—cannot be dissociated from its vicinity to Johns Hopkins's Medical Campus. Yet all of this could not be seen from this particular window.

I had left the office and was waiting for the elevator to take me down again when I was afforded my second view: through large windows on my right I could see blocks of dilapidated row houses, about half of which had been boarded up. I had seen them before, of course, but never from this angle. There they stood, some of them burned-out or partly collapsed, only a block or two away from campus grounds and perhaps a block more from the lavish outdoor pool I had just observed with a mixture of desire and discomfort. The feeling of discomfort grew exponentially after witnessing how closely juxtaposed these two realities actually were, and it was this crude contrast that pushed me to question their shared conditions of possibility. Only much later did I realize how symbolic my location had been: the building that had afforded me these views was occupied by the Center for Immunization Research, a leading institution in vaccine research that has also played a major role in several HIV clinical trials. Next to its world-renowned contributions to the science of biological immune systems, however, Johns Hopkins has been advancing its own immunization project through physical, legal, economic, and financial means. If, as Roberto Esposito (2008: 55) has argued, the paradigm of immunization has given birth to modernity as an apparatus that is intensely preoccupied with the negative protection of life from what threatens to undo it, then Johns Hopkins's role in the shaping of Baltimore's modernity illuminates what Mbembe knows but what seems to escape Esposito—namely, the extent to which this paradigm is structured and made possible by the systemic violence of anti-Black racism. This may seem like a rather counterintuitive and even slanderous statement, given that the university and its hospital was founded by a fervent abolitionist who, before his death, explicitly instructed the board of trustees to provide free medical treatment and care to the city's poor Black population while leaving funds for an orphanage for Black children (Gallant 2015). Yet despite the generous and humanitarian intentions behind its inception and all of the charitable, color-blind medical services provided by its hospital ever since, Johns Hopkins's celebrated history of growth and success has been entangled with the displacement, exploitation, and abandonment of primarily low-income African Americans. The great number of vacant properties in the Middle East neighborhood, many of them bought up by Hopkins over the years, formed a decaying and soon-to-be-destroyed or -refurbished testament to the Janus-faced legacy of the institution locals for many decades have referred to as "the plantation" (Ross 2013).[3]

Johns Hopkins, which has become a significant player in Baltimore's real estate market, started its aggressive expansion into East Baltimore in the early 1950s, displacing 1,100 largely Black low-income families from their homes under the moniker of "slum clearance" and with promises of new homes and neighborhood revitalization. After the 39 acres of land were cleared, however, they were left undeveloped for four years. When building did start, it was decided that all new development would benefit solely the Hopkins community. Instead of new homes for Black residents, Johns Hopkins built housing for students and staff, a shopping center, a hotel, and a medical office building, all fenced off and guarded by campus security (Gomez 2012: chap. 2; Ross 2013). Since then, a pattern of forced displacement and subsequent neglect has established itself as the Johns Hopkins Medical Institutions (JHMI) further expanded its territory at the expense of the local community, which saw few of the new homes and jobs it was promised and has had very little input in the redevelopment projects that deeply affect the lives of those targeted for relocation, as well as those left behind. One notable exception has been the resistance of the Save Middle East Action Committee (SMEAC) against what is by far the largest and boldest project to date: a $1.8 billion urban renewal project—then the largest in American history—that in 2001 set out to raze and rebuild 88 acres of land largely coinciding with the parameters of the Middle East neighborhood. To coordinate and manage this project, which initially included a new biotech park, a parking garage, and a series of housing complexes for students and staff, Johns Hopkins University teamed up with Mayor Martin O'Malley and the Anne E. Casey Foundation, a private charitable organization serving disadvantaged children, to create East Baltimore Development Inc. (EBDI), a public-private venture that was responsible for the demolition of two thousand properties and the forced relocation of 750 households. This was achieved by appealing to eminent domain legislation whenever Johns Hopkins could not acquire property owned by local residents (Gomez 2012; Jacobson 2013). Whereas eminent domain laws originally allowed governments to expropriate private property for public use, often when the property was considered "blighted" or a health hazard, the increasingly broad interpretation of eminent domain in the United States enables cities to take "non-blighted" property and transfer it to private developers, who can then build new structures and thereby ostensibly increase municipal tax revenues in the future (Kerekes and Stansel 2014). It is this speculative rationale that has driven the giant redevelopment scheme in East Baltimore since its inception and explains why a cash-strapped city government would allocate well over $200 million in public funds to private enterprises via the EBDI.[4] The City of Baltimore, like Johns Hopkins University, desires growth and the influx of capital, both of which require the creation of designated zones of entrepreneurial experimentation that radically alter the racial composition and community dynamics of the neighborhoods on which such zoning plans are superimposed.

In the Middle East neighborhood, many residents learned about their forced removal from their homes in the *Baltimore Sun*. The shock and dismay over such blatant disregard for community involvement gave rise to SMEAC four months after the redevelopment plans were announced, and for a nine-year period the committee struggled to secure a better future for community members by pushing for fair and sufficient compensation for those who had to leave; safer demolition methods that did not endanger the community's health; and renovated homes for those who wished to return after the redevelopment was finished (Gomez 2012). While the protests and negotiations yielded considerable successes in the form of equitable relocation packages and more stringent monitoring of potential health hazards during the demolition process, only a very limited number of renovated homes—about forty—were made available to Middle East residents (Jacobson 2013; Ross 2013). Instead of turning more vacant properties into affordable housing for low-income community members, the EBDI focused on building student facilities, market-rate housing, and retail space in the newly developed area, which was renamed Eager Park in an attempt to erase the name "Middle East" and its negative connotations from the minds of future home owners and entrepreneurs. Over time, the construction of planned residential and biotech buildings was repeatedly delayed, which helps to explain why only about two thousand of the projected eight thousand jobs had materialized by 2012—eleven years after the EBDI launched its redevelopment plan. The great majority of these jobs have been short-term construction positions that often did not get filled by local residents, as subcontractors were not held accountable for their hiring practices (Gomez 2012: 139–140; for an updated account of the developments in the area, see Mitter 2018).

The reason I highlight this case is that it is at once exceptional in its scale and common in its perpetuation of a familiar pattern of immunization by way of publicly subsidized displacement and (dis)investment. Following its aspiration to stimulate new economic activity, raise tax revenues, and curb crime rates, Baltimore's municipal government continues to facilitate and support Johns Hopkins as its main "anchor institution" and thereby proliferates pockets of science-driven wealth and privilege whose revitalizing effect on its surrounding environment remains limited. Even though the Middle East neighborhood—now partly rebranded as Eager Park—is surely a safer area due to the presence of campus security and intensified police patrols, a recent study concludes that criminal activity has merely moved to adjacent neighborhoods, many of which are populated by residents who were displaced from Middle East (Linton et al. 2014). With most of the 750 African American low-income households having been removed and only a small number having been able to return, it becomes clear that this public-private security apparatus serves mainly to protect Johns Hopkins's elite (visiting) scholars and students, in addition to the small number of new businesses that have settled thus far in the neighborhood. Inside their/our securitized bubble, members of a cosmopolitan class of (aspiring) academics and medical professionals from around the globe enjoy the benefits of their/our flexible citizenship while the hospital's service, maintenance, and technical staff are stuck in often precarious positions that do not pay a living wage (Gallant 2015; Ong 1999; Shen 2014). As Maryland's largest employer—which also makes it Baltimore's largest employer, if you don't count the city's extensive organized drug trade—Johns Hopkins systematically exploits this contingent of its workforce, many of whom are African Americans living in East Baltimore, by letting workers slip below the poverty line and thus forcing them to supplement their wages with food stamps, to apply for Medicaid, and to find additional employment. When the union representing these workers threatened to organize a strike, Johns Hopkins released a public statement informing the public that "contingency staffing plans" were in place, making clear that this class of employees is considered expendable (Shen 2014). This is one of the ways immunity and superfluity intersect in Baltimore, orchestrated by the city's most powerful private nonprofit anchor institution whose feeding hand nobody can afford to bite.

It is, in fact, this nonprofit status that also makes Hopkins immune to the bulk of municipal, state, and federal taxation, even though its various components are run like enterprises with revenues that add up to $7.62 billion annually.[5] Were Hopkins's revenue and property to be taxed, this would amount to about $12.5 million annually, which is a significant capital injection for a city that has been struggling with a dwindling tax base for more than five decades as it sees the affluent—including several generations of Hopkins executives—flee to surrounding counties. Yet due to its dependence on the medical and life sciences as pillars of Baltimore's economic growth, the city government has refrained from taking steps toward tax reform (Gallant 2015). This once again illustrates the enormous impact Johns Hopkins has on Baltimore and points to its ambiguous position in the city's historical present. While it is widely praised for its medical care, its charitable work, and its contributions to the economic welfare of both the State of Maryland and the City of Baltimore, it also continues to shape the city in its image while depleting public resources and perpetuating the exploitation, segregation, and abandonment of poor Black communities.

For many of the city's most vulnerable residents, this ambiguity is most viscerally experienced when they enroll in one of the many clinical trials conducted by Hopkins in exchange for monetary compensation, which provides eagerly anticipated short-term financial relief even as they know such trials may expose them to additional health risks and they do not really trust the institution to which they are leasing their bodies. For many African Americans in Baltimore, "the plantation" has become associated with folklore, passed on from generation to generation, telling of "night doctors" and "needle men" who abduct unsuspecting Black residents in the area around the hospital on the hill. While much of this folklore is rooted in slavery-era practices of grave robbing, medical experimentation, and intimidation by southern slave owners who spread rumors about these practices to prevent freed slaves from moving to the North, it also reflects realities closer to home. Johns Hopkins has a little publicized history of unethical medical research on poor African American populations, whose most famous case is undoubtedly Henrietta Lacks and her immortal cells that brought the JHMI so much wealth and fame (Skloot 2010) but that stretches well into the age of informed consent and includes a controversial lead paint–based experiment on "inner-city" children between 1993 and 1995 for which Hopkins was sued (Gallant 2015; Moisse 2011). Yet even when all ethical standards are observed, as is the case in the vast majority of today's clinical trials, the persistent sense of mistrust and cynicism with respect to Hopkins among Baltimore's Black residents is far from unwarranted. Aside from their crucial position in "life-sustaining and life-administering apparatuses," such trials constitute a mode of exploitation in which Black bodies form both a pool of "experimental labor" and a standing reserve of biocapital, which allows for the extraction of value—in the form of medical data, blood, and the like—from a population that in other ways has been structurally devalued and rendered superfluous (Opondo 2015: 115; Sunder Rajan 2006). This is another way the new biotech park in Middle East Baltimore is set to bring scientific progress and route capital flows into certain privileged parts of the city at the expense of Black lives.

Getting Around, Getting Stuck

It is likely no coincidence that one finds a great number of advertisements for clinical trials on the city's public buses, given that metropolitan bus services in the United States cater predominantly to the urban poor and underserved. This is especially true for Baltimore, whose public transport system is notoriously dysfunctional, making car ownership pretty much mandatory if you need to get around town without too many transfers and delays. Even though my fieldwork required a lot of travel throughout the city, I could not afford a car when I moved to Baltimore, so I found myself warily depending on public transit during my entire stay. I also walked a lot and tried biking a few times, but I quickly decided that the number of potholes and cars exceeded the comfort level I had built up in Amsterdam, my hometown, which is replete with bicycle lanes. It didn't take long before I learned that, despite my inability to explore my new environment by bike, riding buses and walking around Baltimore likewise introduced me to places an outsider otherwise would not encounter, and I found that such transitory experiences can tell a great deal about a city's social and material organization. Aside from public transportation and walking, my privilege as a Johns Hopkins fellow also allowed me to use the free Hopkins shuttle service, which transfers students and staff between the East Baltimore Medical Campus and the university's Homewood Campus, northwest of the city. I decided to take the shuttle after my interview with the Lighthouse doctor at JHSPH that day, knowing it would drop me off near my Homewood office in less than fifteen minutes, whereas a public bus would take me about three times as long.

The shuttle, in contrast to city buses, mostly leaves on time and drives westbound through East Baltimore without stopping until it reaches the Peabody Institute, a Hopkins-affiliated conservatory and prep school located in the majority-white and stately historic neighborhood of Mount Vernon. From there it drives north on North Charles Street, which, along with the adjacent, southbound St. Paul Street, functions as a corridor colloquially known as the "white way," vertically cleaving the inner city into its majority-Black East and West sections, up to Penn Station, the city's train station and main transportation hub. Here the commuters get off, after which the shuttle speeds farther up North Charles and crosses North Avenue, one of the city's longest uninterrupted east-west thoroughfares, which was once thriving but has experienced ongoing decay since the 1960s. This decay intensified after the riots of 1968 following the assassination of Dr. Martin Luther King Jr. (Elfenbein, Hollowak, and Nix 2011), and, when riots erupted again during protests against the police brutality that killed Freddie Gray, North Avenue was once again a scene of much destruction. When riding the shuttle, however, North Avenue is just another hurdle to be crossed on your expedited transit to Homewood's 33rd Street stop, rushing through the still struggling Barclay and "Lower Charles Village" neighborhoods. When you reach your destination and look out over the manicured campus lawns, it can therefore seem as if Baltimore is compact, transparent, and easy to navigate—a city living up to its Charm City brand moniker.

Indeed, one gets a similar feeling when riding on one of the color-coded lines operated by the Charm City Circulator, a city-funded public transit service—operated by a private company (VEOLA)—that offers residents and visitors free transportation between a number of tourist destinations, historic sites, parking spaces, and businesses throughout downtown Baltimore. Clean, dependable, and (environmentally) friendly, the Circulator certainly provides a valuable public service that is accessible to everyone and avoids downtown congestion. But once again we should ask where these buses take riders and where they do not go, because this tells us something about the city's composition and the identity to which it aspires. In Baltimore's ongoing efforts to brand itself as a tourist destination, one of the Circulator's crucial functions is to accommodate visitors and keep them within the relatively secure borders of the downtown area, where they can circulate vertically between Penn Station and Federal Hill on the Purple Line, or horizontally among several tourist attractions along the Orange Line that runs from Hollins Market to Harbor East and Historic Fells Point, where out-of-towners and locals alike gather to watch sports and drink beer. While the Green Line moves beyond the downtown business and entertainment bubble, connecting City Hall to Johns Hopkins's East Baltimore Campus, it avoids reaching too deep into (North) East Baltimore and neatly follows the thoroughfares Fallsway and Broadway as much as possible. This means that a very large and predominantly Black contingent of the city's population, living farther up in West and East Baltimore, are not served by the Charm City Circulator's services, and because residents of the more impoverished neighborhoods in these areas are less likely to own cars, they have few other options than to take a bus operated by Maryland Transit Administration (MTA) or to walk to where they need to go. You will find a lot of Black and brown people walking Baltimore city's streets, on sidewalks when possible but often on the side of the road. Many other underprivileged Baltimoreans take buses to get to work or access social services, but even those who can afford the bus fare cannot always afford the extensive delays, hassle, and aggravation that can come with being delivered to MTA's volatile service and complex system of routes. How many times can you arrive late for work before you are fired? Despite their dysfunctionality and opacity, however, MTA buses at least service the entire city, which cannot be said about Baltimore's other public transit systems. The Metro Subway is infamous for being limited to a single east-west line, although a total of six lines were originally planned in the 1960s. By the time the plan was approved for funding in the early 1970s, only two lines were left, shortly after which the remaining "south line" from downtown to Glen Burnie and BWI International Airport was canceled by the MTA following concerns of Anne Arundel County residents about increased crime rates if their county was made accessible to inner-city (read Black) crowds. Eventually, after a few extensions in the late 1980s and early 1990s, Baltimore was left with just one line that takes riders from Owings Mills in Baltimore County to the Johns Hopkins Hospital, which does allow West Baltimore residents to commute to Hopkins's East Baltimore campus but does not enable any direct transfer to either the Light Rail or the MARC train, the city's two other public transit systems.

The Light Rail is a product of the original 1960s mass transit plans in that its first line replaced the canceled "south line" running along a right-of-way that had been used in the early twentieth century by streetcar and commuter rail routes. Initiated by Mayor William Donald Schaefer in the late

1980s with the intention of creating a rail transit link to the new downtown baseball stadium being built for the Baltimore Orioles at Camden Yards, a former dockyard where slave pens had stood until the mid-nineteenth century (Clayton 2000), the line opened in 1992; after a few extensions, it now connects the suburban malls and business districts of Hunt Valley, in the north, to Glen Burnie and BWI Airport, in the south. While the Light Rail thus spurs urban development, entrepreneurship, and connectivity in affluent white areas, West and East Baltimore remain disconnected from its trajectory, which cuts right through the middle of the city on Howard Street. Once a thriving retail center known as "Antique Row" for its concentration of antique shops, the street has been struggling against decay and vacancy for decades, and the presence of the Light Rail has exacerbated this trend rather than halting it due to the rail's awkward alignment and obtrusiveness in the relatively narrow space through which it has to move, discouraging pedestrian and retail activity (Urban Land Institute 2010). The few times I rode the Light Rail through Howard Street I was struck by the lack of life on many of the blocks I passed until I reached Pratt Street farther downtown, next to the Baltimore Convention Center and within walking distance—or one stop on the Orange Circulator—of the Inner Harbor. It became clear that only areas that have seen previous investment are set to benefit from the city's limited and highly uneven public transit network, while neighborhoods suffering from prolonged abandonment are much less likely to leverage this network for positive social change and will often be bypassed—if not uprooted—during transit-centered urban development.

At the same time, however, developers of upscale residential areas such as Harbor Point, between Harbor East and Fells Point, are working to *avoid* having public transit connections to these future parts of the city, just like the residents of many wealthy towns in the counties have done in the past, out of fear that their insulated safe havens will become easily accessible to unwanted (again, read Black) populations that threaten their carefully cultivated privilege. Here we return to the importance of having a car in a city such as Baltimore, which from the mid-1940s onward has seen a steady increase in the creation of roads and highways that radically transformed its urban landscape. Like many cities in the United States, Baltimore exchanged its extensive streetcar and trolley system for a new bus fleet after National City Lines, owned by General Motors, Firestone Tire, and several oil companies, took over the Baltimore Transit Company, whose ever worsening operational problems eventually pushed more middle-class Baltimoreans into buying cars (Pietila 2010: 220–221). By the mid-1950s, this had set in motion a process of suburbanization and white—and, later, Black—middle-class flight into the counties that the city still has not been able to counter fully or recover from. In this sense, the proliferation of car ownership was one of the main factors that contributed to the city's postwar downfall.[6] Cars meant physical, social, and economic mobility, which allowed people to escape their inner-city confinement. Still, this hasn't stopped successive city administrations from spending millions in public funds on large infrastructure development projects over the past five decades, seeking to stimulate economic growth by attracting businesses and bringing back jobs to Baltimore. Many of these projects have been less than successful, however, sending more capital out of the city—via private developers and (sub)contractors from surrounding counties—than they generated in terms of tax-base expansion and permanent employment for residents. Moreover, some projects have had devastating effects on the neighborhoods and communities that had to make way for redevelopment.

The best-known and most maligned example in Baltimore's history is the 1.39 mile stretch of U.S. 40 commonly known as the Franklin-Mulberry Expressway, or the "Highway to Nowhere," that was intended to link the western edge of downtown Baltimore to Interstate 70, which would run through part of the city. While its development between 1975 and 1979 resulted in the demolition of twenty blocks of row houses and churches, destroying entire Black neighborhoods and displacing three thousand residents from their homes, it was eventually rendered superfluous after environmentalist groups managed to halt the construction of the I-75 within city limits (Shen 2010). The only function this short stretch of expressway between Franklin and Mulberry streets still has is to serve as a bulwark that isolates impoverished Black communities, living in public housing projects to the west of the redundant transit corridor, from Mount Vernon and the downtown business district to the east. Together with the six-lane Martin Luther King (MLK) Boulevard, with which it intersects and that partly runs parallel to it, the Highway to Nowhere thereby forms a testament to the architectural "arsenal of exclusion" the city has inherited and continues to augment, allowing it to govern capital and population flows while protecting the pockets of wealth that enable it to compete with rival cities (Schindler 2015; cf. Winner 1980).[7] As previously mentioned, these pockets are often astonishingly close to disinvested neighborhoods, and the level of residential affluence and safety can vary block by block in Baltimore. Yet to keep proximity from developing into propinquity, these contrasting environments are in many cases segregated by strategically built and regulated buffers that see to it that people remain in their designated areas.

Race, Religion, Real Estate

I remember the first time I crossed Greenmount Avenue, another infamous bulwark that is to East Baltimore what the Highway to Nowhere and MLK Boulevard are to the west. In each case, the patchy, corrugated pattern of block-based wealth inequality and segregation is overlaid by a boundary-defining corridor that, for all intents and purposes, straightens out the geographical ambiguity of Baltimore's quilt-like neighborhood composition. Yet Greenmount Avenue also differs from these infrastructures in that it has a much longer history as a dividing line between Black and white, going back at least a century. It also is much more extended spatially, especially when you add the long stretch of road after Greenmount turns into York Road in North Baltimore. Both parts seem to have fully blended into their lush green environment to the point of feeling "natural" and thus are rather inconspicuous as racial wedges, at least for unsuspecting newcomers. But on further inspection, as you cross the road from west to east and keep walking, the starkness of the contrasts in color and wealth are quite frankly astounding. You would need to actually walk to experience this, however, given that there are few opportunities for cars to cross Greenmount Avenue from Guilford, which is a traditionally affluent white neighborhood, into working-class Waverly or the impoverished Pen Lucy neighborhood, both of which are predominantly Black. There are even fewer streets that allow cars to drive into Guilford from Greenmount Avenue, as some are blocked by concrete posts while others are either dead ends or one-way streets directing traffic eastward. Wealthy Guilford has turned its back on its eastern neighbors for a long time, even those who are fortunate enough to have access to a car.[8]

I regularly visited this area east of Greenmount Avenue because I was doing fieldwork at the Unity Fellowship Church of Baltimore (UFCB), an African American Pentecostal congregation with a gay and same-gender-loving (SGL) clergy that convened in a small storefront church. I would leave my Homewood office and walk up North Charles Street into Guilford until I reached 39th Street, one of the few broad streets in the vicinity that runs all the way east into Greenmount Avenue. Crossing Greenmount, itself not a very broad avenue, is to traverse two entirely different worlds—to leave a bastion of plenitude and guarded civil contentment and to enter an area dealing with crime, poverty, drug addiction, and other public health problems, such as diabetes, hypertension, and HIV. Most blocks here have at least one vacant house—either boarded up or intermittently used for all kinds of activities—and from the outside it is not immediately clear whether the UFCB's building is in use, because there are no windows on its front. The UFCB's clergy didn't like the idea of my walking around the area, especially after dark, and someone was always insisting that I accept a ride downtown after Spiritual Development class. I think that some clergy members were themselves still getting used to the idea of being stationed in this neighborhood, even though they had been there for about four years when I arrived. The UFCB got its start at the city's gay and lesbian community center in 2000 but soon needed a larger space that could be accessed twenty-four hours a day, seven days a week, necessitating a move into a new building a couple of blocks down the street. However, after six years of services in Baltimore's majority-white, middle-class "gayborhood" of Mount Vernon, problems with lease payments forced the church to relocate. Attendance then quickly dropped because people were intimidated by the new location, which was much rougher and harder to reach by public transit than the centrally located Mount Vernon. Living in Mount Vernon, I recurrently had firsthand experience of the hassle and frustration that came with attempts to reach the church in time for the 11 o'clock service on Sunday morning. While the Spiritual Development classes on Wednesday evenings would be only a twenty-five-minute walk from campus, my Sunday commutes could take up to seventy-five minutes.

I discuss my experiences at the UFCB in Chapter 4. Here I want to briefly examine the ambiguous position of the Black Church with respect to the long history of systematic exclusion, displacement, and dispossession of Black communities in Baltimore through both legal and extralegal means. The Black Church, as a multidenominational assemblage of African American congregations, has functioned as a vital catalyst for the social, political, cultural, economic, and spiritual well-being of Baltimore's Black communities since the late eighteenth century, when the city harbored the largest population of free Blacks even as slavery flourished in the State of Maryland (Crenson 2017; Phillips 1997).[9] Building on this long legacy, it came to play its most significant role in the early twentieth century when, in 1910, the city issued the nation's first residential segregation ordinance, thereby pioneering "the use of government legislation to achieve systematic, citywide race separation" (Pietila 2010: 23; see also Power 1983). For Baltimore's privileged whites, this legal codification of American apartheid was justified by the argument that it secured property values and improved the city's quality of life. The ordinance was challenged and invalidated several times until its fourth iteration was eventually passed in 1913, making it illegal for Black people to move into a block in which more than half of the residents were white—and vice versa. Although this ordinance was effective for only four years before it was definitively struck down in the U.S. Supreme Court's unanimous decision in 1917 in *Buchanan v. Warley,* which eliminated Louisville's residential segregation law and thus set a precedent for the nullification of all other such laws in the country, it gave way to a host of extralegal measures to ensure continuing segregation. These measures included restrictive covenants in the real estate business and redlining in banking and insurance, as well as land-use controls and zoning legislation enforced by the city government.

All of these practices, individually and often combined, enforced the enclosure and containment of Black populations in overcrowded, increasingly disease-ridden areas that lacked everything from running water to clean air and sufficient space.[10] As Antero Pietila (2010: 54) has argued, "Whites' unwillingness to relinquish any established blocks or vacant land made the creation of additional Black residential areas nearly impossible." Even if a Black family could find access to a piece of property beyond its racial enclave, redlining practices made sure the family was barred from getting a loan or a mortgage. Yet it is here that the Black Church—or, at least, its most prominent congregations—was able to intervene and help its community. It had been accumulating property in different sections of the city since the end of the Civil War and continued to do so after official segregation took hold of Baltimore, since the elite churches were typically incorporated and were thus treated as "neutral" legal persons rather than as raced natural persons. As a result of such legal exemption, "Redlining and violence did not have the debilitating impact on the Black church that they did [on] Blacks generally," and "the inapplicability of racial[ly] restrictive covenants to incorporated Black churches gave them a relative advantage in acquiring and developing properties in urban communities" (Brooks 2002: 38). This exceptional status therefore allowed these churches to assist community members in their efforts to find livable and affordable housing, both in terms of providing financial services and engaging in property management.

It is this history that needs to be taken into account when looking at the current entrepreneurial activities of large Black churches in Baltimore and other cities, which often have strong affiliations with so-called community development corporations (CDCs). More recently, the powerful position of these elite churches justified the second Bush administration's push to increase federal funding for faith-based initiatives in neighborhood development, further consolidating the role of the Black Church in urban revitalization projects. This move made sense from a policy perspective, given that many of these churches possess a high level of experience, commitment, and skill in this area, and it was welcomed by many of Baltimore's community-based organizations, whose bad experiences with the strategies of Mayor Schaefer in the 1980s vividly lingered. During the 1980s, most urban housing and poverty programs were being dismantled by the Reagan administration, and federal funding for urban development was reduced to community development block grants—a significant portion of which Schaefer managed to divert away from the underserved communities the grants were intended to aid and toward his high-profile and much celebrated "Renaissance" of Baltimore's Inner Harbor (Berger 2007; McDougall 1993: 87–88). Community-based organizations, among them many churches whose leaders had worked closely with City Hall, felt betrayed by Schaefer's development schemes, which not only perpetuated a long history of disinvestment in the city's poorest, majority-Black communities but also exacerbated housing inequality by raising the price of real estate in adjacent neighborhoods.

George W. Bush's decision to directly fund faith-based urban revitalization initiatives was thus considered a great improvement that would foster the ability of church-affiliated CDCs to serve the contingent of their communities most in need of better housing. However, as demonstrated by Omar McRoberts (2003) and Derek Hyra (2006), such CDCs are commonly rife with intramural class conflict to the extent that they are dominated by the upper- and middle-class interests of their staff and community partners, which include clergy and church members who do not live in the impoverished neighborhoods targeted for redevelopment. Instead of aiding low-income families by improving their living conditions, efforts to create "mixed-income" neighborhoods or blocks have actually contributed to the displacement of poor residents when they can no longer afford the elevated rent and monthly expenses. While members of the Black upper- and middle-class advocate the merit of these projects in the name of urban revitalization and racial uplift, what is actually uplifted in the process are the property values of blocks previously considered derelict and superfluous. This no doubt benefits the prosperous segment of the Black community but does so at the expense of the most vulnerable residents, who find themselves forced to leave their newly upgraded neighborhoods[11]—that is, *if* their neighborhoods are targeted for upgrading at all, because church-affiliated CDCs are increasingly involved in a process of triage during which they have to make decisions about which blocks have "tipping" potential and thus warrant investment and which blocks have to be further abandoned because they have no marketable assets (Philipsen 2015).

Aside from its shifting historical role in the ongoing *enclosure* of poor Black communities, the Black Church has been involved—albeit unwittingly—in the *foreclosure* of thousands of Black-owned Baltimore homes in the wake of the 2008 mortgage crisis. After the Clinton administration publicly committed itself to stricter enforcement of federal laws that prohibited racial discrimination in the provision of housing and credit by launching a "fair lending" initiative in 1993, financial market actors swiftly invented new asset securitization devices that "transformed *exclusionary rationing* into *stratified inclusion*—drawing more and more consumers into exploitative loans that could be sold quickly through Wall Street investment circuits" (Wyly 2010: 512).[12] Whereas redlining, or what Elvin Wyly terms "exclusionary rationing," functioned as one of the primary governing tools in the era of racist liberalism, reverse redlining, or the practice of "stratified inclusion" that pushes subprime mortgages on low-income minority consumers, has become the hallmark of racial neoliberalism. As David Theo Goldberg (2009: 354) asserts, under neoliberalism "race is purged from the explicit lexicon of public administrative arrangements and their assessment while remaining robust and unaddressed in the private realm." Furthermore, neoliberal reason treats race as an issue from the past that has been overcome and rendered insignificant as merely one of many human differences that a post-racial society has to navigate, while it simultaneously continues to devise new market-based methods for the extraction of value and profits from the systematic devaluation of Black life (cf. Melamed 2011).

This is exactly what transpired in Baltimore between 2002 and 2008, when the city—like the rest of the country—experienced a virtually unprecedented real estate boom that eventually proved to be a bubble inflated and overextended by widespread predatory lending practices. The proceedings of a federal lawsuit by the City of Baltimore against Wells Fargo show the extent to which Black churches served as a conduit for selling subprime mortgages to unsuspecting Black customers who were repeatedly targeted by loan officers after recommendations from church leaders eager to support the bank's charity program, which provided a donation of $350 to a nonprofit of the customer's choice for every loan he or she took out with Wells Fargo. Such high-interest loans were commonly called "ghetto loans" by Wells Fargo loan officers, who also referred to Black customers as "mud people" and actively preyed on working-class Black people's desire to be part of the nation's rapidly growing share of homeowners—while leaving white churches alone (Relman 2010). In this way, the status of the Black Church as an institution of care and trust in the community was severely exploited by a financial institution responsible for the massive extraction of housing wealth from Black Baltimoreans, which subsequently cost the city tens of millions of dollars in taxes and city services (Powell 2009; Wyly 2010).

Yet at the same time I do not think that Baltimore's Black churches can be completely exonerated in this case, as they occupy a more ambiguous position with respect to the calculated dispossession of Black communities in Baltimore. To be more precise, by propagating entrepreneurial attitudes and beliefs among their congregations and extolling the virtues of property ownership, these churches encouraged churchgoers to take out loans even when it may not have been financially responsible to do so, thereby facilitating the predatory transactions set in motion by Wells Fargo loan officers. Lester Spence (2012: 146) has argued that we should understand the entrepreneurial spirit of today's Black Church within the context of what he calls "the neoliberalization of Black politics," which "increasingly creates conditions in which racial inequality is managed through Black elite-promoted techniques designed to get Black people to act according to market principles, in which intraracial inequality is increasingly posited as being the function of an inability to properly exercise self-governing capacity." Here we return to the class antagonism within CDCs and prominent churches, some of which are located in impoverished areas of West Baltimore while a sizeable share of their clergy and staff live in middle-class neighborhoods at the edge the city or in one of the surrounding counties. In Spence's terms, such community-based nonprofit organizations participate in a process of "secondary governmentalization" in which marginalized populations are expected and encouraged to "problem-solve their own condition" by being more self-reliant and economically assertive, often guided by community experts or religious leaders whose actions tend to take for granted and perpetuate intraracial class inequalities rather than fighting them (ibid.: 155).[13] Moreover, this proliferation of neoliberal reason within Black communities converges with the increasing popularity of neo-Pentecostalism since the 1990s, which emphasizes spiritual healing through a personal relationship with God, the well-being of the "whole person," and a buoyant vision of self-improvement and personal transformation (Rivera 2002). I noticed elements of these developments during my fieldwork at the UFCB, whose clergy regularly preached and praised the value of self-assertion, emotional reflexivity, and personal growth through Bible-assisted scrutiny of the problems that detract from the quality of congregants' lives. However, as I discuss in Chapter 4, despite my initial skepticism of—and resistance to—the neoliberal subtext of the ideas espoused during its services and classes, my experiences with the church and its members eventually pushed me to rethink the value of their particular uptake of this Pentecostal mode of pastoral power.

The Value of Creativity and (White) Queerness

The expansion of "secondary governmentalization" and the concomitant popularity of vernacular neoliberal discourses within Black communities in Baltimore cannot be disentangled from how the city has marketed these discourses while enacting public policies that differentially target its residents, as well as the places in which they live and work, by monitoring and punishing some while promoting and valorizing others. Ever since the urban "renaissance" inaugurated by Mayor Schaefer in the early 1970s, the imperative of every elected official in Baltimore has been to "revitalize" the city by creating a climate that will attract international investors and businesses. After Schaefer's mix of fiscal austerity, corporate tax incentives, and public-private development projects rebranded Baltimore as "the most exciting, fiscally sound port city on the Atlantic,"[14] which had overcome deindustrialization and now welcomed outsiders to partake in its rebirth as a tourist destination, his successor, Kurt Schmoke—Baltimore's first Black mayor, who resisted the war on drugs and did much more to help underserved communities—invested another billion dollars of public and private funds in the downtown area. Favoring high-profile projects that would foment public goodwill, he built sports stadiums and brought the Ravens to town as the new football team that would alleviate the public's grief over losing their beloved Colts to Indianapolis. When it was Martin O'Malley's turn, his policy agenda from 1999 through 2006 was marked by an intensification of established entrepreneurial governance strategies, as well as an increasing emphasis on punitive and disciplinary measures to control unwanted and superfluous populations. As state and federal funding steadily declined, the O'Malley administration enacted its governing power "through a regime-like network comprising the mayor, city government and an array of private interests including philanthropic foundations who enjoy a prominent role as policy-setters" and who have been instrumental in steering the city away from what city officials have described as Mayor Schmoke's needs-based revitalization toward market-based or "asset-based" development strategies promoted by influential nonprofits such as the Goldseker Foundation (Davies and Pill 2012: 2204–2205). This introduced the process of triage, coined "working from strength," that "adopted property values as the main criterion for investment, focusing the city governing network on developing the so-called middle neighborhoods showing evidence of economic viability" while the most distressed areas were prepared for demolition and clearance (ibid.: 2206).

O'Malley's governing rationale of managerial efficiency through selective investment was scaffolded by the performance-based and data-driven agency CitiStat, hired to evaluate city policy and ostensibly improve its accountability, as well as a zero tolerance "broken windows" approach to policing, both of which shored up Baltimore's new "sovereign machine of governmentality" (Mezzadra and Neilson 2013: 167; Philipsen 2015). As some "emerging" neighborhoods received incentives to develop real estate, market their communities, and improve their overall "quality of life," historically disinvested Black neighborhoods were exposed to the revanchist flip side of O'Malley's efforts to turn Baltimore into the "Greatest City in America."[15] Residents of these neighborhoods were unable to escape the police surveillance and harassment that "extends the processes of carceralization beyond the institutional borders of the penal system" by criminalizing people for petty violations that enable them to survive in the "circuits of capital exclusion" (Silk 2010: 150; cf. Shabazz 2015).[16] In this way, Baltimore, during O'Malley's tenure but continuing under his successors Sheila Dixon and Stephanie Rawlings-Blake, has perpetuated and intensified the city's long history of treating Blackness as a problem and turning poor Black residents into noncitizens, or what Silk and Andrews (2011: 455) term "anti-citizens," whose disposability and potential threat have to be managed and, when possible, monetized. This was not only achieved through spatial containment, however, but also translated into discursive disciplinary techniques that promoted neoliberal values such as self-sufficiency and community responsibility. One central technique mobilized to promote an optimistic vision of the city and its residents while inculcating the moral imperative of civic participation was Baltimore's "Believe" campaign, rolled out in 2002. The $2.1 million campaign, O'Malley's pet marketing project, originated as a means to induce Baltimoreans to believe in their own capacity to contribute to the city's fight against staggering crime rates but soon expanded its purview with an appeal to the public's obligation to improve the general quality of life in their neighborhoods (Silk and Andrews 2011). One of the bitter ironies of "Believe" is that its message of shifting responsibilities, from the increasingly immunized city government toward residents and community-based organizations, primarily targeted communities with long histories of being at once hailed and abandoned by the civic institutions that were supposed to administer care and support—which is, again, to say mostly Black communities. During my time in Baltimore I frequently noticed how the values and logics at the heart of this extensive campaign continued to reverberate among the various Black queer groups and individuals with whom I engaged, which is something I return to in the next two chapters.

While O'Malley's policies, during his time as Baltimore's mayor and as Maryland's governor, maintained the city's political legacy that renders Blackness a problem, they also turned white queerness into an opportunity. To understand how this was accomplished, one has to examine the role of cultural production and consumption within Baltimore's fragile postindustrial economy. Alongside tourism and bioscience, Baltimore's city government was eager to cultivate a more speculative pillar of economic growth in the early 2000s: creativity. Like many other cities across the United States, it was persuaded by Richard Florida's (2002) thesis that a generation of young, well-educated, and highly skilled creatives and knowledge workers constitute a new "creative class" whose presence can revitalize postindustrial urban regions by fostering a "new economy" based on creative industries. While Baltimore was already home to a large and international—yet mobile and thus transient—population of elite academics and medical professionals, O'Malley subscribed to Florida's argument about the potential long-term value of city-sponsored creativity and in 2002 paved the way for its institutionalization by establishing the city's first official arts district, in close cooperation with the State of Maryland and a network of nonprofit partner organizations. The Station North Arts and Entertainment District, representing a patchy area that stretches from Penn Station up to North 20th Street and has Howard Street and Greenmount Avenue as its western and eastern boundaries, was imagined as an incubator of creativity and thus of social, cultural, and economic activity that would regenerate the dilapidated yet salvageable neighborhoods around North Avenue and eventually leverage their real estate value, as well as the city's tax revenues. To achieve this goal, however, the city made available several placed-based tax incentives to developers, businesses, and artists willing to invest in, refurbish, or settle into properties located within the newly inaugurated district, thereby granting predominantly white middle-class newcomers certain financial immunities inaccessible to so-called legacy residents—most of whom are poor, working-class African Americans. As more artists, schools, and businesses have relocated to the area in recent years, these residents are experiencing the burden of increasing property taxes in their neighborhood via rising rents, as well as more stringent housing code enforcements (Zaleski 2014).

Although the presence of gays and lesbians plays only a marginal role in Florida's account of the creative city, whose "gay index" purports to provide an indication of a region's level of tolerance and diversity, which in turn are taken to be indicators of economic competitiveness, the recent history of Baltimore's Mount Vernon neighborhood illustrates the extent to which gay communities and organizations have been at the forefront of the "governmentalization of culture for urban policy ends" (Ponzini and Rossi 2010: 1052). Mount Vernon was home to Baltimore's wealthy cultural elite from the mid-nineteenth century until World War II, bolstering many prestigious institutions, such as the Walters Art Museum, the original campus of Johns Hopkins University, and the Peabody Conservatory. While suburbanization had already begun to leave its marks during the interwar period, white flight from the neighborhood accelerated in the 1950s and reached its peak in the aftermath of the race riots of 1968, resulting in the decline of the city's first tourist destination and once exalted space of cultural production and consumption. As Davide Ponzini (2009: 439) sums up, "In the coming decades the historic buildings were preserved, the cultural institutions continued their lives, and, despite being the physical and symbolic center of Baltimore, Mount Vernon became a low-income residential area." As many residents were leaving the neighborhood in the late 1960s and early 1970s, Baltimore experienced the first organized social and political activity of gays and lesbians, who flocked to Mount Vernon, Charles Village, and Waverly for their abundance of cheap and spacious housing. Whereas the latter two neighborhoods were home to a very active scene of (predominantly white) socialist feminist lesbians between the late 1960s and early 1980s (Clark 2007), the initiatives of a small collective calling itself the Baltimore Gay Alliance (BGA) would eventually establish Mount Vernon as the city's publicly recognized "gayborhood." I return to the BGA's emergence below, but first I want to address how the gay community's initial need for a safe urban environment, and its attendant efforts to develop various avenues for gay culture in Baltimore, have been co-opted and instrumentalized since the 1990s by an entrepreneurial city government whose revitalization strategies are part and parcel of its racialized "revanchist urbanism" (N. Smith 1996). At the core of these strategies is the idea that white queerness, in direct contrast to Blackness, embodies a set of assets that can be leveraged to create market value.[17] Thus, white queers are positioned as deserving of—and are encouraged to actively seek—monetary investments and protection from Black incursions that threaten to devalue these assets, which have come to be associated with creativity, culture, and commerce.

After the AIDS crisis spurred a widespread cultural backlash against gays and lesbians in the 1980s, damaging their slow and highly uneven emancipation in the preceding two decades, the mid-1990s saw the advent of a new gay movement advocating an agenda of respectability and assimilation that sharply distinguished itself from the radical sexual politics of activist organizations such as ACT UP (Duggan 2003). This majority-white liberal movement inaugurated a rights-based model of gay sexual citizenship rooted in consumption and private domesticity, which also affected Mount Vernon's cultural and political landscape at the close of the twentieth century.[18] As the collective energies and interests of its gay community increasingly congealed around commercial initiatives in the neighborhood, such as the opening of new local businesses, the promotion of tourism and nightlife, and the organization of large sponsored events such as the annual and ever expanding Gay Pride festivities, political activities gradually shifted from a strong focus on HIV/AIDS and social justice activism toward local and statewide legal battles for sexual and (later) transgender equality, as well as the enactment of stricter hate crime laws intended to curb violence against LGBT individuals. Propelled by state-level and national LGBT civil rights advocacy groups such as Equality Maryland and the Human Rights Campaign, these efforts to advance LGBT inclusion and safety were increasingly successful and created an urban environment in which a growing number of organizations were ready to pursue punitive measures against anti-LGBT violence and discrimination, while public and private institutions began to position themselves more explicitly as community "allies" and appointed LGBT liaisons to their advisory boards.[19] Concurrently, at the neighborhood level middle-class gays and lesbians also joined local community boards such as the Mount Vernon–Belvedere Association (MVBA) and the Midtown Community Benefits District, both of which are dedicated to securing the area's quality of life, and thereby its property values, by way of various revitalization initiatives that focus on neighborhood beautification and safety—including measures intended to keep out vagrants and other unwanted city dwellers.[20]

Writing about the convergence of calls for safer neighborhoods by "social minorities and property owners in the eras of postwar urban decline and neoliberal development in the United States," Christina Hanhardt (2013: 7–9) has argued that "central to this history is the assessment of risk—the risk of violence associated with gay vulnerability that calls for crime control, as well as the risk of lost profit associated with real estate speculation—and how it shapes the conditions of possibility for normative gay community belonging and the land market." Indeed, this dual risk assessment has increasingly been taken up by neoliberal city administrations like those headed by O'Malley and his successors, which have rebranded Baltimore as one of the nation's gay-friendliest cities while also capitalizing on the kitschy "white trash" queerness of Hampden—a historically poor working-class neighborhood made (in)famous by the early movies of the Baltimore native John Waters, which has experienced intensive gentrification over the past two decades.[21] In their strategic engagement with the place-based politics (and political economy) of violence that firmly ties an individualized notion of threat or risk to a desire for arbitration by state or market institutions, these administrations have advanced policies that promote and protect white gay cultural production and consumption—predominantly focused on nightlife, theater, and the performing arts—in areas considered vital to the economic health and growth of the city. At the same time, they withhold such investments and protections from Black low-income neighborhoods and keep their residents at bay unless they come to work in the service industry that supports these cultural/creative industries.

The question of whose risk—and *what kind* of risk—the city is willing to absorb is especially pertinent for its Black LGBT community, who have long known that resources for the creation of urban safe space are unequally distributed (see Hanhardt 2013: 187). Although Baltimore's racially tense and segregated LGBT community has been increasingly successful at raising transgender awareness and securing legal victories that prohibit gender-based discrimination in housing and employment within the city's jurisdiction, this has done very little to protect or improve the precarious position of Black transgender prostitutes for whom Mount Vernon's "gayborhood" is inaccessible territory and who thus work farther up in the Old Goucher and Barclay neighborhoods right above North Avenue, which are much less safe at night.[22] Likewise, since the widely publicized and debated suicides of a number of gay teenagers, including the high-profile case of Tyler Clementi in 2010, several community initiatives have been founded and funded to assist LGBT youth with issues such as bullying, mental health, and housing, yet these efforts tended to isolate and emphasize sexual minority identity at the expense of its intersections with race and class. While the community was quick to jump on the national "It Gets Better" media campaign bandwagon, it left the "care" for Black queer youth deemed at high risk of HIV infection and homelessness to the city's Health Department and its anchor medical institutions, thus depoliticizing their situation by containing it as a public health issue with little immediate bearing on matters of social/racial justice.[23] Even as the gay establishment frequently paid lip service to the plight of these youths, they have been effectively relegated to what Marlon Bailey and Rashad Shabazz (2014) have termed "anti-Black heterotopias," where their bodies are at once invisible to the general public and eminently available for surveillance, regulation, and clandestine consumption.

Although Mount Vernon's white queerness continues to function as a valuable asset for local entrepreneurs and property owners, as well as for the city more generally, and despite the fact that the neighborhood is still being marketed as a top gay destination for tourists and residents alike, some of the edgier and less respectable aspects of its gay culture are fading. If this is occurring because an outside threat has finally managed to intrude, that threat is not the tightly surveilled usual suspect—Black, poor, and unruly; neither have there been many concerted efforts to keep this creeping force out. On the contrary, most businesses and homeowners have welcomed the looming advance of gentrification, given that it is expected to bring new investments to the neighborhood, which still has its (decreasing) share of vacant buildings and storefronts. Another shift that may explain the waning of Mount Vernon's more deviant gay activity is the progressive integration, if not complete assimilation, of white, middle-class, gender-conforming gays and lesbians into mainstream civil society and its increasingly "tolerant" institutions, which has purportedly rendered superfluous the need for urban gay enclaves and the safe spaces they harbor (Sullivan 2005). Together, piecemeal gentrification and the normalization and subsequent diffusion of gay households and lifestyles have contributed to the recent transformations of Mount Vernon's cultural landscape, forcing a number of community mainstays to reinvent themselves or close their doors permanently. The most prominent venue to close was the Hippo, one of the first gay clubs in the city when it opened on the corner of North Charles and Eager Street in 1972. It served as a popular social space in which drag performance, dancing, and AIDS activism combined, developing a particularly strong relationship with the leather community that lasted until it shut down to make way for a CVS Pharmacy in the fall of 2015. Nearby Leon's, the city's oldest gay bar, is still around, but the adjacent Leon's Leather Lounge has been renamed Steampunk Alley and stopped catering specifically to a gay leather clientele. Before this, Baltimore's leather scene had already been doing without its most cherished and notorious hangout, the Baltimore Eagle, after it shut down for extensive renovations in December 2012. Located less than a mile north of Mount Vernon, the venue offered a space where white leathermen would regularly mingle with Black locals, including transgender sex workers operating in the area, but such nightly encounters have become much less likely since the Eagle reopened in 2017. Whereas the old Eagle's dark, windowless architecture provided patrons with a measure of protection and anonymity, and its cheap drinks ensured that everyone could have a good time, the revamped Eagle prefers a different kind of accessibility: its large windows give the newly added bar and restaurant a bright, airy vibe that seems to be at odds with the leather aesthetic that it continues to memorialize and market to its expanded clientele—consisting of, in the developers' words, "everybody—gay, straight, bisexual, everybody" (Meehan 2015). Meanwhile, back in Mount Vernon one of the few leather boutiques, Chained Desires, had to fold after its owners could no longer afford to pay the bills, and in its small English basement space one now finds a cleaning company.

But it is not just gay leather culture that has been disappearing from the area. "Regular" gay bars have also been forced to close due to declining patronage and raised rents, thereby following a national trend. Many older gay men I met blamed the Internet and the younger generations for the slow but steady demise of their favorite watering holes, lamenting how gay bars have become obsolete in the age of Grindr hookups and initiatives such as Guerilla Gay Bar, a series of events organized by two friends, an attorney and a lobbyist cruising the upper echelons of Baltimore and DC gay life, who staged monthly "takeovers" of different straights bars in the city to promote gay visibility and get patrons to leave their Mount Vernon comfort zone to drink among a "mixed crowd."[24] Even though they admitted that their events took business away from gay bars, often drawing well over a hundred people to straight and largely upscale venues in Fells Point, Canton, and Federal Hill, and while recognizing how they thereby perpetuated a broader trend that may eventually render the "gayborhood" and its nightlife obsolete, both men insisted that they also gave back to the community through fundraising events that benefited various local charities, as well as Gay Pride. Yet even the Gay Pride parade and block party was moved just outside of Mount Vernon in 2014, after tensions among business owners, residents, and the organizers about overcrowding and alleged drunk and disorderly conduct during the preceding year resulted in the designation of a new location for the first time in its history. In 2015, the events were back in Mount Vernon, but not without several regulations that were introduced by city officials and supported by members of the community board the year before, such as the restriction of open-air drinking through the installation of circumscribed beer gardens. This was one of the moves intended to make these festivities more family-friendly and decrease the likelihood of having to deal with what some residents took to be an "uncontrolled mess" (Rector 2014).

"We Embrace and Celebrate Our Blackness Every Day"

Another reason for Gay Pride's temporary move in 2014 was the lack of managerial capacity at the GLCCB, the city's LGBT community center, which is in charge of organizing the annual event. At the time, the GLCCB was experiencing one of its many leadership transitions and had just moved into a new space after having spent thirty-four years at its former location on the corner of West Chase Street and Brexton Street. That building was purchased in 1980 by the then recently incorporated Gay Community Center of Baltimore (GCCB), founded by the Baltimore Gay Alliance in 1977.[25] The BGA had formed in 1975 and was the city's first gay collective whose composition was diverse in terms of gender, race, and class. While, as previously mentioned, a vibrant and tightly knit community of socialist feminist lesbians had been operating out of Charles Village and Waverly since the late 1960s, its politics and lifestyle did not appeal to gay men—or to many lesbians of color (Clark 2007: 2–3).[26] A chapter of the Gay Liberation Front was also fairly active in the wake of the Stonewall riots, yet this initiative ended abruptly after its members decided to pack up and move to San Francisco around 1970. The BGA drew about twenty-five aspiring members when it assembled for the first time on March 20, 1975, in the apartment of the pastor who headed Baltimore's Metropolitan Community Church (MCC), which was established in 1972. Without a space of its own during its first years, it organized various projects and resources from the apartments of its members, including a switchboard that provided a directory service for people with questions about gay-related issues and a newsletter that would become the *Gay Paper*, the city's first steady source of news and opinion for an inchoate gay public and the precursor of the now defunct *Gay Life* newspaper. After founding the GCCB and electing Paulette Young, an African American lesbian, as its first president, the BGA rented different office spaces until one of its other driving forces at the time, Harvey Schwartz, managed to raise enough money to buy a building in the neighborhood where he and many others lived: Mount Vernon. This marked the start of the Gay Community Center on West Chase Street, which also became home to the Gay Health Clinic that the GCCB initiated in 1978, after having received funding from the City Health Department to run a sexually transmitted disease clinic (which it took over from the MCC). The clinic, one of the first of its kind in the country, eventually incorporated as Chase-Brexton Health Services and split off from the GCCB in 1989, which had added "Lesbian" to its name in 1985 and from then on was known as the GLCCB.[27]

The year 1978 was also the one in which Louis, one of the BGA's founding members, co-founded the DC-Baltimore Coalition of Black Gays, one of the nation's first Black LGBT organizations. The initial idea for such an organization took shape in 1977, when Billy Jones, a DC-based activist, came to speak at a BGA meeting and suggested that some of its members should start a collective representing the specific interests of Black gays in Baltimore, as he had recently done in his city. Feeling that such interests and needs were not properly served by the BGA or the GCCB, Louis connected with Jones and co-founded the coalition, which split into two separate organizations—the DC Black Gays and the Baltimore Black Coalition—in early 1979. These organizations formed the first two chapters of the nascent National Coalition of Black Gays (NCBG), which represented a larger platform for political activism and advocacy initiatives that resisted state-sanctioned homophobia, racism within and beyond the LGBT community, and, in the 1980s, the Reagan administration's neglect of African Americans during the ensuing AIDS crisis (J. Bailey 2016; C. Cohen 1999: 94–101).[28] In October 1979, the NCBG not only actively supported the first National March on Washington for Lesbian and Gay Rights but also was responsible for co-organizing the first National Third World Lesbian and Gay Conference that took place in the city on the same day. At the time, Louis was "wearing two hats" as both a member of the BGA/GCCB and the chairman of NCBG's board of directors, and he recalls how he missed Audre Lorde's keynote speech at the Third World conference because he had volunteered to be a bus captain for the center: "We had school buses, and we had people we were bringing. I brought my busload of people, and then I headed, I backed up 7th Street, where the people from the Third World conference are coming down to meet the March on Washington. . . . So that morning, the morning of Audre's keynote, I was over in Baltimore bringing a busload of people. And I remember thinking, 'How did I miss her speech?!'"

According to Louis, Baltimore's chapter was considerably less radical than the National Coalition or its DC chapter, even leaving the word "gay" out of its name: the chapter was known locally as "the Coalition." The rationale behind this decision, he said, was that "if you were too out, people were fearful to join because they would be labeled and wouldn't be protected. It was a very difficult time to be out." He himself had not come out until 1974, at age thirty, despite having very open-minded and supportive parents. By the time his employer—he worked as an electrical engineer—transferred him from Norfolk, Virginia, to Baltimore in 1970, he had had some minor homosexual experiences, but "nothing under that name," and he had always been careful to "keep those desires in check." He had never seriously conceived of himself as gay until he got depressed after a male roommate with whom he had built up a nonsexual friendship relocated back to Spain. Did this mean he *was* gay? he wondered. From that moment on, he felt committed to explore what was going on with him, helped by articles that were coming out in *Time* magazine. He also found out that his coworker and best friend on the job, another African

American engineer, was gay, which encouraged him to be more curious and "out." When he heard other coworkers talk about a drag show that would take place at the Hippo on Halloween, he was excited to go and give it a try, remembering that he had visited the Hippo once before with the woman who was his girlfriend back in 1972; they had expected to find the Chanticleer, a cocktail club that had previously occupied the building since the 1930s. That was the first time Louis saw gay people, and they were dancing together. While he did not attend that particular drag show, he and his coworker would eventually end up in the Hippo together many times, although his enthusiasm for this club would significantly wane over the following years. Hippo staff were known to use tactics such as extensive identification requirements for Black patrons to enforce de facto racial segregation, and Louis remembers how angry he was when the bouncers would not allow his own mother to enter the club without fourfold proof of identification: "She came out with me one evening, and she had left her purse at home. She wasn't allowed in because the Hippo had a policy [that] people of color, and especially women, . . . needed three, four IDs, and they were the only people required to have all this. I was furious, because my purpose for going to the Hippo was to show my mother where I socialized. So there was me throwing a temper tantrum over this." He also knows that the Hippo was not the only gay establishment that discriminated against Black patrons, as bars such as the Torch and the Porthole up in Waverly used the same tactics and—like the Hippo—were later sued for doing so (cf. Drabinski 2015).

People would regularly refer to Baltimore's LGBT community as a "microcosm of society," which is an accurate statement insofar as it indicates how this community reflects and reproduces the city's long history of parochialism and racial segregation. While Mount Vernon has featured as the city's central hub of gay cultural life since the 1970s, its majority-white venues by and large have alienated queer communities of color, which have therefore had to find or create alternative spaces for social life and political organizing on the cultural and geographic margins. Guided by Louis and some of his contemporaries, I learned that most of Black LGBT nightlife in Baltimore has always taken place outside of Mount Vernon, with bars and clubs concentrating in the vicinity of Pennsylvania Avenue (historically the central location for Black entertainment and community life until the late 1960s), along North Avenue, and around Lexington Market (two other once thriving hubs that have experienced rapid decline over the past five decades). Yet in the 1970s, curious newcomers had a difficult time finding out about these establishments, given that the BGA's switchboard did not include them in its resource guide until Louis started to fill this gap. At the time, a number of Black bars were "straight" during the day and would cater to a gay crowd at night or on some nights, such as the Paradise Inn, located in Sandtown-Winchester (West Baltimore), also nicknamed "Jones's" after its owners. As Louis recalls, the Paradise Inn was the place to be if you were Black and gay: "They leased the bar from the liquor store that was next to it, that was like a carry-out selling liquor, and that was very . . . everybody went there." Then there was Odell's on East North Avenue, which had a popular "gay night" on Mondays, as well as Children's Place on Howard Street, a bar run by two lesbians. Another spot with a large Black clientele was (and continues to be) the Gallery, a former leather bar on the corner of Maryland Avenue and East Lafayette Street, where Louis used to meet his coworker's gay friends. This was in the 1980s, when Baltimore witnessed a brief "explosion" of new Black gay bars and clubs. As Ralph James Peay (1996b) writes in a retrospective published in the *Baltimore Gay Paper*, "By mid-decade Baltimore's Black gay bar scene was at a new height. A strip of three bars on Lexington Street behind the Lexington Market became the focal point for Blacks who were gay and went out. The three bars, Tikkis, Burger World, and Our Place, had interchangeable clientele. Also in the same general area was HATS, located on the corner of Paca and Franklin Streets."

The 600 block of West Lexington Street became known as "the Strip," where everyone would go for happy hour before moving on to HATS for dancing and cocktails, after which many would continue their night at the Last Stop, an after-hours club on MLK Boulevard. Kenten, one of Louis's longtime friends, was no stranger to this routine, but he also emphasized that a lot of the nightlife—and social life more generally—happened in people's homes, where people gathered for house parties that often featured not only dancing but often other activities, such as card games. Kenten is a native Baltimorean who grew up in an African American neighborhood in Baltimore County. He came out to his high school girlfriend sometime around 1977, the year his mother died. It was a confusing time, but luckily he had a childhood friend who was already more or less out and introduced him to gay life in the city, taking him to his first gay bar in Fells Point. He remembers standing there, to the side, and just looking—he did not dare to dance yet—and being amazed that people could be that free. He said, "Now, I had a few encounters 'on the low' with some guys in my neighborhood, but we just said it was a 'man thing,' not connecting it to anything else, you know, just messing around. We all had girlfriends. But that there was actually a space that you could go and . . . , I mean, they were all, like, dancing and having a good time, and I was, like, 'Wow!'" He couldn't really talk about his newfound excitement at home, but he did have a high school teacher whom he could confide in and turn to for questions. At first, Kenten kept insisting that he wasn't gay, couldn't be gay, because he had a girlfriend and they were having sex, but his teacher knew otherwise. After a while, he became a mentor to Kenten and would drive him around the city, teaching him about cruising—even though Kenten wasn't familiar with the term at the time:

> I learned the city from him. We had the entire summer, we smoked marijuana all summer long and just drove, and I learned the city. He showed me the cruising spots. He knew some of the guys and would say "hi," and people would come to the car, and he'd introduce me. He just taught me how to really *look* at people physically and assess what type of person appealed to me. . . . [M]y first impression of gay people was this very flamboyant person I saw in my neighborhood, and I knew that if that was gay, then that wasn't me. I learned that most of the guys I was attracted to didn't look or "act" gay.

That summer at the end of the 1970s was a transformative experience in Kenten's life, acquainting him with homosexual scenes and lifestyles beyond the predominantly white gay culture he had been introduced to only shortly before. He found out that Baltimore was home to a relatively small but closely knit group of African American men and women who were openly gay and who, along with men on the down low, hung out in places other than the high-profile spots in Mount Vernon and Fells Point. The 1980s promised to be an exciting decade, and it had gotten off to a good start, until the AIDS epidemic hit Baltimore. At first, many in the Black gay community believed it to be a white gay disease, but after their friends started dying, they didn't know what—or who—to believe. People became fearful, making changes to their lifestyles and routines, which had a devastating impact on the bars and clubs that were flourishing only shortly before (Peay 1996b).[29] Especially in those early years, organizing around issues involving homosexuality and HIV/AIDS in the larger Black community was an enormous challenge due to the stigma attached to both (C. Cohen 1999), and because many African Americans consequently did not identify as gay—they just "messed around." Kenten, who has been an HIV/AIDS activist since 1985, experienced all of this firsthand through his work on a long-term clinical study at Johns Hopkins, but also by conducting HIV tests at the GLCCB, doing educational outreach with his music ensemble, and running a support group for Black gay men living with HIV. In 1988, his group was one of the very few HIV/AIDS-related services in the city that focused on this demographic, whose specific needs were still largely neglected by public health and medical institutions, as well as community-based service providers such as the GLCCB, AIDS Action Baltimore, and HERO—Baltimore's oldest and largest nonprofit organization dedicated to HIV/AIDS care and prevention. The latter did provide Kenten with a space to host his group and sponsored Baltimore's first conference on AIDS in the African American community, back in 1984 (two years before the national conference held in DC), but this event ultimately failed to spur the sustained commitments and resources for which Black queer activists had hoped. Meanwhile, the NCBLG (which added the "L" to its name in 1984) had all but officially folded by 1988, leaving its Baltimore reincarnation—the recently formed Blacks United for Gay and Lesbian Equality (BUGLE)—with a tremendous challenge to meet the community's needs.[30] It was a time marked by death, insecurity, and ignorance, which also took a heavy toll on the city's Black LGBT political organizations.[31] Kenten commented, "I literally had a funeral every week. . . . Nobody had any spaces to turn to, because if they were living at home with their families, who's gonna talk about it? It was still so unknown, not only to the families but to you, too. I mean, I didn't know, but like I said, I started reading stuff. I started asking questions."

This process of discovery and empowerment was not an individual trajectory. Eventually, it was the Black LGBT community's vibrant social life that also enabled the composition of a response to the quickly expanding crisis.[32] As Kenten explains:

> See, a lot of times we would do things like host parties, house parties, card parties—these we[re] more like social groups that linked themselves to HIV issues. Because now all of a sudden, the folks in those social groups are starting to get sick. So there were people always doing things like having social things, but when HIV came along, it was really making an impact, and some of those folks realized "we gotta do something different [*inaudible*] because this HIV thing is starting to infiltrate our social [groups]." . . . And it came from the standpoint of "we have to take care of our people; we don't really hear much about our people."

From the early 1990s onward, a lot of plans and initiatives in Kenten's social circle would be somehow connected to Club Bunns, known as Burger World before the arrival of a new co-owner and still one of the last surviving Black gay clubs in town.[33] Here one could frequently hear talk about the need to "do something different," something tailored to the needs of Black queer Baltimoreans who were being marginalized by majority-white institutions. Along with Kenten; Dana, a co-owner of Bunns; and their friend Leroy, Carlton was a driving force behind the projects that were being conceived during a time when their people needed them most. Carlton, who is originally from New York City but had studied in Baltimore at Morgan State University before his job at Amtrak eventually stationed him in DC, returned to Baltimore in the early 1990s after a close friend who was dying of AIDS convinced him to move there together. He met Kenten at the support group Kenten was running at HERO, which he initially felt apprehensive about—he didn't even want to be in Baltimore at that time. Yet to his surprise he felt really comfortable, and their conversations inspired him to become more active. He got his first experience doing advocacy work for the People with AIDS Coalition of Baltimore, but things really got started when Kenten, who was working at the Baltimore City Health Department's AIDS Education/ Outreach Program, introduced him to a coworker who asked whether he would be interested in joining a new program created to educate minority men about HIV/AIDS: the Men of Color AIDS Prevention Project (MOCAPP). The program, which received funding from the U.S. Conference of Mayors in August 1995 and was led by the local Black activist and shop owner Dale Madison, gathered "men of color representatives" from organizations such as HERO, Chase-Brexton Health Services, the People with AIDS Coalition, and the Black Educational AIDS Project (which targeted the Black churches) to provide outreach specifically to men who did not identify as gay or had not migrated to one of the popular gay neighborhoods, thereby falling below the radar of standard HIV-prevention strategies (Jensen 1996; Peay 1996a). Despite its struggles and internal strife, MOCAPP was a vitally important early initiative that would sustain itself for a number of years and inspired related groups such as MOCAA (Men of Color against AIDS) and, later, MOCHA (Men of Color Health Awareness).[34] Kenten and Carlton were actively involved in all of these programs.

Even though HIV/AIDS absorbed most of their activist energies in the 1990s, the friends also frequently discussed the need for a broader cultural platform and an alternative to the annual Pride festivities, where they did not feel fully represented. Dana had been throwing Pride after-parties for the Black queer community in and around Club Bunns since 1991, when he took part in organizing the first Black Pride festival in St. Mary's Park (a few blocks north of Bunns), and there had been a few attempts to establish a Black gay community center on the 600 block of West Lexington Street, but a more durable institution would have to wait until the next decade. According to Kenten:

> They [the GLCCB] would include us, but you didn't feel included. . . . It was its own, self-contained entity that for the longest time dominated the culture, because there was nothing in place, and there was nothing to go up against it, because we weren't organized to that level yet. We were just doing social [things]. . . . It wasn't until some of us started saying, "You know what? They're not really better than us. The bottom line is we just need enough people to organize, to make something concrete that makes us stand out as a community. So guess what: let's start something!"

Carlton added:

> Dana was doing Blacks Together in Pride and having the block party. So then Dana put the cry out to say, "Hey, why can't we have, like, other [events and] be nationally known?" And I looked at him and said, "I'll take it on." I was involved in a lot of Black gay men's stuff and saw how I could, because I knew the resources, I had a sense of where the money was coming from in Baltimore, and I knew who could get involved.

By the late 1990s, Carlton had built up an extensive network on the municipal as well as the state level and was active in multiple HIV/AIDs-related organizations, doing MOCAA with Kenten and serving on the board of directors at HERO, so he had learned how to fund-raise. "And once I'd learned that, it was like [*snaps fingers*]," he said. "It took a while, but once I learned how to do it and had people to help me with the paperwork, that was it." When his friend told him that he was getting ready to form an organization called the International Federation of Black Prides, Carlton jumped at the opportunity to formalize Dana's Blacks Together in Pride festivities by integrating them into a larger institutional framework. They would finally have their own thing. Carlton noted, "There was a cultural need for Black pride in the community. It affirms us. As our saying goes, 'We embrace and celebrate our Blackness every day.'" By joining the federation in 2002 and becoming officially known as Baltimore Black Pride (BBP), the intention was to no longer focus on male-centric HIV/AIDS issues or throw an annual block party but to improve the visibility and well-being of the entire Black LGBT community by organizing a variety of other events throughout the year, such as monthly seminars and forums, fund-raisers, vigils, and get-togethers. Another important objective was to pursue partnerships with other organizations and programs, both locally and statewide, as this ensured the continuation of funding opportunities. Moreover, Carlton and his friends were always committed to cooperation and reaching out to potential allies, wherever they could be found and no matter what color their skin was. To them this did not infringe on their aim of Black queer empowerment. This did not sit well with everyone in the community, however, and the same year that BBP got its start also saw the Portal opening its doors and claiming its position as Baltimore's African American LGBT community center. The Portal was run by an acquaintance from back in Carlton's Amtrak days who wanted to have a durable space dedicated to Black men and did not think the BBP was doing enough to create one. The two did not see eye to eye on a number of issues, including the extent to which majority-white organizations should be involved in the operation of Black queer projects, which kept them from sharing resources and information. For this reason, the two organizations did their own thing in Baltimore during the first decade of the twenty-first century, and the rift only widened when—as I mentioned in Chapter 1—the Portal merged with Black Men's Xchange and Cleo took over. The Black radicalism espoused by Cleo was something Carlton could never get behind, as its racial negativity conflicted with his ideal of openness and mutual affirmation.

Carlton regrets the public perception of the BBP as "those party people" who are mainly concerned with organizing Black Pride festivities, although he also acknowledges that they often came up short with respect to relevant and consistent community outreach: "You heard from us in June and October, but other than that . . . , we did some things here and there, but most of our time was put into Pride." This was one of the reasons the federation's board of directors, including Carlton, decided to restructure and rebrand the organization as the Center for Black Equity (CBE) in 2012—shortly before I ended my fieldwork. Baltimore's chapter of the CBE became operational in 2013, with the objective to dedicate itself year-round to social justice advocacy, HIV/AIDS awareness, and Black LGBT community empowerment. The new structure also allows the center to forge more diverse alliances with other programs and organizations, enabling new funding opportunities, even though in practice the vast majority of funding sources have been connected to HIV prevention and treatment. This brings us to a persistent and fundamental problem for Black queer community organizers who aim to create sustainable infrastructures for collective flourishing in the city: as Carlton and his peers know very well, HIV/AIDS remains a crucial issue facing the community. Yet it is far from the only one, and far more resources are needed to really make a difference and allow their people to thrive. However, given that such resources are largely unavailable, community organizers see no option other than to collectively jump on any opportunity that will bring in prevention or treatment money, with its circumscribed deliverables and ties to the pharmaceutical industry. Carlton once referred to this as "getting in bed with the devil" and admitted:

> It's really hard to fund-raise. And when you don't have. . . . I'm not a grant writer. I'm a hustler. I know how to get the money. . . . It's getting to the point where you're doing a song and dance just to get money from the pharmaceutical people. It's like, "Don't pass us by!"—you're selling your organization. And we have to, because we don't know how to build infrastructure, at least not independently. The biggest thing is capacity building, and for that we're dependent on prevention money.

This dependence also returns us to Baltimore's three main features, introduced at the start of this chapter: ambiguity, immunity, and superfluity. Carlton and Black queer activists like him know intimately well what it's like to operate in "ambiguity city," where one often cannot be sure what the right decision will be because what looks like the best initiative to empower the community may well turn out to hurt people in unforeseen ways. Nobody I talked to wanted to be so dependent on funding for HIV prevention or treatment, but neither did anyone dare to bite the hand that feeds. Perhaps the situation is best encapsulated by the aptly named Paradox, a long-running club with a Black queer clientele that opened in 1991 and closed in 2016. Around the time I was doing my fieldwork, the Paradox served as a site for Black Pride events as well as HIV testing booths targeting youths and young adolescents—two interdependent initiatives insofar as the former gathered the bodies to test while the latter would (co-)fund the events. Many saw this as a mutually beneficial situation that would save the community by safeguarding the health of its youth. But despite this general consensus, an increasing number of people started to sense the tensions and shortcomings of this immunitary social contract between the city's Health Department and the community. As I detail in the next chapter, various programs welcomed Black queer youths as sexual citizens responsible for their own health and safety while failing to provide the resources and support required to sustain their collectively crafted form of life. Those who did not or could not be integrated into the new "Test-and-Treat" regime were essentially considered superfluous and consequently abandoned. Yet Chapter 3 also starts my exploration of how Black queer folks compose alternative modes of belonging, survival, and flourishing in response to their exclusion from—or selective and partial inclusion in—protective bureaucracies predicated on the notion of citizenship as a set of state-sanctioned privileges and immunities. In other words, it begins to examine the composition of civic intimacies.

Coda: Entangled and Uncertain Futures

At the start of 2015, the GLCCB—then led by a new Black executive director—received two grants sponsored by the pharmaceutical industry, together worth more than $45,000, to provide community education about pre-exposure prophylaxis, or PrEP. As noted in the local press, this renewed its aspirations to play a more active role in Baltimore's LGBT community via public health services and increased its chances to attract more federal funding in the future (Rector 2015). However, the center's opportunity to reassert itself through this new HIV-prevention initiative may have come at the expense of the most vulnerable segment of the community it is trying to protect. PrEP was a new development sweeping through the United States and causing controversy among Baltimore's prevention community around the time I was finishing my fieldwork. Hailed as a paradigm shift that would radically decrease HIV incidence rates, it severely intensifies the logic of biomedicalization that governs contemporary prevention programs by prescribing that HIV-negative populations judged to be "at substantial risk"—read young Black queer men and (trans) women—take a daily dose of antiretroviral medication to prevent infection. In other words, treatment thereby becomes the primary, if not the single, mode of prevention. Not only are those living with HIV constantly implored to act responsibly and take their medication so that their viral loads remain "undetectable," Black queers—at risk *because* they are Black and queer—are now expected to adhere to a strict regime of heavy drug therapy that could previously be avoided by those who managed to remain uninfected. PrEP thus turns the mass-medicalization of precarious minorities into public health policy, thereby not only discarding prevention methods that tackle the compounded socioeconomic problems that actually endanger these groups but also relegating their future to no more than the continual vigilance and dread of self-contained risk management. While the next chapter does not discuss PrEP, focusing instead on the various conditions and developments that heralded its emergence, it should serve as a cautionary tale about the entangled futures of the GLCCB and the Black queer youth who have shown up on its radar, yet do so primarily as a target population. As the GLCCB figures out how best to use its PrEP money while it lasts, Black queer Baltimoreans are increasingly facing the moral pressure to ingest a noxious drug as the preferred way to secure themselves in the toxic environments to which the city has consigned them.

3

Capture, Containment, Composition

Walking Time Bombs

As I noted in Chapter 1, I first met Cleo at one of the monthly HIV-prevention/care coordination meetings convened by and at Maryland's Infectious Disease and Environmental Health Administration (IDEHA). One of the few people who would frequently counter his criticism during the meetings was Margaret, who always displayed as much zeal for her objectives as Cleo did for his. Margaret, who is white and in her fifties, has been working for the Centers for Disease Control and Prevention (CDC) since 1978. As a public health adviser assigned to local jurisdictions, she has seen many health challenges throughout the country, but to her mind nothing compares to Baltimore: "The reason Baltimore's worse is that we have worse poverty, worse crime, worse drug abuse." Sitting in her cramped, windowless office at the downtown headquarters of the Baltimore City Health Department (BCHD), we talked about her experiences during three decades of HIV/AIDS and how she has been able to cope with the immense amounts of grief and loss. "I'm not numb, she said. "I am passionate about what I do, but it's like, . . . you know, when I was twenty-one, I probably thought I could change the world. And probably when AIDS came along, when I was about twenty-eight, I started realizing quickly that I couldn't save the world. So you adjust, and at some point in my life I got to the point where as long as I'm making a difference, that's all that matters." From her current perspective, making a difference means getting people tested, something in which she is extraordinarily invested: "We sure don't solve all the problems. We know that, and we have no hope of solving [them]. What we try to do is go out into the community and do outreach, make sure people know that testing is available, try to get everybody we possibly can tested for HIV." This objective also drives the Health Department's decision to target more of its outreach and testing resources at the city's Ballroom community, which has only recently registered on its radar.

The Ballroom community, or House Ball community, is "an alternative queer kinship system that is organized to meet the needs of its members for social solidarity and mentoring in a racist society largely hostile to sexual and gender expression differences and that has as one of its ritual expressions the dance and performance competitions called the balls" (Rivera Colón 2009: 26; cf. M. Bailey 2009, 2013, 2014). Originating in New York City during the 1960s but with roots going back to the "Faerie Balls" of the 1920s, so-called Houses have provided a refuge for young Black and Latinx queer youth who often were excommunicated by their families and living under the continual pressures of a punitive heteronormative society. These Houses, which were inspired by—and took their names from—the famous haute couture fashion houses of Paris, cultivated an alternative kinship structure in which experienced and respected House mothers and fathers "adopted" their "kids" and took them under their wing, often taking them off the streets and into their House.[1] Along with providing shelter and a sense of familial belonging, House parents perform other kinds of "queer cultural labor" (M. Bailey 2013: 16), guiding and taking care of their children in a variety of ways—from teaching them how to walk Balls (i.e., teaching them how to dress, move, and conduct themselves at a Ball) to helping out with job interviews and occasional financial support. The everyday relationship between parents and children varies among the different Houses, however, and some parents are predominantly interested in grooming their kids for Balls. Here, members of the various House families compete—mostly head to head—in battles that can win them prizes in a virtually endless number of performance categories, such as European and American Runway, Butch Queen Vogue Femme, and different types of Realness. These categories emphasize the fluidity and performativity of gender and sexuality, as well as participants' sense of style, grace, and fierceness.[2] Winning prizes at a Ball is the most important way to garner respect from peers and climb the social ladder to attain the status of Star, Statement, and, eventually, Legend or Icon.

From its inception and growth in New York City, the Ballroom community spread to other urban areas with large African American populations, such as Baltimore, where the New York Houses started their chapters and new Houses entered the scene. When the HIV/AIDS epidemic hit Black and Latinx communities in New York City and other urban centers across the United States in the 1980s, some activists saw the Houses as key venues for education, prevention, and, eventually, research (M. Bailey 2013; Rivera Colón 2009). In 1989, the Gay Men's Health Crisis, the largest HIV/AIDS prevention and care organization in New York City, responded by creating the House of Latex to do prevention and education in the Ballroom community, promoting sexual health among the House families and training members to become peer prevention specialists. Over time, the interaction among funding sources, community-based organizations, and the Ballroom community has become more widespread, and the House of Latex annually hosts the largest free Ball in the country, also attracting some Baltimore youths.

Yet Baltimore's own Ballroom community is less organized than its New York City counterpart, and unlike New York City, Baltimore has no history of cooperation between local HIV-prevention services and the community. In fact, the BCHD became aware of its existence only after STAR TRACK, a clinical care and prevention program connected to the University of Maryland, hosted a free mini-Ball in 2007. It would take three more years before Margaret hired Anthony, a community liaison, to start making inroads into the Ballroom scene. She told me about the infighting and the idea of getting some Houses a nonprofit status, which was quickly dropped "because they can't get their act together, and there's no point in putting money in something when they fight among themselves." As our conversation progressed, I got the feeling that the BCHD was less interested in investing in a vibrant and healthy community than in finding ways to secure the contagiousness of its individual members. When I asked Margaret about the value of the department's connection to the Ballroom community, she brought up the Free Ball it had recently sponsored at the Sheraton Inner Harbor Hotel:

> We found new cases of HIV there in November. But it's troublesome because it's very expensive. The Free Balls aren't free for us. But when you sponsor these events, then you got a hope of getting in there and getting some of them tested. Then when some of them test positive, you can get them into care, start the whole process. Our main focus is finding out who has HIV and getting them into care, and the only

way we can do that is by testing. It's absolutely prevention because if you can get their viral load down . . .

She didn't bother to finish her sentence, as if suggesting that we shared the biomedical knowledge that validates this particular approach to public health interventions. I could just as well have finished the sentence for her, because it is supposed to make perfect sense: when you lower people's viral load, you lower their infectiousness, which means that you lower the chances of HIV transmission. "They're walking time bombs for their own personal health," she said. "It's a twofold thing: we want to be compassionate about the person as well as the public health." But what about the space between the individual and the population? What about community, kinship, and social justice? Can the Ballroom scene expect some form of reciprocation on the side of the Health Department, something that can strengthen this Black queer community in its struggle to deal with a disease that has ravaged generations of House families, or is it merely expected to deliver new bodies for testing purposes?[3] And what happens after the House children are "taken to care"? "We're an interpoint [sic] for them," says Margaret. "We want to turn them over to a case manager that's going to be dealing with them through their illness. We basically try to get them to the door."[4] What concerns me in this chapter is this door and what transpires once one passes through it. In other words, I am interested in what happens to national prevention goals when they are scaled down to a plane of existence on which a public health "crisis" often feels less exceptional than ordinary, something commonly experienced as an extended impasse rather than an emergency. Moreover, I ask what conception of "life" circumscribes governmental and biomedical efforts designed to save it. I engage these questions through an examination of how Baltimore's HIV-prevention initiatives are courting the city's Ballroom community in an attempt to materialize their "target population" for testing. Previously ignored by municipal and medical institutions, members of the Ballroom community now find themselves addressed as responsible sexual citizens who are expected to protect their bodies as well as their loved ones by getting tested and making informed decisions about how to safely manage their "risk behaviors." However, these moralizing prevention messages about sexual health and safety starkly contrast the precarious environments that many Black queer youths are forced to navigate on a daily basis.

I begin with an overview of what has been heralded as the "new paradigm" in HIV prevention, which intensifies the institutional connections among testing, treatment, and clinical care, before examining how this paradigm is shaping

Baltimore's response to the ongoing epidemic. I then focus on the affective "cultural labor" of HIV prevention performed by members of the Ballroom community (M. Bailey 2013), demonstrating how the new prevention approach becomes a polyvalent object that attracts a host of optimistic investments in collective and individual prosperity, which nevertheless threaten to remain unrequited under the conditions of the established arrangement. This leads to a reflection on the fundamental incongruity between the biomedically defined life of the "Black MSM" as an epidemiological category captured by the national HIV-prevention apparatus and the collectively cultivated form of life that enables Ballroom community members to persevere under arduous circumstances. After assessing what is saved and what is sacrificed under the current Testing and Linkage to Care Plus (TLC+) regime, I close the chapter by suggesting a different take on HIV prevention, inspired by Ball culture's vernacular intimacies, care, and creativity.

A New Paradigm

Recent transformations in HIV prevention reflect a series of biomedical innovations that inform contemporary HIV/AIDS epidemiology. For example, a widely cited international clinical study corroborated previous trial-based evidence that antiretroviral therapy (ART) reduces the risk of HIV transmission in serodiscordant couples by lowering the viral load—and thereby the infectiousness—of the HIV-positive partner (Cohen et al. 2011), while other studies have demonstrated that early and wide-scale implementation of ART among people living with HIV/AIDS can significantly reduce HIV incidence in "high-risk populations" by suppressing so-called community viral loads (Das et al. 2010). An influential study that used mathematical modeling to predict the ostensible public health benefits of an extensive scale-up of HIV testing has further contributed to the appeal for Test and Treat and Treatment as Prevention approaches (Granich et al. 2009). These approaches, which focus on the identification, surveillance, and viral suppression of people living with HIV/AIDS and thus turn what used to be called secondary prevention into a primary objective, have been widely heralded as "game changers" (Stephenson 2010) that position us "at an important crossroads" (AIDS Foundation of Chicago et al. 2011) and represent "a tipping point in AIDS history" (Hofmann 2011). Indeed, as the Black AIDS Institute (2011: 77) proselytizes: "Some of the recent advances are so radical that they upend many historic assumptions about how to address AIDS. Indeed, to capitalize on these new tools, it will be necessary to adopt entirely new approaches to control the epidemic."

The most striking thing about claims such as this is their technocratic reasoning, in which the advent of "new tools" provides the rationale for adopting "entirely new approaches" against the backdrop of three decades of "disappointing results in HIV prevention" (Black AIDS Institute 2011: 77). While responses to the epidemic have always been driven by biomedical in(ter)ventions, and many of these ostensibly new tools and approaches should be seen as a continuation of earlier initiatives rather than as presenting a break, the current push to transform HIV prevention in light of new clinical outcomes should nevertheless be regarded as exceptional. This is warranted due to the unprecedented scale of the administrative infrastructure assembled to enact this "paradigm change," spearheaded by President Barack Obama's National HIV/AIDS Strategy (NHAS), which was revealed in July 2010 and is implemented through the CDC's new High Impact Prevention approach. Hailed as "the most comprehensive federal response to the domestic HIV epidemic to date" (Yehia and Frank 2011: e4), the NHAS represents an extensive biopolitical intervention into the existing public health infrastructure dealing with HIV/AIDS. To realize its three main goals (reducing the number of people who become infected with HIV, increasing access to care and optimizing health outcomes for people living with HIV, and reducing HIV-related health disparities), the strategy aims to reorganize and tighten the relationships among prevention, treatment, and medical care, as well as focusing the available resources on areas most affected by the epidemic. While it is careful to avoid some of the negative connotations attached to the Test and Treat moniker, the TLC+ (the plus sign referring to treatment) that has informed many of the policy directives included in the NHAS nevertheless emphasizes the importance of clinically driven viral management, facilitated by expansive testing initiatives and the provision of treatment adherence counseling to people living with HIV/AIDS.[5]

This becomes more concrete when we look at how the CDC advances the NHAS through the High Impact Prevention approach, which mobilizes "scalable, cost-effective interventions with demonstrated potential to reduce new infections, in the right populations" (Centers for Disease Control and Prevention 2011). Structured as a five-year HIV-prevention funding opportunity for health departments in states, territories, and select cities, the approach is designed to allocate "core HIV prevention resources" in a way that better matches the "geographic burden of the U.S. epidemic today" (ibid.). In addition to increasing the number of cities eligible for direct funding, as opposed to indirect funding via the state, this entails the provision of guidelines that stipulate which specific prevention interventions should be prioritized. In this way, the federal government has inaugurated a system that expands its power at the expense of state and local governments' decision-making capacities, which are now delineated through national funding criteria. The prevention activities that deserve priority, according to the CDC, largely follow the new rationale prescribed by TLC+, which combines a more aggressive approach to testing with an intensification of the links among prevention, treatment, and "care."[6]

In Baltimore, the trajectory of the HIV/AIDS epidemic is starkly delineated by the racial boundaries that historically have segregated the city. The areas most affected by HIV consist of some of the city's poorest and most underserved neighborhoods—such as those surrounding Johns Hopkins's Medical Campus, discussed in Chapter 1—which are primarily inhabited by African Americans, who constitute 64 percent of Baltimore's population while accounting for close to 90 percent of the city's HIV and AIDS cases (German and Latkin 2012).[7] In addition to a high concentration of HIV infections, these neighborhoods suffer from compounded problems informed by drug addiction, gang-related and domestic violence, homelessness, unemployment, incarceration, and a lack of access to health care, resulting in elevated rates of obesity, heart disease, diabetes, hepatitis C, and syphilis (see, e.g., Cohn 2010; Walsh 2010). It is under these conditions of pervasive racial disparities in health and safety that a generalized epidemic among African Americans has been able to take hold of the city, which had the nation's second highest number of AIDS case reports in 2006 and continues to be one of the most heavily HIV-burdened urban areas in the United States (German and Latkin 2012; Hall et al. 2010). Baltimore's epidemic was predominantly driven by injection drug use, but as a result of the city's successful needle exchange program, heterosexual transmission has become the dominant mode of infection (Hall et al. 2010). However, due to the perceived epidemiological overlap between Black "high-risk heterosexuals" and men who have sex with men (MSM), as well as the rapid increase in HIV infections among MSM over the past years, the federal response to the city's epidemic remains largely guided by concerns about the "unsafe behaviors" and infectious bodies of "Black MSM."

Right before I started my fieldwork, in September 2010, the CDC provided funding to IDEHA to develop an Enhanced Comprehensive HIV Prevention Plan (ECHPP) for the Baltimore-Towson metropolitan area to identify "the optimal combination of coordinated HIV prevention, care, and treatment services" that would lead to a reduction of new HIV infections in the region (Infectious Disease and Environmental Health Administration 2011). The development of the ECHPP, which was the first federal effort to implement the national goals of the recently launched NHAS in Baltimore, was largely prompted by a local longitudinal study reporting rates of unrecognized HIV infection among the city's "Black MSM population" that far exceeded national incidence rates (German et al. 2011).[8] According to one IDEHA employee, the outcomes of the study were considered so alarming that the CDC prioritized the City of Baltimore's eligibility for direct funding at the start of the 2012 fiscal year. Less than a year after it funded IDEHA to develop the ECHPP, the CDC thereby effectively sidelined the State of Maryland and transferred authority over all future HIV interventions in Baltimore to its Health Department, albeit under the strictures of the High Impact Prevention guidelines that aim to strengthen the CDC's core strategy: TLC+.

Despite its administrative shakeup, this development did little to change the sedimented power relations in Baltimore's highly research-driven prevention system, with Johns Hopkins University and the University of Maryland serving as important "community partners" running clinical services and behavioral surveillance studies that double as prevention interventions. Aside from the historically dominant position of Johns Hopkins University, particularly its medical facilities and School of Public Health, the shape of the city's HIV-prevention landscape can be attributed to the "post-crisis" climate that emerged globally in the wake of the biomedical normalization of HIV/AIDS as a more-or-less manageable chronic condition in the late 1990s (Race 2001). This, together with a shift from the epidemic's close association with white male homosexuality to a situation in which (heterosexual) men and women of color have become the public face of the HIV/AIDS crisis (Fenton 2007; Hall et al. 2010), has contributed to a national decline in the number of white gays and lesbians engaged in community advocacy and activism. In Baltimore, community-based organizations have not had much institutional power at least since the bankruptcy of HERO in 2008. None of the underfunded and understaffed community-based organizations (such as the GLCCB, Baltimore Black Pride, the Portal/BMX, and AIDS Action Baltimore) had sufficient resources to independently develop alternative outreach activities that could scale, while Equality Maryland (the state's largest civil rights organization) was preoccupied with its campaign to get gay marriage approved in the State Assembly. This has created an environment in which HIV/AIDS prevention and care are largely left to the two research universities and the BCHD, which recruit their own community liaisons and convene various coordination groups for service providers, like the one I attended at IDEHA. As mentioned earlier, the organizations represented there were often vying for the same scarce funding opportunities, which was a recurring source of frustration for many providers and community members.

The Ambiguities of Peer Outreach

Some months before my arrival in Baltimore, the Health Department hired Anthony to establish sustainable connections with the Ballroom community. A friend had forwarded the job posting, thinking the position would fit him like a glove, given that he is an active House member who regularly participates in Balls and because he would talk a lot about what the city needed to do better in terms of serving its African American youth. At twenty-five, Anthony had already accumulated a lot of experience doing public work, and it showed in the confident way he carried himself. He told me, not without a sense of pride, that he worked as a youth commissioner for the Mayor's Office around the time he was finishing high school, focusing on health issues, which "kind of put a spark" in him and led to a number of other volunteer jobs for the city. "I just really wanted to help the community. I really wanted to do something. At first I started out doing youth development and then juvenile justice works, which led me to education and then education led to—. So I basically volunteered everywhere around the city." At the time there weren't many young Black community leaders who would speak out publicly on important issues because they felt their voices weren't heard, which was something he wanted to change. One issue on the top of his list was the HIV epidemic among Black gay and SGL youth, which up to that point had received insufficient attention from the city, as well as from the community itself. "Nobody knew what was going on," he said. "It was, like, OK, everybody knew someone who was infected with HIV, but there really wasn't too much talk about building resources or anything. . . . There kind of wasn't any talk at all; it was kind of taboo. It was kind of like . . . you know what's going on but you didn't talk about it." This impasse hit close to home when two of his good friends and two family members who were gay and around his age were all diagnosed with HIV within a short period of time. After he had somewhat processed these events, he decided to really get involved and joined the city's Commission on HIV/AIDS while also volunteering as an outreach worker for the BCHD. By the time he applied for his current paid job, Anthony was thus more than qualified.

You could call Anthony a "trust broker," someone dedicated to the cultivation of spaces and relationships built on trust. This has taken a lot of work, however, and many of his initial efforts were focused on what he saw as "damage control." Given Baltimore's intense racial disparities in healthcare access and the structural abandonment experienced by the majority of its African American inhabitants in general, and its Black queer residents in particular, many have lost their faith in governmental and medical institutions: "So, you know, taking all those negative things that people have thought about all the time and trying to turn it around and say, 'That's not true, and this is why,' that's the hard part of changing people's minds and opinions." One of the recent avenues for Anthony's mission to promote the BCHD in the community is his mediation between department and the Baltimore Ballroom Coalition, a loosely organized assembly of fathers and mothers representing the different Houses in the city. With their help, he organized the BCHD's first free Ball, modeled on New York's Latex Ball and likewise centered on HIV-prevention messages. It was a huge success, especially in terms of turnout and testing, with more than five hundred youths in attendance. One of the service providers with a table that night was the prevention program that had hosted the first free HIV-themed Ball three years earlier. When I asked Anthony why the BCHD had refrained from collaborating with the program in organizing its Ball, given the opportunity to share resources, he suddenly seemed annoyed. Perhaps I shouldn't have talked about "reinventing the wheel," because he seemed particularly irked by that wording. "I don't believe we were reinventing the wheel at all," he said. "Also, our Ball was more of a Ball/conference. It wasn't just a Ball. Like, we also had, you know, we had testing going on. As soon as you came up the escalator, it was like, 'Hey, come on,' you know?"

His effort to dissociate the BCHD's Ball from its predecessor is emblematic of the fragmented and competitive HIV-prevention landscape in Baltimore. This time, the BCHD seemed to have won the favor of the community. "With the partnership we have now, you know, if there's a major Ball coming up, we are asked to do testing," Anthony said, "and if there's events coming up, we are asked to do testing, as well, or provide information. And that shows that people are really pushing for our services." I mentioned the emphasis on testing and asked whether he thought the relationship between the BCHD and the Ballroom community was one-sided, with community mainly functioning as a site for data collection and surveillance. His slightly evasive answer suggested the extent to which peer outreach work is limited by a biomedical prevention approach invested in viral containment and managed care: "No matter how you look at it, you do need to get tested. It's for your own good, so it's not a one-way street. And most of the things we do, we invite community members to help plan, to try to be a part of it.

And then we offer free linkage to care. We help people with their doctor's appointments. We even give incentives to get tested." He was bothered by the fact that, unlike Johns Hopkins, which paid study participants $50 to complete a survey and take an anonymous HIV test, the BCHD could offer only T-shirts and $5 Safeway gift cards. This tied in to his more general frustration with the lack of resources he confronted, which he illustrated this way: "When you're there in the ocean, you may just see a tip of the iceberg, and that tip may be HIV, but you have to think [that] what's under that tip is a whole range of issues . . . , because it's just so much. . . . I wish there's more that I can do." Despite these discontents, Anthony loved his job. Accomplishing change in his community, even within the given limitations, is what drove him. He saw the need every day that he went out and talked to his peers, for whom the Ballroom scene in many cases provided shelter from violence and exclusion. He said, "So what happens is, lots of times, [there are] these kids that may be put out of their house at the age of thirteen or fourteen, and then they have to support themselves, which often leads to prostitution and things like that. Now these people, being young, they're still in need of parental guidance. They don't get it from their real parents, so they seek it from people in the Ballroom scene. . . . So it's a safe space to grow, but it can be hard, because they really don't trust too many people."

Building this trust, as a House father and a mentor, is what Anthony's friend Deon does daily. Now thirty-six, Deon got involved with the Ballroom community at age twenty. He had his "transition into the gay life," as he called it, a year earlier, right after he finished high school. He thought of himself as a "spoiled brat" back then in the sense that his parents continued to love and accept him after he told them he was gay, he said, but also because nobody could tell him what to do. He thought he knew everything, and wasn't really receptive to others, but he also felt a little lost. "You know, it took an army of positive people to show me a different way," he said. "I had a lot of guidance. People gave me a chance and never gave up on me. This is why I have to do the same for others." Many of the people who took him under their wing were involved in the Ballroom scene, which led him first to attend, and after a while to participate in, Balls. His category of choice was Realness—in particular, Butch Queen Realness—because he was attracted to the idea of being able to pass as a straight man when walking down the street. The expression of masculinity, in the multiple forms available to him, is a very prominent concern for Deon. In his view, being a man means taking responsibility for yourself and your family, however defined: "Like, I raised a family, almost, so I had to be a man first and foremost. You know, I might be a gay Black man, but *I am a man*. It comes with a lot of responsibilities to be a really grown man." Deon is talking about his House family here. When he became Legendary—the highest social status in Baltimore's Ball scene—young kids started following him around, asking questions, which eventually led him to take on the role of father of the House he represented. As much as he loved this role, he admitted that it consumes a lot of time, creative energy, and money: "It takes a lot of time helping my House family, my kids, keeping them organized and keeping the House organized, making sure they have their meetings, everything a father should do. And most people make their own outfits, so it's a big creative process." What a father "should do" is something that Deon learned from his own House father: "My father actually is the one that helped me to grow into a better man. Like, he installed a lot of positive feedback in me. He showed me that anything is possible as long as you put in the hard work."

This positivity and affirmation is now central to how Deon raises his House kids, who, he said, he teaches to love themselves no matter what: "You can't love nobody else unless you love yourself. Always understand your worth. You are worth more than society is pointing at you saying 'that's all you're gonna be,' you know what I'm saying? Know your worth, that's what I always install in them. Like, never give up on anything that you wanna accomplish." In his book-length study of Detroit's Ballroom community, Marlon Bailey (2013: 19) argues that when members of the Ballroom scene engage in what he calls "kin labor," which is part of a broader spectrum of queer cultural labor dedicated to "care, service, critique, and competition," they are performing the indispensable work of maintaining family and community ties, otherwise composed. As he writes: "Conditions of marginalization within and exclusion from Black communities and society necessitate an alternative terrain for members of the Ballroom community" (ibid.). Building this terrain, generation after generation, is hard work, as Deon could attest: he even had to take a yearlong break so that he could focus on his relationship. It is also work that thus far has received little appreciation, either in the form of remuneration or scholarly attention. Still, Deon said he kept going because he knew that, without the support structures he and his peers continued to compose, Black queer youth would have few places to go. He had already witnessed too many homeless kids roaming around the city and continued to believe in the truth of his House father's words that "anything is possible as long as you put in the hard work." So he was proud of how well structured and "family oriented" his House was, pointing out that some other Houses lacked this kind of commitment. "Most of those Houses, most people are together that way because they get high together," he said, something he disapproved of because he had seen how it could lead kids to prostitute themselves in exchange for drugs and thereby put themselves at risk of becoming infected. Marijuana was allowed in his House, but nothing stronger.

Deon was also a member of the Ballroom Coalition. The reason for coming together, he claimed, was "to try to bring more positivity back, more fun, more of the— [Trying to] stop some of the unnecessary stuff that's going on here in Baltimore, the fighting, the stigma. The whole point of the coalition is to put Baltimore back on the map." He supported Anthony's work because he felt it allowed them to accomplish these goals. He didn't like to think of the Ballroom community as a target population and instead preferred the term "empowerment movement." "I don't look at it from [the BCHD's] perspective," he said. "I look at the community aspect, because in this day and age, we need outlets, we need *something*, and I commend people who're putting forth efforts to try to make a difference." As I was in my interactions with Anthony, I was struck by the unremitting sense of optimism and hope that inflected Deon's words in the face of so many obstacles, the most pertinent of which were nearly always financial. "We don't have the funding, we don't have the outlets, but, like, that's why I love Anthony," Deon said. "He's a go-getter. We keep saying, 'We're gonna make a difference.'" Yet when it came to his own contributions, he was less optimistic and realized the institutional limitations: "The only thing I can offer really is more strength in numbers as far as testing and knowledge. . . . We offer them gift cards, Safeway cards, you know, because some people can't afford food. But it's also about knowing how to talk to people, how to feel the vibe." As a House father, Deon has learned how to feel the vibe, how to perform the affective labor of mentorship and teach boys how to be proud Black gay men. In his role as a volunteer, he draws on this tacit knowledge when delivering prevention messages and connecting youth to service providers. He mentioned that he wouldn't mind working in HIV prevention professionally, like Anthony. It would definitely mean more money, and he liked the work. Anthony was trying to get him a job with the BCHD, but he hadn't heard back from the department during the time I was speaking with him.

For many members of Baltimore's Ballroom community, finding employment in the field of HIV prevention provides an attractive alternative to unemployment or a minimum wage job. Yet given the abiding lack of funding for community-based prevention work, these positions remain scarce. Marlon, who was twenty-three and identified as SGL, was keenly aware of this and considered himself lucky. Many of his friends had been asking him to hook them up with a job at one of the organizations he worked for, but it was hard to get a foot in the door. In addition to being an outreach worker at a clinical care and prevention program run out of the University of Maryland, Marlon worked for Black Men's Xchange and was starting a new job as a recruiter for a Johns Hopkins study, where he would be taking surveys and doing testing. Nearly all of his time went into prevention work, and he often felt exhausted, but he was not complaining. A gregarious person who loved to be the center of attention, Marlon enjoyed all of the opportunities he had to socialize with his peers, many of whom were his friends, and he said his activities often didn't feel like work at all. Also, he said, his life was so much better than it had been a few years earlier. Like many other young Black gay and bisexual men, Marlon was thrown out of his home by his mother and stepfather at an early age, and for about a year he struggled to retain a roof over his head. After many months of sleeping on different couches in various cities across Maryland and, when he had to move out again but wasn't able to find a new host via Facebook, spending some nights in public parks, he hitched a ride to Baltimore to stay with a man he met online and had talked to by phone a couple of times. This was a sketchy move, he admitted, but since the man lived with his mother, Marlon figured the situation was safe enough. And it was, at least for six months, before the man started touching Marlon against his will, and he knew he had to leave that house. From there, he moved around a number of times, roaming West Baltimore neighborhoods that initially scared him but that he eventually got used to. "I had to adapt," he said. "I had no choice. I had nowhere else to go." While in perpetual transit he managed to keep his job at a clothing store, which he got when he moved to Baltimore, but it was very difficult for him to do so because he was dealing with such an insecure and chaotic personal situation. Then one day, while sitting on a bus on his way to work, he began conversing with another young SGL man who was active in the Ball community and did prevention work for the University of Maryland. They hit it off, and Marlon was invited to attend a meeting, which opened up a new world. He immediately applied for a vacant position and got the job. Shortly after that, he moved in with his new colleague, who is now also his roommate, although they are really more like brothers.

Marlon was optimistic about his future and trying to decide what was next for him. "What I really wanna do in life is I wanna be a choreographer," he said. "I want to be a dancer and choreographer, but I love the community. I love love love helping the community! . . . This [prevention] work, I could see it as being a career for me. Because I already said I'm twenty-three; I'm tired of having a job, [and] I wanna start a career." A colleague was trying to help him combine his two professional aspirations by having him perform at outreach events across town, which Marlon had done six times when I met him, and on each occasion he had received a lot of praise and positive feedback. I saw him perform twice and thought he was great, but when I spoke with him afterward, he told me that all of his gigs had been unpaid. He couldn't ask the community for money because he knew how cash-strapped everyone was, and even though he didn't mind performing for free, it was making him rethink his chances of starting a career as a dancer or choreographer. He would eventually have to make a career decision, and all signs were pointing in the direction of prevention work. During one of our last conversations, I asked him for his thoughts on the mobilization of (former) Ballroom members like himself by service providers such as BCHD and Johns Hopkins, to which he responded with a frank analysis:

> At first, they [Ball kids] didn't see community activists who looked like them, and they were like, "Why are they here? We're not test subjects." But with younger people, when they see us, it's more something like, "OK, if you're involved with it, it must not be so bad." With older people, they just walk right past you, but when it's us, they are more prone to listen, or take a test or a survey. But I actually call it manipulation because it's still the same thing, but more so. . . . I am conscious of it, but I know it needs to happen. Yes, it's wrong to manipulate somebody, but sometimes a little manipulation can help.

Marlon clearly felt ambivalent about the current prevention model. While he, like others involved in peer outreach, was committed to TLC+ and believed that venue-based testing would prevent new infections in the community, he was also skeptical about its increasing ubiquity. He repeatedly stressed that the most important aspect of peer prevention was the continuing guidance on issues such as safer sex, but in a way that engages with the specific needs and circumstances of the youths who associate with and through the Ball community. "There doesn't always need to be testing," he said. "That's just gonna push them away, because HIV is not the only issue on our list."

It is tempting to argue that Anthony, Deon, Marlon—none of whom has HIV—are merely being used to meet the testing quotas set by the CDC, which has designated Baltimore one of its primary sites to test-drive the national TLC+ approach. Yet even though this may be the case, it certainly does not *feel* this way to them, not because they have been duped or cannot see "the bigger picture," but because it reveals something about the complex situation in which they find themselves and from which they need to navigate their often incremental next steps. Frequently they have to just roll with the punches, something that everyone—including Margaret—is growing accustomed to but that also continues to generate contradictory and ambiguous feelings. For many outreach workers, especially those without high school diplomas or college degrees, employment in the field of HIV prevention provides a measure of access to a stable, ordinary life without the constant pressures of survival by way of minimum wage service jobs or other, more informal economic activities such as prostitution and the drug trade. From the perspective of social status, it also enables them to gain a sense of recognition and value that comes with being part of a professional workforce, especially when the labor performed serves a humanitarian purpose. Beyond the realm of individual prosperity, a job as peer outreach worker provides members of the Ballroom scene with an opportunity to relate to their community in a different register, reaching out to friends and relatives who are stuck in some of the same debilitating situations that once trapped them. In other words, it holds out the promise of being able to give back to the community that has offered them a safe haven and a creative outlet for the pressures of being Black, queer, and poor in America. A job in prevention might provide them with ways to contribute to the health of their community, even if "health" just means the absence of HIV.

We can thus see how the TLC+ model comes to function as a multivalent promissory object that is able to absorb many different optimistic attachments and investments, such as the hope for better health, better reciprocity, better community, better recognition, better agency—in sum, a better life. When Deon preferred to see his community as an "empowerment movement" rather than as a target population and welcomed the BCHD because, as he said, "in this day and age, we need outlets, we need *something*," he was not being naïve or misguided but insisted on negotiating the potential good(s) that such a new connection might deliver. The chance that the BCHD's involvement might improve the integrity, well-being, and image of his community was something he could not afford to detach himself from, regardless of the particular means used to achieve the end. This does not mean that the means were irrelevant to Deon or to his friends and colleagues, who were all sincerely invested in the biomedical prevention model that posits TLC+ as the only viable option for stopping the spread of HIV/AIDS in their community. Yet it is the form, or structure, of the optimistic attachment, rather than its content, that granted it its adhesive power. As Lauren Berlant (2011a: 48) writes, "Any object of optimism promises to guarantee the endurance of something, the survival of something, the flourishing of something, and above all the protection of the desire that made this object or scene powerful enough to have magnetized an attachment to it." For Berlant, however, an optimistic attachment becomes cruel when "the object/scene of desire is itself an obstacle to fulfilling the very wants that bring people to it: but its life-organizing status can trump interfering with the damage it provokes" (Berlant 2011a: 227). I believe that her notion of cruel optimism can help us to better understand how the new HIV-prevention paradigm, with its expanded and intensified emphasis on viral containment, is able to mobilize members of previously neglected "high-risk populations" such as the Ballroom community. Deon's and Anthony's attempts to support their community are often frustrated by a lack of funding and other resources, which is a direct result of the prioritization of prevention activities guided by TLC+ that focus on epidemiological surveillance and individual risk management. But despite this recurring impediment to their world-making efforts, the optimism of their attachment to this very model is not easily relinquished, because such an interruption would threaten to collapse the cluster of affective investments that constitutes the infrastructure of their unrelenting drive toward ensuring a healthier and more vibrant future for themselves and their community. Although they frequently feel conflicted about the shortcomings of the TLC+ approach, they cannot give up on its life-sustaining promise and the resources it makes available; compromised world building is still better than no world building at all.

Life—Sacred and Abandoned

"Compromised world building is still better than no world building at all" would actually be a fitting subtext for HIV Stops with Me (HSWM), a multifaceted national social marketing campaign that has been running since 2000 but did not reach Baltimore until May 2011, where it focuses exclusively on Black gay and bisexual men. As its website states, the campaign's aim is to "prevent the spread of HIV while also reducing the stigma associated with the disease. The campaign features real HIV positive people talking about real issues" (HIV Stops with Me 2011). But what exactly is the reality promoted through this campaign (which is one of the CDC's best-evaluated HIV-prevention campaigns and has won a Webby award for Best Health Website)? At its core, the HSWM campaign addresses people living with HIV/AIDS as the most crucial node in their respective social and sexual networks, encouraging them to take responsibility for stopping the transmission of the virus by protecting themselves and, by proxy, their partners and communities. This is illustrated by the theme of the most recent phase of the campaign in Baltimore, which uses the slogan "We're Still Here, Still Taking Care of Ourselves, Still Protecting You" to emphasize the presumed causal direction of effective prevention: from the HIV-infected individual outward to the community. In this prevention rationale, rooted in biomedical science and technology, the onus of halting the spread of HIV is on those who are already infected, who have a responsibility for keeping their viral load down to the status of "undetectable" (Race 2001). When treatment is prevention, as is suggested here, the individual management of risk through viral suppression becomes the most efficacious and laudable measure of sexual citizenship.[9] But where does this immunitary logic of viral containment leave those who are not infected yet are persistently exposed to the normalized presence of HIV? As the fight against HIV is led by people living with HIV/AIDS who are "empowered" to protect the life of their community by insulating their bodies with various forms of prophylaxis (e.g., antiretroviral drugs, condoms), the resources that could increase the agency of Black queer youth who remain uninfected are severely diminished. Moreover, what kind of life is being protected here, exactly?

I argue that the TLC+ approach and the HSWM campaign embody a contemporary biomedical iteration of the paradigm of immunization that, according to Roberto Esposito, inaugurated modernity as an all-encompassing apparatus orchestrated to deal with the perennial problem of life's preservation.[10] In Esposito's reading, this problem always contains its own ineradicable negativity, since "immunization is a negative [form] of the protection of life. It saves, insures, and preserves the organism, either individual or collective, to which it pertains, but it does not do so directly, immediately or frontally; on the contrary, it subjects the organism to a condition that simultaneously negates or reduces its power to expand" (Esposito 2008: 46). The immunitary protection of life is thus a fundamentally paradoxical and precarious endeavor, also when it pertains to the life of a community: "To survive, the community, every community, is forced to introject the negative modality of its opposite, even if the opposite remains precisely a lacking and contrastive mode of being of the community itself" (Esposito 2008: 52).[11] This profound ambiguity is intimately familiar to my interlocutors, from community icons such as Carlton to relative newcomers such as Marlon, for whom TLC+ represents an appealing *pharmakon* whose effects are nevertheless impossible to gauge in advance: will it save or sacrifice their community? As my research progressed, the latter possibility started to seem increasingly plausible.

I also became increasingly aware of the need to situate Esposito's sweeping account geo-historically: to position the paradigm of immunization and the modernity it created within the history and afterlife of slavery in the United States and to acknowledge their roots in a plantation apparatus devised for modes of anti-Black capture, containment, and dispossession that continue to haunt the fabric of cities such as Baltimore. As it inaugurated an incipient modernity, the deeply racialized and racializing paradigm of immunization was itself predicated and cultivated on the plantation, which is to say that, as Alexander Weheliye (2014: 38) writes, "Racial slavery represents the biopolitical nomos of modernity." Conceiving of the plantation as the biopolitical *topos/nomos* of modernity affords a critical lens for analyzing how the racialized logics of immunity, ambiguity, and superfluity shape not just Baltimore's spatial organization—examined in the previous chapter—but also the federal HIV-prevention policies and campaigns the city has adopted/adapted. Just as it has a past, the plantation has a present and a future, all of which are entangled. Katherine McKittrick's (2013: 2–3) notion of "plantation futures" sensitizes us to this entanglement in that it "tracks the plantation toward the prison and the impoverished and destroyed city sectors and, consequently, brings into sharp focus the ways the plantation is an ongoing locus of anti-Black violence and death that can no longer analytically sustain this violence." At the same time, however, the notion of plantation futures also impels us to imagine and generate other futures in which Black life is not defeated by the violence perpetrated against it and continues to forge alternative modes of care, belonging, and well-being by *working through and against* the conditions realized by this violence (ibid.: 10–15). Imagining and creating such futures is what the Ballroom community, at its best, is about. Outreach workers such as Anthony, Deon, and Marlon know this, they *feel* this, which is why they continue to welcome any support they can get, despite the potential violence it may do to their peers.

On different occasions, Margaret expressed excitement about a new local campaign that would replace (or augment—she seemed not to be sure) the HSWM campaign in Baltimore at the start of 2012. Called "Status Update," it specifically targeted Black queer youth affiliated with the Ballroom community by playing on the double meaning of the term "status" as a position defined by both the HIV test and the social hierarchy of the Ball scene. In an effort to reduce the high number of unrecognized HIV infections among young Black MSM, the campaign aimed to raise awareness about the importance of getting tested by evoking an affective association between Ballroom status, as an object of intense investment, and HIV status. According to Margaret, it would mainly revolve around a Facebook page with information about the local Ballroom scene and places to get tested, which would be moderated by community members. "It will be social, with the health slid in there," she said. "It's not going to be like HIV Stops with Me, because it's going to be less noticeable. It will be more of an underground marketing campaign." Aside from its different mode of affective capture, Status Update was unlike the HSWM campaign in that it focused on youth and young adults considered "at risk" for HIV infection rather than on those already infected. There are, however, important similarities between the HSWM campaign and Status Update, whose launch augmented the national Testing Makes Us Stronger campaign, funded by the CDC, that had recently been rolled out.[12] Like its predecessor, Status Update made a strong moral appeal to Black queer youth to take responsibility for their own health, as well as the health of their community. Sexual intimacy here is primarily viewed as a risky sphere requiring careful scrutiny and management rather than as a source of creativity that can combine pleasure with health and well-being. Furthermore, both campaigns mobilize a reductively narrow conception of "health" as essentially the absence of HIV viral load, either in individual bodies or on the "community level." In the case of the HSWM campaign, an emphasis on longevity through viral suppression often veils the attritional effects that still accompany many antiretroviral drugs, while Status Update implicitly equates a "negative" status with the achievement of a healthy body.

Again, I wonder what other forms of health, care, and agency are available to uninfected youth in this particular prevention model—forms that exceed getting tested (and getting tested again). Paradoxically, many of these youths are unable to access even the most basic health-care and social services, while their HIV-positive peers receive these services free of charge or at low cost due to the entitlement rights associated with their illness. Case workers told me that this lack of access had even motivated some of their clients to intentionally contract HIV; at least this way they would get some health insurance. Here we can discern at once the practical necessity and the severe limitations of what has come to be known as "biological citizenship" (Petryna 2002) or "therapeutic citizenship" (Nguyen 2010), where rights claims and responsibilities are derived from an individual's biological impairment, whether it is a sustained injury or a chronic illness such as HIV/AIDS. Although this mode of biopolitical citizenship affords entitlements that provide a level of social and somatic security otherwise unavailable to the dispossessed and outcast, the act of politicizing the biologically damaged body and thus making it available to governmental capture and regulation excludes those who do not share the biomedical condition on which these entitlements are founded.[13] Within the present context, this means that the Health Department's TLC+ approach to HIV prevention, whose main biopolitical concern pertains to the rights (e.g., to medical care and treatment) and responsibilities (e.g., treatment adherence, self-monitoring) of youth who test positive, fails to provide a viable infrastructure that allows for creative and enduring interventions *for* and *by* youth who have managed to remain uninfected. Insofar as members of the Ballroom community retain their negative status and are unable to find employment as peer outreach workers, they find themselves in a liminal space where they are both hailed and abandonment as the state encroaches on their biological life while withdrawing from the environments that both violate and nourish it.[14] Unable to make claims predicated on the need for managed HIV care, their only other means of access to civil society's legal and medical provisions is to offer up their (still) uninfected yet risk-infused bodies as speculative objects for clinical surveillance, turning their blood into a tenuous form of biocapital that will have increasingly little value as it becomes more abundant when the TLC+ approach reaches scale (Opondo 2015).[15] Immunity, ambiguity, superfluity: these are the features of the plantation logic that drives TLC+. Yet as Marlon kept reminding me, HIV is merely one of the many problems facing his community, and it is not the most acutely demanding. Homelessness, unemployment, police harassment, and homophobia are much more immediate threats, which tend to overwhelm one's capacity to attend to more creeping dangers. Moreover, with respect to HIV-positive youth, these threats severely limit what is perhaps the most pivotal aspect of TLC+: treatment adherence. To quote Marlon: "It's hard to take your medication when you don't have a roof over your head, or when there's nothing to eat."

To be sure, treatment can be a valuable component of HIV prevention, and given the high rates of unrecognized infection among Black queer youth, it would be injudicious to deny the importance of targeted testing initiatives. Neither am I necessarily opposed to the fact that service providers are taking an interest in Black queer communities such as the Ballroom scene. However, this involvement becomes problematic when it is unilateral and devoid of structural investments that benefit the well-being of the Ball community *as a collective.* As I have been suggesting, there is an incongruity between the kind of life— and, by extension, the kind of health, care, intimacy, and citizenship—that the U.S. government seeks to preserve through its immunitary HIV-prevention policies and the form of life constitutive of the Ballroom community in all of its cultural specificity and splendor. That this discrepancy is fundamentally about different racialized conceptions of the meaning and value of life is something that Deon, Marlon, and Anthony experience daily as they struggle to procure funding for their world-making efforts. At stake in the biomedical-*cum*-humanitarian rationale driving Baltimore's HIV/AIDS governmentality is "the sacredness of life as such," whose securitization and preservation are of the highest value (Fassin 2009: 50). As Gil Anidjar (2011: 716) writes, echoing Hannah Arendt, this is a modern understanding "according to which life—sacred life—is institutionalized as biological and where the survivor has long become the ultimate political ideal, the ideal (life above all) whereby the world is not what must be made through political action but what must rather be survived." While Anidjar offers a crucial insight here, he fails to appreciate how the life of the survivor is always already caught up in the violence of biopolitical racism. Instead, he asserts that life, within this understanding, "is sacred even if (and perhaps precisely because, precisely when) it is bare of all attributes, political or others, and utterly abandoned" (Anidjar 2011: 716), which seems to suggest that once life is fully rendered disposable, it transcends racial, sexual, and gender specificity. In contrast, I am arguing that the epidemiological capture of the racial, sexual, and gender specificity of Baltimore's Ballroom youth, abstracted into the category "Black MSM," is exactly what enables the biopolitical production of Black queer life as "at once sacred and abandoned" (Anidjar 2011: 723). While saving the species life of "Black MSM," the immunitary strategies of TLC+ sacrifice the Ballroom community's particular, complex, precarious yet enduring *form of life*. Here, too, we should heed Esposito's (2010a: 33) warning: "Sacrificing life to its preservation is the only way of containing the threat that menaces life. Yet this is the equivalent of preserving and perpetuating as well life's capacity to be sacrificed; to 'normalize' the possibility if not the reality, of its sacrifice."

From Lifesaving to World Making

So what about this rich form of life that animates Baltimore's Ballroom community and that elicits so much affective investment from its members? How does its formation manifest itself, and how might it provoke us to rethink the value and meaning of concepts such as health, care, intimacy, and citizenship beyond their respective associations with individual rights, surveillance, risk, and biology? Finally, are there ways to harness the vibrant and creative forms of expression—the "performance labor" so characteristic of Ballroom culture (M. Bailey 2013)—for engagements with HIV prevention that offer an alternative to the current paradigm of immunization? For a provisional answer to these questions, I want to turn to a place that may initially seem to hold little promise: the Sheraton Inner Harbor Hotel, located in the heart of Baltimore's most ambitious project of neoliberal urban revitalization. As previously mentioned, this location was the unlikely (and, one could argue, unseemly) host of the Free Ball sponsored by the Baltimore City Health Department on November 20, 2010. While its purpose was to gather the members of the Baltimore Houses and other affiliated youth under one roof to "raise awareness" about HIV/AIDS and provide them with the opportunity to get tested, the event exceeded these intentions, and those present that night could catch a glimpse of something far more capacious and radical.

Riding up the Sheraton escalator, the first thing I noticed was the large number of service providers who had lined up, table by table, in the second floor lobby. Clearly, the BCHD had used its resources to widely promote its first Free Ball, and the promise of having hundreds of "young Black MSM" in one place proved to be a compelling incentive for the many organizations that came out that Saturday night. I spent the first hour or so roaming around the lobby and collecting booklets from the different tables, meanwhile scanning the space for familiar faces. Later than planned, but still with few people in attendance, the Ball was opened by the two emcees—called Commentators—who took turns paying tribute to the Legends and Statements present that evening. As they walked to the center of the dance floor and gave away a brief performance to exhibit their widely respected skills, each received obligatory and rather lukewarm applause from the slowly accumulating crowd of spectators. The various messages about safe sex, testing, and available health-care services, dutifully delivered by the Commentators, were welcomed with a similarly underwhelmed response. Most of the youth seemed preoccupied with other things, such as socializing over the free snacks that were strategically placed at the entrance of the main hall, which now functioned as one of the spots for the exchange of hugs, gossip, accessories, and other tokens of affection. Perhaps it had to do with the formal and restrained ambiance of the Sheraton Hotel, or maybe it was the oversized hall that allowed people to spread around, but it took a few hours—and several categories—before the Ball really got started. When it did, the now extensive crowd of mostly Black queer youth amassed around the dance floor to loudly support their family members or participate in one of the categories themselves. The atmosphere quickly turned dense.

Each battle, in which competitors contend for cash prizes in many categories, is an intense event that evokes the passionate and sometimes caustic exchange of commentary among the Commentators, the judges, and the audience, who all are deeply invested in scrutinizing the performances and the performers. Propelled by the boisterous house music, with its deep bass thumps that resonated throughout my body, the Commentators heightened the intensity by rhythmically commanding the DJ and competitors to "gimme that, gimme that, gimme that vibe! Gimme that, gimme that, gimme that vibe! Gimme that, gimme that, gimme that vibe! I, want, tha *VIBE!*" In response, the DJ pumped up the volume, and the competitors showed their best moves as they walked, coiled, stretched, vogued, threw their bodies to the floor, and displayed the most stylized hand gestures to please the judges, as well as the Commentators and the audience. Everywhere around me spectators hollered comments at both the competitors and the judges, sometimes running onto the dance floor or up to the judges' table to express their discontent with a decision. Occasionally, controversy would ensue, and the crowd in the back would climb on their chairs so as not to miss anything that transpired in front of the judges' table. As the night progressed and the seemingly endless list of competition categories was worked through, the space of the initially oversize hall appeared to contract as the number of people invading the dance floor increased, leaving less and less room for the competitors. The Sheraton's management had already announced that it would soon close down the event by the time we got to the final few battles, in which competitors showed off their most extravagant HIV-themed creations—most notably, a giant helmet made of inflated condoms that topped a bright red, tight leather coat and silver stiletto heels. Nearly five hours after opening the Ball, the MCs were still conducting the show with vigor, and the crowd's enthusiasm wasn't letting up. In the meantime, many of the service providers had packed up their materials and left the hotel.

Equal parts exhilarating and exhausting, balls provide a space of affirmation for Black queer youth whose lives are marked by racist, heterosexist, and homophobic exclusions and displacements that not only position them beyond the parameters of white civil society but also alienate them from their communities of birth, often at a very young age. By staging competitive encounters in which participants can mobilize and artfully reassemble conventional notions of gender, sexuality, and race, these events function as a safe platform for the creative experimentation with identity and belonging. In the case of HIV-themed Balls, they also open up an aesthetic and political space for addressing how HIV/AIDS continues to permeate the experience of being young, Black, and queer in the United States. As Bailey (2013: 20) argues, the "performance labor" at the heart Ballroom culture forms a crucial response to the HIV/AIDS crisis "insofar as it challenges the dominant discourses that construct the epidemic," by making possible "alternative representations" and thereby "charting a new course for community action against it." I agree, although I want to emphasize here that the potential of Balls—and of Ball culture more generally—to function as an effective form of "intravention" exceeds their representational and discursive impact.[16] Balls also engender a temporality that deviates from the claustrophobic time inhabited by many young Black queer folks who are forced to imagine their lives under the constant threat of HIV/AIDS, in addition to many other social and economic pressures. In contrast to the suffocating temporal framework of a racist, heteronormative society that has largely excluded them from institutionalized visions of the good life and its viable future, Balls offer these youths a reprieve that extends their temporal horizons beyond the parameters set by parents, caseworkers, schools, clergy, service providers, and epidemiological statistics. This reprieve may often feel like a new breath of life, as illustrated by the Ballroom community idiom of "giving/given life" to describe the audience support in response to an impressive performance (Rivera Colón 2009). When an audience "gives life" to an amazing performer by cheering on her or him and loudly bestowing their praise, there is an exchange of energy that allows both to flourish and increases the vitality of everyone involved, with the term "vitality" here understood in decidedly more than biological terms.

This brings us to the affective force of Balls and Ball culture, which I think could offer resources for a different take on HIV prevention. While a Ball always starts out with a ritualized recognition of respected people in the scene, and battles take place between two or more individual competitors representing their respective Houses, this is only the most visible part of what happens during the event. Permeating these status-based rituals is an intensive layer of affective attachments that tends more toward the collective than the individual and whose political potential does not arise from the realm of the person but is rather of the *impersonal* kind.[17] Beyond personal recognition, or individual rights, an impersonal politics is invested in enhancing the pleasures and powers that emanate from the interstices of bodies, complicating the heavily policed boundary between self and other (Sharp 2009). As Esposito (2010b: 130) formulates it, "If right belongs to the person, justice is situated in the impersonal. It is that which reverses what is proper into the improper, the immune into the common." During its drawn-out trajectory, a Ball becomes exactly this reversal of the immune into the common—a process in which the proliferation of diva behavior, statuses, and familial factions makes way for the ecstatic enunciation of a sense of community, no matter how fragile, antagonistic, or transient it may be. Instead of securing life through immunitary strategies of biospatial containment, the expressive form of life that keeps Ball culture alive requires circulation and contagion. Consequently, intimacy here becomes a vital interstitial sphere where vulnerable bodies hesitantly open themselves up to new, erotically charged and potentially empowering affects, rather than being safeguarded as a carefully managed zone of statistically inferred sexual risk. This is an impersonal kind of intimacy, one that does not hinge on the desire for individual sovereignty and transparency but emerges from a shared aspiration to articulate a joyful being-in-common.[18]

Bypassing the self-contained, rights-claiming, and responsibilized sexual citizen, whose subjectivity and access to care are increasingly mediated by biomedical criteria, the impersonal dimension of Ball culture also alludes to a different mode of citizenship. If, following Esposito, "right belongs to the person," the depersonalizing violence against Black queer youth has made the redemptive power of the law largely unavailable to them—unless they become infected with HIV. When, however, "justice is situated in the impersonal," it becomes possible to reimagine citizenship as a practice of composition: the precarious fabric of the Ballroom community, woven from feelings such as fear, joy, shame, anxiety, pride, and other conflicting affects, needs to be continuously recomposed so it can persist as a space of affirmation and shelter against anti-Black/queer persecution. It is important to stress here that these are *political* feelings, in the sense that they form the visceral, affective response to the multifarious injustice that Black queer youth have to bear on a daily basis, and because their force may be mobilized for the development of a more critical and creative model for dealing with HIV/AIDS—one that, in Arendt's words, would give Black queer folks "a place in the world which makes opinions significant and actions effective" (Arendt [1951] 1979: 296). Still, notwithstanding the strategic importance of pushing more capacious approaches to HIV/AIDS prevention on the public agenda (cf. M. Bailey 2013), the most pertinent political contribution of Ball culture is another world-disclosing practice altogether, one that affirms Black queer forms of life that have been deprived of their worth, if not their humanity, in the civic world Arendt never ceased to defend. This is also where it becomes important to recall that, according to Esposito, no community can survive without a certain measure of protection: immunity is the negative condition for the survival of life. Yet in contrast to immunitary strategies that insulate the person, the individual, or the organism, the civic intimacies so central to Ball culture help us to imagine a "common immunity" that is cultivated within House families and protects the form of life immanent to the collective cultural survival *and* flourishing of the Ballroom community.[19] This form of life is at once irreducibly biological, sexual, racial, gendered, spiritual, aesthetic, and political (and, and, and . . .).[20]

But how, then, can this reconceptualization of intimacy and citizenship inform an attempt to do HIV prevention differently? First, I want to suggest that Balls and Ballroom culture exhibit a different kind of magic from the "magic bullet" proposed by the current TLC+ approach to prevention. The fact that large groups of Black queer youth have managed to build and sustain a kinship infrastructure that allows them collectively to express their particular inflection of queerness in a creative manner, despite all the precariousness and violence that surrounds them, is nothing short of magical. That a great number of them have also remained uninfected is an equally miraculous accomplishment, given the plethora of insecurities that expose them to HIV/AIDS—which far exceed any reductive explanation preoccupied with "risky behavior." The efforts that have enabled this accomplishment are certainly affected by the disruptive force of new policies and protocols being pushed on young outreach workers at a rapid pace, yet the work of maintenance and repair that keeps this fragile community together exhibits a more protracted temporality. Such observations should give us pause to consider how prevention work can become more attuned to the vernacular world-making capacities of the Ballroom community, instead of merely mobilizing its members as a standing reserve of biomaterial for testing purposes. What is needed is a more engaged, sustained, and well-funded dialogue among service providers, peer outreach workers, and the different Houses—a dialogue dedicated to learning, to studying how Black queer kinship structures and their communal events inspire youth to circumvent the virus in a *convivial* relationship with their environment, rather than in opposition to it (Puar 2009). Trust is a vital element in this process, as it forms the congealing substance that holds these structures together. Yet as everyone I talked to knew very well, trust is also an utterly fragile currency circulating among these different actors, and it threatens to become exhausted when the city's investment in the Ballroom community remains limited to free HIV tests, T-shirts, and Safeway gift cards. Moving within the parameters of the federal TLC+ approach to the war against HIV/AIDS, the "cooperation" between the Baltimore City Health Department and the Ballroom community is bound to go bankrupt as long as it employs a narrow range of depoliticized biomedical weapons to fight a disease so intricately tied up to the ongoing war on the Black, the queer, and the poor. Meanwhile, Baltimore's white bourgeois LGBT community and its mainstreamed political institutions for the most part have kept their distance from any of these wars, as they have been preoccupied with more respectable causes, such as marriage equality, over the past two decades. Perhaps, then, the cruelest aspect of the affective labor that fills the days of many un(der)paid outreach workers is that little currently exists to which they can realistically attach. It is this poignant fact that needs to be addressed if we are to move beyond the reductive idea that we can treat our way out of this epidemic and instead refocus our attention on HIV prevention as a social justice struggle embedded in the complex assemblage of disease ecology, political economy, and racist hetero/homonormativity.

This brings me to my second and last suggestion: if anything, HIV prevention methods need to become *more* promiscuous.[21] If we trace back the etymological root of the term, the Latin *prōmiscuus* designates that which is mixed, rather than separated, or something "made up of various disparate elements."[22] Likewise, I believe that for HIV prevention to be effective, it has to deploy an assemblage of heterogeneous interventions able to respond to the epidemic from a variety of different angles. HIV testing and treatment will certainly form elements in this assemblage but cannot be its main focus, as I have argued here. They have to be combined with approaches modeled on a Black queer relational sense of the world that works against the norm of immunitary self-defense, thus allowing for a more capacious conception of health and life, which, like kinship, are phenomena not solely explained by biology (Sahlins 2013). Interestingly, it is Georges Canguilhem—one of the preeminent philosophers of the biological—who points us in this direction when he, in his most Spinozist moment, describes health as "the feeling of a capacity to go beyond initial capacities, a capacity to make the body do what it did not initially seem to promise" (Canguilhem 2008: 474). In the face of Black queer lives that historically have been debilitated by HIV/AIDS and many other violent injustices, federal, state, and local governments should not exempt themselves from the task at hand: a critical reassessment of the racialized biomedical model of life that is currently being promoted and continues to reinvent and thereby shore up the *nomos* of the plantation. At the same time, community members, activists, and scholars must anticipate alternative futures that inevitably emerge from the (s)pace of the plantation yet exceed its logic and means of capture by conjuring—thinking, reading, writing, and celebrating—Black queer culture as a catalyst for the political expansion of bodily capacities beyond what has been promised.

4

Forces of Faith

It's true that there are constraints from the Church which operate on the painter, but there is a transformation of constraints into means of creation. They make use of God in order to achieve a liberation of forms, to push the forms to the point where they have nothing to do with an illustration.

—GILLES DELEUZE, "Seminar on Spinoza"

One of the main conclusions of the previous chapter is that there is an incongruence between the Centers for Disease Control and Prevention's immunitary investment in preserving the biological life of young Black queer men and the forms of life that these youths actually need to survive and to flourish. These forms of life cannot be sustained solely through HIV prevention, treatment, and managed care focused on individual cases; they need more creative and collective commitments inspired by the intimate attachments, expressions, and rituals cultivated in Baltimore's Ballroom community.[1] As I have argued, Balls offer these youths a reprieve from their daily pressures by staging a carefully curated series of intense and intensely pleasurable competitive performances that forge a sense of empowerment and community. Besides these ecstatic events, the Houses—many but certainly not all—provide a different kind of support structure in which fathers and mothers guide their children and help them to take care of themselves and others. While they are not always the most stable households, these Houses nevertheless answer to the widespread need for safe spaces in which Black queer youth can experiment with who they are and aspire to become, creating environments of care and affirmation that establish a precarious "common immunity" (Esposito 2011). Yet even the best Houses and Balls cannot provide what many young Black queers are looking for: the cultivation of a religious spirituality. For this reason, you can find a good number of them in church on a Sunday morning, even after attending a Ball that ended a couple of hours before the start of service.[2] Despite the fact that they either have to hide their sexuality from their congregation or risk the recurrent threat of scorn, ridicule, or (worse) damnation, they still return at least intermittently because they desire to sustain a relationship with God.[3] But what does this mean, exactly? How do Black queer folks, many of whom have been and continue to be subjected to religious bigotry and exclusion in their home communities, maintain an investment in their faith and find solace in a divine presence?

To answer these questions, this chapter sets out to examine what it means for a Black queer community to cultivate relationships of mutual and critical care in the face of chronic social insecurity when these efforts are mediated through religious practices and attachments. The intersection of religion and queerness has become a burgeoning topic of academic interest over the past decade, especially as it pertains to themes such as Christian theology, (post) secularity, (neo)liberal governmentality, sexual regulation, and Islam (see, e.g., Althaus-Reid 2003; Gold 2010; Jakobsen and Pellegrini 2003; Jivraj and de Jong 2011; Stychin 2009; Wilcox 2009). Likewise, a small but growing body of social-science research exists that focuses on the role of religion and spirituality in queer people's everyday lives (Browne, Yip, and Munt 2010; Hunt 2009; R. Miller 2005; Wilcox 2012).[4] Meanwhile, however, studies on religious experience in *Black* queer lives remain conspicuously scarce, especially when compared with the enormous wealth of literature on the position of religion and the Black Church in the shaping of African American culture and Blackness more generally.[5] Apparently, to rather clumsily riff off Michael L. Cobb's remark in his study on James Baldwin and the queer uses of religious words, religion is not supposed to say much about queer Blackness/Black queerness—or vice versa.[6] With this analytical blind spot in mind, I look at how divine presence informs Black queer practices of self-formation and world making at the Unity Fellowship Church of Baltimore (UFCB), a Black LGBT/same-gender-loving (SGL) Pentecostal church briefly introduced in Chapter 2. I thus present an account of how religion, as a personal experience as well as a collective sense of transcendence and belonging, affects the lives of the UFCB's congregation, which moves alongside the threshold of the spiritual and the worldly, while its members shift between enduring and celebrating life in a city with a church on every corner.

A Pedagogy of the Otherwise

As noted above, the UFCB is an African American congregation led by an LGBT/SGL clergy. While the majority of the congregation identifies as LGBT or SGL, heterosexual friends and family members regularly attend, as well. The UFCB was established in 2000 and grew out of the national Unity Fellowship Church movement, which was founded in Los Angeles by the Reverend Carl Bean in 1982 to provide a place of worship for openly gay and lesbian African Americans. Even though the UFCB is interdenominational in outlook and practice, its services have a distinctly Black Pentecostal flair due to the backgrounds of the movement's archbishop (Pentecostal-Apostolic) and the UFCB's founding pastor (Pentecostal-Baptist). The charismatic style of preaching, the call and response, the exuberant musical praise, and the two-and-a-half-hour services all speak to a worship experience that I hitherto had no experience with as a white agnostic European with a Roman Catholic background. In addition, the services often incorporate African influences, such as various forms of percussion and elements from the Yoruba religion, as well as a libation ceremony to honor ancestors and those who have passed away more recently.[7] The mix of these non-Western traditions, augmented by elements from different Christian denominations, is part of the church's explicit aim to be inclusive and welcoming to anyone who needs a safe space to worship and is emblematic of their pragmatic approach to the various ways the divine can be made present. "While we have the [Pentecostal] style, we don't necessarily subscribe to all of the doctrine," Shawn told me while driving me home after Spiritual Development class. "You can feel God and experience God in different ways." Because he came from a Pentecostal-Apostolic background, Shawn said, part of him felt right at home when he first attended worship at the UFCB and felt a familiar atmosphere. Still, that first service proved to be a struggle to sit through. Flying in the face of all that he had been taught in the conservative environment of his home church, it united "God talk" with "gay talk," which were two aspects of his life he wasn't yet prepared to experience together:

> I counted: they actually said the word "gay" eight times. I was, like, "This church, this doesn't work for me." It was liberating and frightening all at the same time. It was bumping up against my past way of knowing, which was still very much alive and existing in me. I was still holding that to be a truth, an absolute.

Shawn, an African American SGL man in his early fifties, had already been in ministry at his home church for twenty-seven years when he came out at age thirty-nine. The decision had severe repercussions for his life, as his own father, who was the pastor of his congregation, consequently put him out of the church. This caused an intense feeling of abandonment, because it severed his ties with not only the home church of his youth but also family, friends, and the nurturing habitat on which he had come to rely. "Coming out just kind of like pulled the rug from under my existence," he said. "Prior to coming out, my life was wrapped in . . . [E]verything that I dealt with related to church, religion, spirituality and so all of my existence was wrapped in this shell called church. And when it broke, it broke everything." Since then, he'd been trying to build his life back up again, initially without any stable attachments to a church or ministry. He occasionally took part in music ministry at different churches, where people were glad to have him because of his beautiful voice, but since word travels fast through the grapevine of Maryland's close-knit Black Church network, he was quickly outed each time that people from his former church found out about his new affiliation. Shawn described the five years he spent without a solid connection to church life as a "very unstable existence" and "a place of emptiness" in which he struggled to find his footing. Reflecting on that period, he attributed his anxieties to his Black Church upbringing, where one is taught that the church is God's home and therefore is the primary place to find his presence on Sunday mornings: "So while we've been told that there's this ongoing connection, . . . it's this plug-in. We were not conditioned to know that we could have the same existence with God in our homes that did not have this title of 'church.'" While he knew that he could access God in his own home and heart, and did have some very spiritual moments in which he connected with the divine outside the conventional worship experience provided by the church, he nevertheless continued to feel a need for a more structured and collective church life.

In 2005, after a friend invited him to a service, he gradually found this life at the UFCB. Following that first ambiguous worship experience he started attending Spiritual Development classes, where he immersed himself in doctrinal and theological questions in an attempt to open himself up to new perspectives that would enable him to reconcile his former teachings with his desire to openly and sincerely practice his faith as a Black SGL man. It was an intensive process during which he forced himself to have internal "critical dialogues" to reassess the knowledge he had accumulated over the years and to work through the guilt he felt about teaching this knowledge to others. "It's been about transformation for me—and reinventing who I am," Shawn told me one afternoon over coffee, "so the challenge for me is, as I develop this new family, this new sphere that I can live in . . . it's not the same as my past sphere." The process of reinventing himself once his habitual footholds were no longer available has been difficult, and he repeatedly made clear that his new familial sphere would never be able to replace his past sphere of "bloodline family." Still, the UFCB gave him a place of safety, rest, and community support in which he was able to cultivate the life he needed, not only to survive but also to flourish. "I crave to be in the presence of people who are so loving, so caring, so full of energy," he said. "That boosts my energy for the whole week. People that will hug you and say 'I really do love you,' and I feel the truth of that statement." Moreover, the church has provided him with a space that encourages critical questioning as an integral part of the collective religious experience, which created a propitious atmosphere for his experimental trajectory and eventually led him back into ministry. It is this critical attitude toward Christian doctrine, ecclesiastical mores, and a host of more mundanely secular topics that formed a red thread throughout my engagements with the UFCB. While the church does not subscribe to any particular tradition of liberation theology, the movement's general emphasis on emancipation and its imperative to question established forms of knowledge, power, and morality were nevertheless recurrent motifs during Sunday services and Spiritual Development classes. What these weekly gatherings made available was a *pedagogy of the otherwise* by showing those in attendance that things could also be different and teaching an awareness of the God-given power to create some change in one's life.[8]

Yet, as will become clear, the UFCB's version of emancipation and faith-based uplifting deviates from Black liberation theology's historical focus on fighting white supremacist structural violence through grassroots activism—including but not limited to radical hermeneutics—to achieve social justice (Cone 2010). Instead, it prioritizes a critical hermeneutics of self-examination and a concern with actualizing personal and collective potentials through education and the cultivation of marginalized truths. From a political-economy perspective oriented toward redistribution, this approach hardly seems apposite, given that the UFCB serves a chronically underserved community, especially since it moved into its new location, where the scarcity of basic resources such as food, clothing, childcare, and medical attention has turned everyday life into survival for many of its inhabitants. My apprehension was exacerbated when I noticed the similarities between some of the central themes addressed in the services and classes, such as accountability, choice, and self-empowerment, and neoliberal narratives that promote the virtues of self-sufficiency and personal responsibility. As I have demonstrated in the previous two chapters, these narratives were widespread in Baltimore—and perhaps even more vibrantly so in Black Baltimore, not only permeating the Black Church, but also forming the discursive and ideological center of large-scale initiatives such as Mayor Martin O'Malley's Believe campaign and HIV-prevention strategies such as HIV Stops with Me. Moreover, the majority of the UFCB's clergy was middle class, and some adhered to entrepreneurial norms and values that were beyond the aspirational radar of many of their congregants. I thus initially had serious misgivings about the UFCB's approach, which, in light of the obvious need for material support, seemed inefficacious and perhaps even complicit in maintaining the status quo. Yet my experiences at the church and my conversations with Shawn and others eventually pushed me to nuance my views considerably and encouraged me to rethink the relationship among religious spirituality, ethical conduct, and political practice.

"The Power, the Change, the Atmosphere"

When I asked Shawn why the church wasn't more involved in grassroots activism and economic outreach in the community—initiatives the UFCB had organized in the past—he explained that the church had seen a dramatic decrease in tithes and other donations since it moved to their its location, because fewer people showed up and those who did come did not have much to spare. This consequently diminished its financial resources and made it harder to recruit church members for activities. But he also raised a more fundamental issue:

> So many people who come out as same-gender-loving folks have these compound issues that are very personal to them. Because we are . . . [T]he majority of our church is working class or border [on] working class, . . . It's hard to get them on the front line, or even in the line, to do activism work when all they can think about is "How am I gonna make ends meet next week?"

Before I could respond, he continued:

> And they're trying to deal with "What am I going to do with my children? How can I get my baby's dad to be OK with me being in a

relationship with a woman? How do I work out family issues?" All of those things are really at the forefront of their minds. So when we make a call for activism, to be active in the community, the number of people who show up is very small. They're trying to get through the week.

Activism, of the kind that lays claim to one's time, finances, or psychic investment remains an unfeasible commitment for many who frequent the UFCB. For instance, Rhonda, an SGL woman in her thirties who had started attending Sunday services about a year earlier, was struggling to pay her bills with the money she earned from two temporary jobs while also trying to juggle her responsibilities as a mother of three kids, a daughter to her sick mother, and a girlfriend to her partner. One Sunday afternoon after service we ended up talking while standing outside the church, as she was waiting for a family member to pick her up. When I asked what drew her to the UFCB, she told me:

> I come to church because it gives me a place of peace—a place where I can find other folks like me, who have gone through similar experiences and are really willing to listen to my problems, to help me work on them. Being here helps me clear my head and get a perspective on things, by praying, singing, and listening to what Pastor has to say [and by] being in the presence of God, you know, really feeling that. . . . People here are just more real and less judgmental than at other churches I've been at.

Rhonda enjoyed the facilities the UFCB offers, such as the Youth and Young Adult Ministry for her kids and the community lunches that often follow the Sunday service. Yet when I asked her whether she wanted to see the church get more involved in community outreach or organize social justice projects in the neighborhood, she expressed concern about the level of commitment this would require from the congregation and wondered who would be able to donate time or money:

> Most folks around here are not in a place for those kinds of activities, mentally and financially, you know? That's not why they come to church. They're struggling to run their own lives, dealing with their problems. So even if they would want to get involved, . . . it's just hard, you know? I wouldn't know where to find the time or the energy.

Before congregants such as Rhonda can even begin to think about committing to causes that are not directly related to the pressure of their own daily obligations, they need some kind of infrastructure that provides a safe space where they can work on themselves in the renewed presence of God to get a better grip on their lives. Surely this requires various forms of material support and sustenance, but in a largely depleted environment, such resources are hard to come by. Rather than focusing on what people do not have and what the church often cannot properly supply, the UFCB's clergy is determined to nurture a different set of potential resources. Through what I am calling a "pedagogy of the otherwise," they are challenging their congregation to pause and critically reflect on their lives in a concerted effort to cultivate modes of agency that were previously neglected or inaccessible without "a detour through God" (Deleuze 1980). As Shawn told me:

> For me, it's about getting people clear about what they possess and what they have. So, not saying to them that there's this bootstrap-pulling-up thing that needs to happen [as I had insinuated], it's about helping to get clear about what's in me about this situation, what's in me that's having me operate the way I'm operating. If I don't know that I have the power within me to respond in the way I want to, . . . are we really challenging ourselves to think about how we're doing this, or are we basing this on what we've been told or what we've heard?

The UFCB's clergy kept coming back to this during service: there is always something "in you" about a situation, which means that you could potentially assert a mode of agency, however minimal, that might change the situation in your favor and improve the quality of your life. During one Sunday service, one of the church's pastors structured his sermon around the message, "God gave us the power to change the atmosphere," which formed a motif woven through his stories about addiction, health problems, and financial issues. These are the problems his congregants come to see him about on a daily basis; now he stood, reaching toward them from the pulpit, to proclaim the loving power of God on which anyone with an open heart can draw when they are ready to make an effort to confront whatever impedes their well-being.[9] He testified that he had been in their shoes; he'd had his own share of drug problems and financial troubles. Most people present that morning also knew about his continued health struggles, which, he told me privately, restrained his mobility and left him stuck behind the pulpit during most of his sermons, whereas he used to be able to hop over the pews whenever he felt the spirit calling him. He'd always been a "theatrical person" with a very charismatic style of preaching, "doing all kinds of crazy stuff" such as moving wildly up and down the aisles, arms flailing, shouting and hollering, led by the spirit that brings forth the word. Sometimes he was led away from his notes, and the sermon became "whatever the Lord is leading," creating a spiritual connection with people in the room, who showed up afterward to tell him he was speaking directly to them. The young people especially loved this, which was a big relief for him when he first started preaching at another Unity Fellowship Church in the late 1990s. Preaching in the new environment was strange at first, because he suddenly had the freedom to say the word "gay" without having to condemn homosexuality. At his home church, where he was ordained as an elder, he had actually felt himself becoming increasingly traditional in his teaching, which was intensifying his internal struggle with his sexuality. He was in a committed relationship with a man and knew that, if something were to happen to him, his partner would not receive the same care and support from his church, which eventually persuaded him to leave and look for another church. His partner was the first to join the Unity Fellowship Church movement, and he followed soon after, determined not to get involved in ministry. The church's bishop had other plans, however, and convinced him to preach one Sunday, slowly setting things in motion. When he and his partner had a commitment ceremony, he was ordained into the movement by Archbishop Bean, who would also ordain him as pastor of the UFCB in 2000.

Pastor told me that the church had a number of community outreach activities when it was still doing services in Mount Vernon. It had an AIDS ministry and offered support and services for sex workers and the homeless, such as a mobile night feeding program and free condom distribution. It also partnered with the Black Educational AIDS Project (BEAP) and successfully applied for a grant so it could provide free HIV testing in a van parked around the corner. When I asked him why all the initiatives had stopped, he echoed Shawn, saying that it primarily had to do with the relocation: "It all sort of died after that. We lost a lot of people in that move, partly because they didn't want to get on the bus to travel that far." But he also reminded me that a lot of the community-based HIV/AIDS organizations, such as HERO and BEAP, had shut down over the past years, and it was harder to organize such projects alone. And then there was the new neighborhood: Pastor mentioned that its community had expressed prejudice against the church for being "gay," and it was difficult to get locals to show up for services, let alone to get involved. Still, he mainly blamed the church for its failure to show more engagement with its surroundings:

> We moved into a new location and then sort of put up a wall around us. And that needs to come down so we can take our community into the community. . . . We need to be more visible, working with people dealing with addiction, because that area has a big addiction problem. We need to work with families, how to parent your kids. We do need to work with HIV/AIDS. We need to focus on youth in the community, after-school tutoring. There's a lot we need to step up with and do. The only thing we would run into is the need for new funding, if things would indeed pick up.

I noticed how Pastor struggled with this issue. He was at pains to reassure me that he planned to "resurrect" the outreach ministry, even if this meant reaching deeper into his own pockets and spreading himself too thin. He told me that he sometimes pondered exhausting himself just to see what the rest of the staff would do in response—a staff that was preoccupied with forging connections to religious and LGBT rights organizations at the expense, some say, of the community. But he was also realistic about the impediments that limited his aspirations. His health was deteriorating; in addition, the church's economic woes had been exacerbated by the move, and he believed the economic crisis that started in 2008 had also left a mark. Like Shawn, he therefore was choosing to focus on what the church *could* do and what *was* possible within the present constraints. While he knew that "you can't talk to a hungry person about God" (the reason the church continued to organize community lunches and dinners), he was resolute that the UFCB's primary task was to help people help themselves in whatever way possible, and that started with loving yourself. As is consistently preached on Sundays, only when you truly love yourself does it become possible to find the love of God in you. This love, in turn, constitutes a vital resource for any effort to acknowledge and subsequently transform the immediate conditions that restrict one's flourishing.

While the imperative of self-love may seem troublingly proximate to calls for self-reliance, I understand what the church was doing less as therapeutic responsibilization than as a mode of activism—a method of actualizing capacities and subjugated truths, embedded in a divinely inspired process of governing oneself and others. Near the end of his 1982 lecture series at the Collège de France, Michel Foucault introduced the notion of *parrhesia*, most often translated as "truth-telling" or "frank speech," to more systematically connect his earlier research on the care of the self to his more recent interest in the ethico-political practice of governing self and others (Foucault 2010). According to Foucault, both hinge on a transformative engagement with the "test" of truth, conceived of as a "game of veridiction" that seeks a harmony between one's words and one's actions (ibid.: 310). Although he would continue to modify his description of *parrhesia* in terms of its features, functions, and uses as his research progressed, Foucault consistently associated it with a courage to tell or to otherwise manifest the truth about oneself *and* about others whom one assists in the process of self-formation. This emphasis on courage as a prerequisite for parrhesiastic practices points to the risk inherent in speaking or acting truthfully without reservations, especially when the manifested truth deviates from the hegemonic normative order. Indeed, marginalized communities constantly run the risk of being persecuted, dispossessed, and subjected to various types of violence because the truth they express through their particular form of life cannot be ignored or incorporated into prevailing visions of the good life. *Parrhesia*, the circuit of truth as it is experienced, spoken, and acted on, thus constitutes a double-edged sword: while it performs a crucial function in the government of self and others, conceived as a reciprocal procedure that cultivates the critical abilities necessary to resist one's oppressive conditions, it also threatens the very existence of alternative social projects and those invested in them.

It is exactly this paradoxical situation that prompts Elizabeth Povinelli (2012: 454) to inquire into who/what survives the test of truth: "If, as Foucault argues in *The Government of Self and Others*, the conditions of the otherwise lie in the radically potential spaces of a kind of a kind of truth speaking (*dire vrai, parrhesia*), what political and theoretical weight will be given to the exhausting conditions of these spaces?" Her central concern is with the conditions of possibility that grant some who are "ethically otherwise" the agency to overcome their debilitating circumstances by speaking truth, while others fail. What exactly are the resources and practices subordinated peoples can draw on to develop certain capacities to "rise above" and express their truth, given that few of them will actually be able to meet this imperative without risking whatever keeps their world together? Povinelli (2012: 472) turns to the pragmatist philosophers William James and Charles S. Peirce for a provisional way forward, but while they point her to the importance of a persistent "effort of attention" that may congeal into "a method of *trying things out* as a manner of capacitating thresholds," she eventually concurs with James that the question of why some actualize their potential to escape or transform spaces of exhaustion while others do not remains unanswerable. While I agree that a universal or definitive answer is indeed impossible, given the situated and singular nature of exhausting environments and the alternative social projects that traverse them, I believe that James's work nevertheless attunes us to how religious faith constitutes one vital resource for the cultivation of capacities that enable the "ethically otherwise" to not only survive their circumstances but also resist and change them.

In Foucault's (post)modern secular approach, Christianity threatens to be reduced to the exercise of a pastoral power that guides and controls embodied souls through techniques of obedience, confession, and self-renunciation, leaving little room for a consideration of why and how people actually practice their faith and maintain a relationship to the divine—however understood. In other words, by treating Christian religion as an institutional apparatus, Foucault effectively evacuates God from its premises. In contrast, William James, as both a pragmatist and a man of faith, chooses to take divine presence at face value. His *The Varieties of Religious Experiences* offers a queerly unmodern account of the value that religion adds to human life, without sacrificing the reality of that which exceeds the human. While his pragmatic approach prioritizes religion's utility to "man," leading him to assert that "the gods we stand by are the gods we need and can use, the gods whose demands on us are reinforcements of our demands on ourselves and on one another," for James this does not imply that divinities lack concrete existence (James 2004: 290–291). Rather, their particular mode of existence depends on the faith invested in them, which means that—like all other things in James's "pluriverse"—their reality is not absolute but a matter of degree: the more they yield their practical "fruits" in the lives of the faithful, the more their existence is amplified by faith. Conversely, when a divinity loses its value or moral purchase in a community of faith, its efficacy is weakened, and it will slowly wither away. In this sense, the divine, plural or singular, needs the faithful as much as the faithful need the divine.[10]

This relationship of mutual dependence is also what concerns Bruno Latour (2011: 328) when he claims that the mode of existence we call God "appears and disappears according to the way he is spoken of, proclaimed, pronounced, or uttered." Since divine entities are highly sensitive to the ways they are talked about, it is of crucial importance to achieve the right "tonality," or "key," which allows one not to merely talk *about* religion but to truly talk *religiously* and thereby enunciate a divine presence. For Latour, who is here inspired by speech-act theory, Christian religion is one specific "regime of enunciation" that is able to produce truth in different cultures around the world, yet, like all other regimes, it has to satisfy certain "conditions of felicity" particular to it before its enunciations can become truthful (Latour 2010b: 100–101).[11] Thus, the same sermon can be delivered in many different ways, but for it to contain any truth—*religious* truth specific to this regime—it needs to delivered in a "tonality" that is able to meet the three felicity conditions indigenous to Christian religion: closeness, presence, and transformation. Despite many claims to the contrary, Latour contends that (Christian) religion has never been about the distant, the supernatural, the infinite, or the sublime; it is, rather, about proximity and the present, the here and now. The central aim of religion is to generate anew each time a sense of presence of what was previously misunderstood or distorted. It has always been about renewing the presence of the divine, and about being present again to one another, to "redirect attention away from indifference and habituation, to prepare oneself to be seized again by this presence that breaks the usual, habituated passage of time" (ibid.: 122). It this in this way that religious truth, enunciated in the right key, becomes transformational—or "spiritual," to use Foucault's terminology. True religious experience causes a "slight displacement in the normal pace of things" (ibid.: 102), which transforms how the faithful inhabit space and time and creates an intensified feeling of what Jean-Luc Nancy (1997) calls "being-with," which traverses the sacred and the secular.

This returns us to James (2004: 52), who, early in *Varieties*, argues for the importance of religious feelings that open up "a new sphere of power" in the face of struggle. When later discussing mysticism, he suggests that heightened states of religious or "spiritual" awareness bestow "a new expressiveness" on previously mundane facts, which allows them to "make new connections with our active life" (ibid.: 370). Mystical states offer us "*hypotheses*" about the potentiality of a "more extensive and inclusive world"; they invite us to think about and act on a *more* to come (ibid.). Finally, in his concluding remarks, James holds religion to be a "postulator of new *facts*" and asserts that the world interpreted religiously is endowed with a different constitution from a disenchanted "materialistic world": "Different events can be expected in it, different conduct must be required" (ibid.: 443–444). Religious experience adds reality to this world by opening it up to "other worlds" that enrich the here and now of concrete existence (ibid.: 444). As he writes, "Not God, but life, more life, a larger, richer, more satisfying life, is, in the last analysis, the end of religion. The love of life, at any and every level of development, is the religious impulse" (ibid.: 435). I think that James captures in these passages how religious faith operates as a resource from which the UFCB's "ethically otherwise" can draw the sustenance and inspiration needed to navigate its frequently exhausting spaces and develop the courage to experiment with new modes of self-formation and world making, which I term "civic intimacies." Far from being a solitary endeavor, learning how to love and stand up for yourself is a *collective* process that involves the entire congregation, whose members are spurred to speak truthfully about what troubles them and to reflect critically on their situation in the presence of others—including God. As Pastor put it, "To truly love yourself, you have to be connected. People that isolate themselves cannot experience the full love, because love is also part of giving and receiving. You can't be fully engaged with love unless you are connected with others."

It was not uncommon for Spiritual Development classes to erupt into heated discussions about particular issues congregants were dealing with and that were brought up during recurrent "What's up?" check-in sessions. Such sessions, which usually opened the classes, provided those in attendance with an opportunity to vent their frustrations and to update one another about recent experiences and activities. On one occasion, Kimberly, a lesbian woman in her mid-thirties, opened up to the room about her inability to detach herself from her drug-addicted ex-husband, whom she had divorced more than a year earlier but who continued to contact her with pleas to borrow money. She told us, visibly upset, that even though she knew that she should not answer his requests and that she wanted him out of her life for good, she just could not get herself to break all ties and had lent him more money than she could spare, which has resulted in not only financial strain but also significant tension with current partner. While some congregants recognized her situation and offered advice, drawing on similar experiences with friends or family members, others couldn't hide their indignation and implored her to be more stern. The adjunct pastor who was leading the class recognized the intensity of the emotions surging through the room and suggested that we spend our remaining time in a collective attempt to make sense of Kimberly's situation in terms of the relationship's structure, the expectations and affective investments it elicited, and the harmful dependencies it generated. Guiding the discussion, he also tied her experiences to broader issues such as drug use, poverty, and heterosexual masculinity, thereby showing how her problem existed within a larger societal framework marked by inequity. Near the end of the conversation, everyone took turns providing their perspectives on how to move forward, often referring to the need to love and respect oneself despite the shame, doubt, and negativity that, for many, had become a part of daily life. When someone expressed the desire to pray, the adjunct pastor led us in prayer and asked God to give Kimberly the strength to persevere and take control over her life. Standing in a circle in front of the altar, we all held hands, and I felt an acute sense of determination in the room, which I was sure Kimberly must have felt, too.

Two weeks later, at a barbeque cookout organized by the UFCB, I sat down next to Kimberley to find out how she was doing and how she had experienced that particular evening. When I asked her, naively, whether she had also felt something during our prayer circle, her face expressed amused incredulity. "What do you think? *Of course* I felt something," she said. "I always feel the love and power of God when we pray together. That's why I come to church. Being there just feels good, something happens to your spirit, you know. . . . It's a small place but it feels so big." Yet the church is more than a place for spiritual development, and Kimberly was explicit about how valuable the congregational support had been for her ongoing efforts to disengage herself from the situation that was wearing her down:

> What happened that night, in that class, really changed how I looked at myself and my relationship to John [her ex-husband] and Monique [her current partner]. Things are real in there; they tell it like it is, and sometimes that's exactly what you need. You just have to have an open heart and not be afraid of what you're gonna get whupped with, you know. And I'm just so grateful for all the love and honesty in that place, because it has allowed me to reconnect with God and to show up truthfully, to really start putting an end to all that craziness.

We returned to Kimberly's situation a number of times during subsequent Spiritual Development classes, checking up on her and using her "case" as a stepping stone for joint reflection on related problems that were brought up by others. Because of this sustained attention, care, and truthful speech, she was able to slowly withdraw from her ex-husband's sphere of influence and learned to be more secure in her new relationship with Monique, who always accompanied her on Sundays. This transformation made available the psychic and financial resources she needed to work on herself within a new familial setting and to cultivate other, more life-affirming attachments, resulting in her decision to volunteer at a local bookstore. Again, I am aware that some readers may be put off by the therapeutic self-help ethos of the UFCB's method—as I was, initially—and that the mundane tribulations recounted above seem remote from radically queer conceptions of political struggle. Nevertheless, I contend that their approach creates an invaluable space for "inventing other forms of pleasure, of relationships, coexistences, attachments, loves, intensities" (Foucault 1988: 116), which open up opportunities for flourishing that otherwise would remain inaccessible to Black queer folks. It is in this way, then, that the ethical care for and government of self and others acquires its deeply political character.[12]

"God Is Love, and Love Is for Everyone"

Much of the UFCB's project of emancipation relates to its Black Church identity and heritage, given that virtually every member of the congregation has roots in an African American Christian denomination. During the services and Bible study classes I witnessed a sustained reflection on the various injurious beliefs and investments that people had taken with them from their home churches, whose moral condemnation of homosexuality was propagated by the pastors they had grown up with and had learned to trust unconditionally. In an effort to begin a process of what was called "healing" or—less often—"deprogramming," clergy responded by engaging in alternative biblical interpretations that emphasized the movement's central slogan, repeated over and over again like a vibrant incantation: "God is love, and love is for everyone." This form of counter-conduct was intended to make God available again to those who had been told that the divine had abandoned them as punishment for their sinful desires. Countering this deep-seated fear and self-suspicion, the UFCB's clergy cultivated a critical attitude toward the regime of truth established in many traditional churches, encouraging its members, as Foucault (2007: 47) expressed it, to "question truth on its effects of power and question power on its discourses of truth."

This focus on the relationship between truth and power manifested itself most distinctly in Bible study classes that historicized and reassessed biblical passages notorious for their alleged denunciation of homosexuality. During one of these classes, Pastor decided to discuss Leviticus 18:22 ("Thou shalt not lie with mankind, as with womankind: it is abomination" [King James Version]). Congregants had repeatedly expressed their concern over what they perceived as the clear prohibition against homosexual acts contained in this injunction, with which they had been confronted so many times at their previous churches. For many, it provided evidence that God does in fact "have a problem with gay people"—as one church member put it. Pastor responded by pointing to the specific religio-historical context in which chapter 18 of the Book of Leviticus should be understood—namely, as part of a section known as the Holiness Code, which covers specific laws that delineate proper behavior for Israelites. As he told us, these laws were meant to prevent Israelites from engaging in pagan ritual practices involving idol worship and homosexual promiscuity, then common among Egyptians and Canaanites. For this reason, he continued, the prohibition of homosexual activities found in Leviticus 18:22 should not be read as a wholesale condemnation of homosexuality, but should be seen as part of a particular set of regulations aimed to preserve to moral purity of the Israelite people at a specific time in history. To substantiate this interpretation, he turned to the term "abomination," which he explained to be an English mistranslation of the Hebrew word *to'evah,* meaning roughly "something unacceptable to local custom" rather than something abhorrent. Again, he argued, this indicates the importance of attending to the situated nature of different parts of the Bible: it contains not one truth but many, each pertaining to different cultural and historical circumstances. As he liked to point out, "The Bible is a book inspired by God but not written by Him," which is why he teaches his congregation always to be critical of its content rather than wielding it as a weapon—as many of his peers insist on doing. Only by adopting this critical attitude in concert with others can one find the most capacitating truth for one's own life. For the UFCB's pastor, the Bible—like Foucault's conception of truth—is a test, one that requires effort and whose outcome is a transformation of the subject engaging with its trying contents. And it is exactly this transformation that is necessary for congregants to reach beyond their fear and self-doubt so they can open themselves up to what the UFCB considers the most important and enabling truth: that God is love, and love is for everyone. This combination of explication and affirmation is what makes these weekly Bible study classes so popular among church members, even those who do not regularly attend Sunday services. Mike, an SGL man in his late twenties whom I sporadically saw on Sundays yet who claimed hardly ever to miss a class, expressed it in this way: "Pastor takes history and brings it into the present. He allows you to take that knowledge and apply it to you own life, you know what I'm saying? He shows that God has always been there for us and always will be there, and that's what many of us need to hear."

Nevertheless, the presence of God was not something that could be taken for granted, and some clergy members also asserted that the worship rituals most people were comfortable with in the Black Church tradition might not possess the right tools to build an authentic connection with God. It was here that the UFCB's ambiguous relationship to its Black Church heritage was most pronounced and where it also touched on another, equally complex association: that between emotion and truth. In Shawn's words:

> The Black Church has been built on emotions. If you look at early Black experiences, it's all about emotions, and the emotions were a sign of being connected to your divinity, to God. If you weren't feeling something, then you weren't connected. It was a sign for the church that you caught the Holy Spirit or it caught you. . . . That's how it manifested itself.

Within the charismatic tradition, visual emotions signal the true presence of God in the person who worships him, and it is this tradition that is still central to the worship experience at the UFCB. Sunday services were always loud, musical, and celebratory, with most attendees standing in the pews with raised hands while singing or shouting their praise. They were deeply visceral events whose intensity was ritually bookended by a series of hugs and the message "God loves you, and so do I." Yet in their efforts to apply a critical pedagogy to all aspects of congregational life, some ministers concurrently treated these emotions as potentially suspect. Far from acting as signs of being truly overtaken by a divine presence, they could well be inauthentic conditioned responses developed during years of animated rhetoric and demagoguery practiced in many traditional Black churches.[13] Shawn was very adamant about this:

> Folks have become so comfortable with the sermon that it's like getting up in the morning, like riding a bike. I am a firm believer that people go to church and they don't think. They just take everything at face value. It's because we get caught up in this emotional thing, so the preacher knows how to whoop or hoop that just creates this energy that just gets people in this place of call and response. But are they really feeling it? And what are you missing when you're so busy trying to find your note and where you can say "yeah," or something?

According to Shawn, true divine presence could not be established by the energetic exchange of surface affects, because this set of routine gestures does not challenge people to actually "think"—that is, to feel the presence of God in a more cerebral way. In other words, this kind of emotional display does not equal true divinely inspired feeling, given that divinely inspired feeling requires critical thinking to be authentic. Rather than trying to "find your note" in a call and response that does not include God, religious speech should search for the right "tonality," to use Latour's expression, enabling people to become truly present to themselves and each other *through the presence of*

God. This right tonality, which consists of a kind of "reflective feeling" rather than depending solely on excitable gesticulation such as whooping, is what most clergy members attempt to achieve during services and classes.[14]

Even so, embodied emotions were also taken seriously at the UCFB. In fact, the most prevalent subject discussed in the Spiritual Development classes was the way people deal with emotions in their everyday social relations. Like Kimberly, many of the regular attendees were struggling with various problems connected to their domestic situations, such as unemployment, addiction, and dysfunctional relationships, which were frequently taking a heavy toll on their mental and physical well-being. To help them in their efforts to get a better grip on the negative feelings that attach to these stressors and to promote a healthy concern for one's self, the adjunct pastor assembled a curriculum in which emotions were the topic of weekly reflection. From the curriculum's perspective, emotions figured as potential expressions of a truth about how bodies—both human and institutional—affect other bodies and are affected in return. Yet before these emotions could actually express this truth, they needed to be turned into objects of rational understanding so they could consequently be acted on. Thus, for four consecutive weeks we gathered to share experiences in which particular emotions had somehow formed a debilitating force that detracted from our well-being and power to act, followed by a collective effort to identify what had brought these emotions about and how we could better work through them in the future. The three emotions most often mentioned were anger, frustration, and disappointment, although they were obviously hard to disentangle. Marcus, a gay man in his mid-twenties, had just been laid off and learned that his best friend was HIV-positive. He told us that he had been feeling intensely angry and had repeatedly lashed out at his environment. Kelly, an SGL woman in her fifties, felt both frustration and disappointment with her family and colleagues for not accepting her sexuality. Peter, a gay man in his fifties, had a difficult time staying sober and felt a lot of anger and frustration toward himself for lacking the determination to finally quit drinking. Naturally, none of these problems could be "solved" within the constraints of these few classes, and neither did this therapeutic initiative do anything to change the complex and sedimented structures of inequity that are frequently at the root of the issues brought up by the members of this class. But by attending to how mundane emotions functioned as "action signals"—as they were referred to by the adjunct pastor—which could tell people something meaningful about their lives and potentially prompt them to address those parts of their problems over which they *could* exercise some control, this curriculum did increase people's capacity to not be defeated by their afflictions. As the adjunct pastor told us during our first meeting: "How you navigate your emotions defines the quality of your life." While this certainly is a simplification, it is also one that makes modest change possible. What the weekly classes offered was a space where attendees felt safe to navigate and could create new, more affirming attachments to people and projects by collectively developing an attunement to how emotions can speak some truth about what inhibits their flourishing. Marcus, for instance, found these classes tremendously rewarding because they helped him get a grip on his emotional life and not be overwhelmed by it. Although he was aware that there was little the church could do to alleviate his financial stress, and he still had to come to terms with his friend's disease, he was grateful for the mental and social support he received at the UFCB. He said:

> Pastor is always asking us, "What's the attitude you're gonna show up with?" and that really made me think on how I approach the things I'm dealing with. Like, I know that many of my problems are bigger than me and I can't control them, but what they tell you here is, like, "Show up with intention and own it; walk in it," you know? That's something I've been trying to do, with the help of God, with His faith. If you don't try to own the situation, if you let yourself be owned by it and let it drag you down emotionally, then there's no way you're gonna progress and move on. You can't walk in your truth with that attitude.

When I asked him what it means to "walk in your truth," he thought for a moment and then replied, "It's about being real with yourself and others, about sticking to your guns and showing up truthfully no matter what, because you know that's how you gotta be." Marcus's response resonates with other answers to the same question. Kelly likewise understood the phrase as emphasizing the importance of being authentic, yet she also pointed to a necessary element of change: "It means asking yourself, 'Am I talking the truth?' and really standing up for who you are, what you wanna get out of your life. But it also means not being afraid to challenge yourself and change your behavior if need be, because if you're not willing to change, then you can't expect to walk in your truth." For his part, the adjunct pastor stressed that walking in your truth is a collective process:

> [The] community is there to help explore and engage a deeper truth that one person may not see by him- or herself. This is what Spiritual

Development is about. It's about creating the opportunity for folks to engage, have real dialogue, ask the tough questions, engage them, to get to what's real for me, what's the truth for me, what do I understand, what do people see that I don't see. All of those things.

In sum, to walk in your truth is the outcome of a process of self-examination and transformation that compels one to be honest with oneself and act intentionally in accordance with what one feels and knows to be truthful at a particular time and place. It is the provisional result of a trajectory that requires the courage to face up to the risks involved in aligning one's life to this truth—about one's sexuality, relationship, dependencies, or financial situation—given that the effort of detaching from unbearable situations and subsequent attempts to reattach to more enabling resources necessarily exposes one to an interval of exacerbated precariousness previously avoided with the familiar crutches still in place. For this reason, one needs to learn how to walk in one's truth in concert with others—including God—without whom the test of truth would be impossible to take on. As Pastor made clear, "None of us arrive at our truth alone, because all our truth is informed by our lived experiences. . . . Within UFC there's still truth to be added, still truth to be explored, still truth to be exposed to, before we can say we're walking fully in it." His words echo James's understanding of religious experience as a "postulator of new facts," or "hypotheses," about the possibility of a more expansive world where different events can be expected and different conduct is required. For Pastor, as for James and Latour, religious truth is pluriform and capacious and adds reality to this world, displacing one's habituated prehension of space and time and bringing one closer to the divine presence whose faith and love need to be made manifest by the faithful.[15]

Moreover, it is this emphasis on truth as involving a transformational relationship to oneself and one's surroundings that invokes Foucault's notion of "political spirituality," or "the will to discover a different way of governing oneself through a different way of dividing up true and false" (Carrette 2000: 137). Truth, here, is inseparable from specific collectives that add, explore, and in turn are exposed to truthful speech and action in a recursive process of governing oneself and others. Rather than an ever receding end in itself, the truth, conceived as a test rather than a target, thus becomes a heterogeneous set of "means without end" (Agamben 2000). Yet whereas Foucault's political spirituality discarded the presence of God, His proximity and accessibility are of vital importance at the UFCB, where He is an integral member of the collective who *inspires* congregants to overcome—or, at least, to better deal with—the exhaustion and anxiety caused by daily pressures.[16] Here we should note that the etymological lineage of the noun "inspiration" traces it back to the "immediate influence of God or a god" that breathes life into the earthly domain of mortals.[17] This divine breath of life, so crucial to the survival and flourishing of the congregation, is then remediated by the UFCB's clergy in the pulpit as well as by those sitting in the pews when they shout, holler, whoop, and sing the praise that fills the church with good vibrations that resonate through the bodies in attendance—bodies that witness and then testify to this vital force. Ashon Crawley (Crawley 2013b: 50; cf. 2017) calls this "aesthetic production of breath" during Black Pentecostal services "*Black pneuma,*" or "the capacity for the double-gesture of inhalation and exhalation as the hint of life, life that is exorbitant, capacious and, fundamentally, social, though it is also life that is contained and engulfed by gratuitous violence." Like the reciprocal gesture of "giving life" during a Ball, which increases the vitality of both the performer and the audience, the Black queer *pneuma* that circulates during services constitutes the dynamic Spirit that gives life—life at once sacred and profane, holy and irreverent. *Pneuma*, in its close etymological contiguity to *psūkhē*, is irreducible to "mere" biological life. Formed from the verb *psūkhō*, "to blow," *psūkhē* likewise denotes the breath of life that later was commonly translated as "soul" or "spirit," yet, as Eugene Thacker reminds us, for Aristotle it figured as "the *archē* of life, the life-principle": "Aristotle takes up the way that the concept of *psūkhē* explains *that* life is and *how* it is, but he also makes the term account for *what* life is. Aristotle raises up this term to mean not simply the facticity of living beings, but that by which such a facticity of life is possible" (Thacker 2010: 13) The "that by which," the condition of possibility for life to exist with and against death and assume its variegated forms through the enunciations of the living, is here nothing other than God's lifegiving breath that animates the world-building practices of the UFCB.[18]

In this light, it is interesting to follow Foucault as he, at the end of his final lecture at the Collège de France, explicitly addresses the issue of divine presence. In his discussion of Christian *parrhesia*, he turns to what he calls the "parrhesiastic pole of Christianity," where "the relation to the truth is established in the form of a face-to-face relationship with God and in a human confidence which corresponds to the effusion of divine love" (Foucault 2011: 337). He opposes this mode of *parrhesia*, as "that openness of heart, that relationship of confidence which brought man and God face-to-face" (ibid.: 333), to Christianity's "anti-parrhesiastic pole," a collection of practices he had hitherto referred to more generally as "Christian ascetics." Here, the truth of the self and its place in the world can be deciphered only through a suspicious "mistrust of oneself and the world, and in fear and trembling before God" (ibid.: 338). Having grown up in a familial-religious atmosphere where the scandalous truth of their sexuality was subject to both shaming scrutiny and shameful silence, many UFCB members had indeed learned to mistrust themselves and their desires in fear of a judgmental God who would abandon them in disgust. Consequently, they tried to hide away, withdrawing into the protective yet isolated realm of privacy—to the extent that they could— while constructing a public persona built on what they essentially knew and felt was a lie. But while lying to oneself is tough, lying to God is eventually unbearable. This is why the UFCB's gospel "God is love, and love is for everyone" presents such a welcome and emancipatory counter-truth: it is a parrhesiastic enunciation proclaiming that LGBT and SGL people are in fact deserving of God's love and that He will enable them to walk in their truth if they have the courage to open their hearts to Him. Furthermore, the truth of this gospel is truly *religious*, in Latour's terminology, given that it meets the three felicity conditions of Christian religious speech: closeness, presence, and transformation. By restoring congregants' "face-to-face relationship" with God, which has been distorted by years of homophobic discipline and indoctrination, it renews their confidence in the presence of God's love in their life, which then becomes a radically *other* life than the existence to which their former churches had condemned them.[19]

However, following Latour, it is important to note that this presence and proximity is always already mediated, and there can be no immediate access to the divine. In other words, the paradox here is that we can get to the "here and now" only by way of several detours. Foucault himself comes close to acknowledging this when, loosely citing Dorotheos of Gaza, he notes that Christian *parrhesia* is in fact "multiform," manifesting itself through "speaking, touching, and looking" (Foucault 2011: 336)—to which I would add listening, for without this mediation, no truthful speech could resonate. Returning to Latour's argument once more, divine entities are highly sensitive to the ways they are talked about, and religious enunciations can be truthful only if they succeed in making manifest, or are able to "transport," the God they invoke, which again points to the value of achieving the right "tonality." At the UFCB, congregants and clergy gather multiple times a week to attain this tonality through various embodied and mediated enunciations, or "sensational forms," such as collective prayer, sermons, call-and-response routines, incantations, hugs, music, and song.[20] These sensational forms demonstrate the variety of objects, objectives, and practices that are enrolled in the parrhesiastic process of walking in your truth, which always involves a curved—or should we say queer?—path rather than a straight line.

The topic of tonality returns us to a second paradox, addressed above: while some of the UFCB's ministers are critical of the emotional "tone" of worship cultivated and normalized in the Black Church tradition on the grounds that it often contributes to a form of routinized and thoughtless conduct, they nevertheless adopt a number of sensational forms and emotive rhetorical devices that firmly tie the church to its Black Pentecostal heritage. There was the call and response, the shouting and whooping; there were improvised musical interludes, moments of testimony, and plenty of exuberant singing, chanting, and praise. Yet, as previously discussed, while these forms and devices produce a worship experience that manages to assemble the congregation through orchestrated displays of emotional testimony and well-worn techniques of affective contagion, they are concurrently folded into a pedagogical project of "political spirituality" that hinges on a critical ethos of conducting oneself and others differently. In other words, the UFCB's clergy enrolls familiar sensational forms, which historically have proved instrumental in achieving the presence-enhancing tonality of Black religious enunciation (Lincoln and Mamiya 1990), yet mobilizes these forms to "change the value of the currency" with regard to the hateful and threatening messages they too often circulate and aestheticize.[21] This process of transformation thus actively draws on the affective pull of evocative ritual and convention in order to create and sustain an alternative spiritual, multisensory infrastructure in which Black queer folks can develop a commitment to one another and to a different, more enabling truth. This is the truth that they are worthy of having a good life, that their life has value, and it is theirs to make, to change, to love. As Crawley (2013a: 35) puts it, "Blackqueer aesthesis, voiced by the voice, displays the viability and tenacity of a life force that is thought to be nothing other than the drive toward death."

For a Faith in This World

Foucault's lectures in *The Government of Self and Others*, in which many of his long-standing concerns are crystallized, are ultimately about citizenship. His engagement with *parrhesia* as a practice that mediates the political relationships between members of a *politeia* is aimed toward a problematization of political power in society beyond the "juridical-institutional system of that society," by examining of the correlations between governmentality and subjectivation (Foucault 2010: 159). As I have illustrated, it is in the space that connects these two concepts that we can most clearly discern the intimate relationship between ethical and political practices, which also makes it a space for the cultivation of forms of citizenship that operate beyond the purview of those political and juridical infrastructures that traditionally anchor a secular faith in state-secured stability and belonging—what I am calling our immunitary citizenship regime. While Chapter 1 addressed the anti-Black heteronormativity that subtends and supports such a regime, this chapter—like Chapter 3—has attended to Black queer experiments with collectivity and solidarity that, in Lauren Berlant's (2011a: 261) words, imagine "the work of citizenship as a dense sensual activity of performative belonging to the now in which potentiality is affirmed." Given that Baltimore is home to countless communities of faith, these experiments, which I call civic intimacies, are frequently permeated and facilitated by religious practices, feelings, and attachments that imbue this "dense sensual activity of performative belonging" with spiritual energies, which are then mobilized in Black queer counter-conducts that fold external forces inward in a way that critically transforms them. In this sense, we can say that the government of self and others takes a "detour through God," whose renewed presence and love inspires a confidence that enables Black queer folks to manifest their truth despite the inherent risk of losing whatever anchors their ongoing survival. This is not a transcendent divinity whose sovereign will decides on the fate of his disciples and who demands obedience and self-sacrifice. Instead, it materializes as an immanent presence that inspires and encourages while the difficult ethical work of transforming one's life has to be accomplished each day anew by the faithful. Like Berlant's "lateral politics" of citizenship, the experiences and activities narrated here are committed to the here and now of the sensual present, as an intimate space-time in which a process of mutual attunement can develop into an enduring sense of obligation to care for, or concern oneself with, the lives of others and so generate new life-enhancing attachments that are mediated by a divine presence. Rather than directing attention *away from* the world, then, religious experience helps Black queers of faith achieve the consistency and courage they need to recalibrate their lives so they can conduct themselves more forcefully *in this* world, thereby expanding the political agency of not only those who are "ethically otherwise" but also those whose Black queerness/queer Blackness has rendered them superfluous to the body politic.

Despite queer theory's epistemological commitment to alternative ways of knowing the world and our place in it, and notwithstanding its persistent advocacy of subjugated, situated, embodied, and oblique forms of knowledge production, it has nevertheless sustained an overwhelming investment in (ostensibly) secular modes of critique and analysis. Even at a time when queer scholars are further expanding conventional conceptions of what it is and what it takes to know, venturing beyond the human body and its affective composition into the nonhuman realm of animals, objecthood, and vibrant matter, there has been very little serious interest in the development of critical thought that is informed or mediated by (faith in) a divine presence.[22] Yet the daily lives of countless Black queer (trans) men and women are marked by a vital and unwavering religious faith that often forms the foundation for the enactment of emancipatory social projects. Far from somehow distorting their analysis, or distracting them from the "real" matters of concern, the ambit of the religious and the sacred provides Black queers of faith with resources for the development of the kind of critical attitude that scholars committed (often tacitly) to the tenets of Enlightenment modernity have conventionally associated with the sphere of secular thought and action—as if these two spheres could be unproblematically separated. In contrast, this chapter has attended to a different, distinctly nonmodern movement by which Black queer worldly experiments with an ethics of self-formation and a politics of being governed differently merge with—and become mediated by—religious problems, practices, devices, and investments. Such convergence defies any clean separation between religious feeling, or "belief," and secular reason, or knowledge.[23] Rather, religiously inflected feelings frequently form the affective framework in which critique can take shape through improvised forms of knowledge production that tie together sacred and profane sources. The UFCB is experimenting with such Black queer modes of knowledge production by capacitating thought that is able to critically interrogate Christian doctrine. It is thus also resisting the transubstantiation of its anti-Black/queer violence into the enlightened epistemologies of secular modernity, whose central political notions, as Carl Schmitt (2005) insisted, are indelibly marked by their theological origins.

Gil Anidjar (2011: 722) writes, "If Christianity is the biotheological surge that brought about the sacralization of life, and if modernity has consisted less in a break with than in the intensification of this particular vector, then Christianity might be more plausibly understood as the unique and complex apparatus that brings into the world this singular division [between blood and soul, flesh and spirit] (along with the specific terms of that division)." Very well, but against the institutional forms of doing and knowing that follow from this political biotheology, which, as I argued in the previous chapter, sacrifice life at the very moment it is saved, the UFCB organizes a different and more capacious vernacular epistemology that is deeply "*an*institutional" in its efforts to resist dominant epistemologies "that seek enclosure rather than porosity, that seek containment rather than permeability" (Crawley 2015: 88). This is not to say that the UFCB relishes its vulnerability—far from it. It functions as an invaluable safe space and support structure that, like the Black gay club, does not separate flesh from spirit but, rather, celebrates the flesh as the site of communal spiritual practice. To know the spirit is to do so *through the flesh*—flesh conceived as that sacred-*cum*-profane common substance animated by God. As a small community of faith whose schism with hegemonic Christianity and the mainstream Black Church has turned it into an outlaw congregation propelled by the divine breath that never ceases to give it life, the UFCB militates against the immunitary temporal logic of sacrifice and sacrificial love that abandons Black flesh and expedites its annihilation.[24] When God is love, love is for everyone, right here, right now. To hell with the future if it does not speak to the Black queer present.

5

Pleasure, Violence, and the Past's Presence

> To survive violence, to find a way forward under its weight: is this less or more radical than to dream of overcoming violence in a final, exceptional stroke?
>
> —CANDACE A. VOGLER and PATCHEN MARKELL,
> "Introduction: Violence, Redemption, and the Liberal Imagination"

While Chapter 3 examined how Baltimore's Ballroom community negotiates and offers alternatives to the racialized biopolitics of HIV prevention and Chapter 4 looked at how the Unity Fellowship Church of Baltimore (UFCB) seeks to affirm Black queer existence by reclaiming God and speaking truth to the power of homophobic institutions—most immediately, the home churches in which many congregants grew up—I have thus far remained largely silent on another of Michel Foucault's major and interconnected interests: the use of pleasure. Here I take up this theme more explicitly by investigating how the ethics of sexual pleasure and violence shape the life-making practices of Black queer women in Baltimore's gay leather and BDSM community.[1] For Foucault (1990a), the radical potential of bodies and pleasures derives from their polymorphous qualities over and against the rigidity of the truth-producing apparatuses that have staged "sex desire" as a psycho-familial drama. In interviews, he expressed his keen interest in San Francisco's leather scene during the 1970s, where he observed the tentative emergence of new, "desexualized" forms of pleasure that forgo genital intercourse for practices and protocols that engage the body as a fragmented and exalted surface—a "body made entirely malleable by pleasure: something that opens itself, tightens, palpitates, beats, gapes" (Foucault 1996: 187; see also Weiss 2011: 118–120). Yet in Foucault's androcentric and color-blind imagination, this body was assumed to be white and male, much like the dominant physiognomy of San Francisco's leather scene. How, then, does Black queer women's embodiment throw into relief, or disarray, understandings of pleasure, power, and violence concomitant to such an assumption, which continues to structure the popular and scholarly treatment of gay leather sex and BDSM? What historical taboos will have to be addressed, and what social boundaries will need to be transgressed, for Black queer women's sexuality to be taken seriously as a cipher for the "tense and tender ties" (cf. Stoler 2001) between pleasure and violence, so carefully choreographed in BDSM performances?

In *The Color of Kink*, her recent critical intervention into scholarly debates on race and sexuality in pornographic representation, Ariane Cruz puts Black queer women's bodies front and center. Employing BDSM as an "apt lens through which to consider Black sexuality and its performance in pornography" (Cruz 2016a: 9), she examines the formative role of violence in the construction of this sexuality while recognizing "the pleasures and power some Black female subjects experience in sexual performances scripted by the memory of slavery" (ibid.: 2–3). Cruz's work attunes us to the ambiguity and complexity of BDSM as a "productive space" (ibid.) with a fraught relationship to this memory, where Black women's sexual practices are dynamic and include both thrill and trauma, submission and dominance. By problematizing conventional assumptions and stereotypes, she presents Black queer women as active agents and legitimate participants in BDSM culture who embody the legacy of racialized sexual violence not solely as burden or abjection, but also as a template for new modes of making and representing the self. While her important contribution informs my argument in this chapter, Cruz's aims ultimately differ from mine. I am less interested in the perverse racial semiotics of BDSM per se and therefore do not engage in the close reading of Black queer women's BDSM performances as pornographic texts (ibid.: 23). Instead, I examine how Black queer women in Baltimore negotiate their relationship to BDSM as a kinky lifestyle and community that offers valuable resources for experimenting with pain, pleasure, and power, despite its historical and ongoing marginalization of Black women's sexuality. I argue that this marginalization, which structurally infringes on these women's erotic self- and world-making practices, persists because Baltimore's gay leather/BDSM community takes for granted its whiteness and attempts to neutralize any racially gendered antagonism by circumscribing it within the sacred space of consensual intimacy and sexual play.

Safety in Numbers

My initial encounter with Baltimore's gay leather and BDSM scene happened when I attended the Mr. Maryland Leather Contest at the Hippo, about six months into my fieldwork.[2] I was invited there by two community contacts who were both members of Command MC, the leather club that was in charge of producing the contest. Next to Command MC, Baltimore's oldest leather club is the Shipmates, which was founded in 1974. As I would soon find out, both clubs have an exclusively male membership and are majority-white, even though the leather contests I attended were more mixed in terms of gender and—to a much lesser extent—racial representation. Baltimore also has a club for leatherwomen: FIST, or Females Investigating Sexual Terrain. FIST started as a social organization in 1994, catering primarily to lesbian and bisexual women, although everyone who identified as a woman was—and still is—welcome. Its most important aim at that time was to create a level of visibility so that women interested in the leather lifestyle would know that there was a place where they could meet one another. Although leather sex and BDSM have always remained a central aspect of club life, FIST also developed a strong focus on community service during the AIDS crisis of the 1990s, exposing it to a broader LGBT public and allowing it to establish closer connections with the men's clubs in the city. This happened primarily at community events such as the leather contests but was also facilitated through Brother Help Thyself (BHT), a community-based organization that redistributes the annual total sum of money raised by the different leather clubs in the form of community grants, awarded during their annual grant ceremony. People of color were most visible at these ceremonies (I attended two), usually as grant recipients, which does not imply that Baltimore's leather clubs had no members of color, but it *does* mean that Black people in the lifestyle were far less publicly visible in the city, which has no Black leather club.[3] Baltimore did see the emergence of Black BEAT (Black Expression Alternative Tastes), the nation's first leather/BDSM organization owned and operated by people of color, which was founded by three African American women in 2003 with the aim of hosting educational conferences and get-togethers.[4] During its twelve-year existence, Black BEAT played a pivotal role in increasing Black visibility within the community and raising awareness about the specific vulnerabilities and concerns of African Americans involved in BDSM.

Yet despite such recent progress, the thing that struck me as I was browsing through the historical materials on display at the traveling Carter/

Johnson Leather Library—curated by Viola Johnson, a Black lesbian venerated nationally for her long-standing service to the community and her knowledge of the culture—is how incredibly *white* they were. While the books, pamphlets, pictures, and magazines cover a wide range of practices and proclivities, spanning roughly four centuries worth of kink and ordered in a way that gives the visitor a good sense of the (pre)history of leather and BDSM culture, they nevertheless showed little racial diversity, let alone a sustained focus on Black leather culture.[5] Gay leather history is largely a history of white men and (later) women, despite the piecemeal influx of queers of color and the establishment of Black leather clubs in the 1990s. Of course, the leather community has been marked by racial segregation since its very foundation, given that the wartime U.S. Army in which the first leathermen formed their intimate bonds was such a deeply segregated institution. These white gay bonds outlasted the war, as did the military rituals and protocols that shaped early club life, whose relatively well-documented aesthetics and codes of conduct became the blueprint for the contemporary leather scene. But no Black or multiracial clubs seem to have existed at that time, and if they did, no documentation has survived as far as I am aware. Beyond the history of modern leather and BDSM, the much longer history of sadomasochism and "kink"—an exceedingly capacious notion (Weiss 2011)—is similarly dominated by (representations of) white deviant sexual practices, which have been documented for as long as documentation has been possible. Indeed, the concept of "kink" is itself white, since nonwhite people for many centuries have figured as the very embodiment of sexual deviancy: exotic and hypersexualized creatures regulated and contained, objects for the prurient gaze of a *scientia sexualis* that governed a Western colonial imagination in which sexual *subjectivity*, whether normative or deviant, was exclusively reserved for white citizens. White citizens could have kinky proclivities, whereas to be nonwhite or, worse, to be (rendered) Black *was* to be queer, abject, and unintelligible as anything other than property or sexual fetish.[6] In the contemporary U.S. context, Black sexual politics and culture continue to be haunted by the histories of chattel slavery, segregation, dispossession, and other kinds of structural violence against African Americans, which in turn cannot be disentangled from other social forces, such as the Black Church experience and the transformed etiology of the HIV/AIDS epidemic (C. Cohen 1999; Collins 2004). This fraught historical context sets the parameters within which Black queer folks experiment with alternative forms of gendered sexual expression and cultivate their own spaces of erotic intimacy and care, such as the nationwide urban network of Ballroom communities that operates largely beyond the purview of the mainstream gay community. Yet this obviously doesn't mean that there are no kinky Black queers. There are plenty, and they are organized, but they continue to occupy a marginal position within the larger gay leather and BDSM community.

Baltimore's racial history is especially fraught, as discussed in Chapter 2, and it has in turn informed the race relations within its LGBT community. Although Black and white queers occasionally mix at social or political events, they still "don't party much together"—as someone phrased it in a conversation once. If you walk by the Hippo on any given night of the week, you will see mostly middle-aged white men and women hanging at the bar, except on Thursdays, when a large crowd of twenty-something Black youths line up in front of the main entrance for the club's hip hop night and there is hardly a white person around. This is one of the few nights that young Black queers—many of them Ball kids—set foot in the gayborhood of Mt. Vernon, which is otherwise too gentrified and remote from the spaces they usually inhabit. For Monica, a twenty-seven-year old African American queer woman who has lived in Baltimore her whole life, the main thing that draws her to this neighborhood is the Playhouse, a former warehouse converted into a multiroom BDSM dungeon.[7] While few of her white peers seemed willing to talk about racial issues in their community, instead seeking to emphasize the affirmative practices and social cohesion of the leather scene, Monica was outspoken about race and repeatedly pointed out how there are actually more Black people into leather and BDSM than one would be able to tell from going to clubs. Being out at a public play party or some other event at a club can be a costly privilege, both economically and culturally, which is why a lot of Black people stay at home and organize small house parties. "The more public you are, the more it is a privilege, because you can just be out with it," she said. "But that's not so easy for a lot of Black people. In the Black community there's this code word, 'freaky,' which means that you're into alternative stuff. So a lot of people have this idea, like, I wanna explore, but I don't want to explore so much that I lose my Blackness." This sense of Blackness is more easily protected in the privacy of a friend's home, together with a small group of other Black people, than when attending a public event at a club whose majority is invariably white.[8] Baltimore's Playhouse is no exception, and while it caters especially to queer women, many of them are what Monica refers to as "white leather dykes." Although she has gone to many events there, she also finds its scene "rather clique-y," and the high entry fees charged at some of its club nights have pushed her to organize play parties at her house: "So doing it at home, that's where I'm at now. I don't need to pay $20 for an event." But she definitely has, and despite her previous assertion, she continued to do so, albeit more sporadically.

Monica said she went to more events when she was younger and just entering the scene, which she had been exploring for about seven years when I met her. At first she did not feel welcome, because there were only a few people of color around, and she had a negative experience at the very first event she attended, where the racial tension was palpable, people kept staring at her, and some men and women hit on her in a particularly aggressive manner. However, being a stubborn person, she decided not to give up on her newfound interest and kept showing up at events to talk to people and learn about the scene and its practices, in addition to finding out who she was. "I never really had to question whether or not I was Black," she said. "There was still an awakening in the sense of what it meant to me, but it was pretty obvious. But I had to constantly question whether I was queer, whether I was kinky, and it was the first time I felt like I was part of a minority I didn't know." Despite this newfound vulnerability, what enthralled her about BDSM was that it was so different from anything she had ever known or done before while at the same time it embodied some of the same moral ideals she grew up with, such as honesty and mutual respect. Monica grew up in a very sheltered, religious household, where, she said, she "was being groomed to be a minister's wife." Sex was something of a taboo in her family, and she was told to save herself for her future husband. So by the time she went to college, where "everyone was gay," she found it difficult to deal with her new environment and initially responded by condemning gay fellow students who would surely be going to hell. Yet during one particular conversation with a lesbian student, she experienced what she called a "break" in her sexual awareness, suddenly recalling that she had had sex with a woman years before but afterward had "created a world where that was not sex." This set her on a path in which she would slowly come to terms with her "lesbian desire," even though she continued to be attracted to men and started dating a man she ended up marrying. He also introduced her to leather and BDSM, which provided her with a new and daunting platform to explore her pleasures and sense of identity, eventually leading her to adopt the term "queer" to capture her fluctuating sexual predilections. After her initial bad experience and other "stupid" and "unsafe mistakes" that she attributed to her ignorance as a novice and no longer wanted to dwell on, Monica decided it was time to school herself properly. She started going to "munches"—meetings at bars and restaurants at which new and experienced peers can socialize over food in an environment whose casual publicness provides a measure of safety for most newcomers. She immersed herself completely in the culture and history of leather and BDSM, as she does with all things that intrigue her, and within a year she was running a munch of her own, going to conventions, and taking up positions in various community-based organizations. An important reason for becoming so involved in the organization of munches was to prevent others from making the same mistakes she did by educating newcomers about the protocols and risks that are at the heart of leather sex and BDSM. As she told me, "I wanted to help new people. I felt an obligation to help other people, so they have a sounding board, because a lot of people in the community get hurt in various ways, some of which can be prevented."

Kris, Monica's "leather mother," had been her sounding board and source of education since they met a few years earlier at a conference. Monica was slightly in awe of Kris's presence, which was indeed radiant and awesome; wherever she goes, she takes her knowledge and attitude with her, and I remember feeling intimidated when we met for an interview. Sitting across from me at a café, she looked me straight in the eye and told me in an intense voice, "I don't care how stoic you are; I don't care how powerful you are. I'm gonna get in there, and I'm gonna turn you into a pile of mush at my feet. I have the ability to get in your mind and have you think for one instant whether or not I really will take this fucking blade and cut your goddamn jugular open [*making the sound of a throat being cut open*]. There's a fine line between fear and excitement." Now *that* was a first impression. Kris, an African American polyamorous woman in her mid-fifties, exuded confidence and pride in her skills as a dominatrix, which she had carefully honed over the previous fifteen-plus years. Although she was Monica's leather mother and the two were very close, they had little in common in terms of their background and how they derived pleasure from BDSM. Whereas Monica preferred to "bottom" (i.e., to take the submissive role during play) and grew up in a religious household where conventional gender and sexual roles were carefully policed, Kris's journey started in a very different place: 1950–1960s Harlem. She said:

> I come from a long line of strong Black women who were heads of the household. And I've always been dominant; when kids would come over, I'd make them clean up my room. I tied kids up; I had to be the cop; I would spank you. . . . The only father I ever knew was a woman. She was a hustler, looking like Nat King Cole, in a suit. We had a lot of hookers hanging around. One, Tulsa, would come into my room and tell stories. I remember her twang, her leather shoes, black stockings, black bra. . . . She smelled so good. She would talk as I fell asleep. And

I remember the attitude; all the women were glamorous. There were drag queens around. It was a very international environment. So it was only when going to Catholic school, by the time I was in fourth grade [because her mother thought this would provide her with a better education] that I knew these things were not normal. They made fun of me because my mother always came to school with a woman.

Despite the free sexual and gender mores Kris grew up with, and her early proclivity for dominating others, it would take another thirty years before she acted on this inclination in a way that eventually led her to explore the meaning and use of her kinky pleasure. It wasn't at all pleasurable at first, however, as she rediscovered what she now sees as her "talent" while she was in an abusive relationship with a man she nevertheless loved dearly. They got together when she was thirty-two, living in Virginia Beach, and what started out good quickly turned sour when she found out he was an alcoholic who would regularly pick fights with her. She later understood these as "games" he played to get her to physically assault him: "He knew I was stronger than him, so the game was to convince me that I was weaker. . . . One day, he caught me right, and . . . I couldn't take it anymore. I grabbed him and, good God almighty, I fucked him up. I had him in a headlock and beat him in the head with an iron brush handle." To her surprise, this turned him on, and for a while she would beat him every two weeks, although she couldn't really share in his pleasure because she felt resentful about the manipulation. "So, something's going on here," she said. "I didn't understand it, and there was no one to talk to." This impasse led her to ask around for information that could help her make sense of her situation, and via friends she heard something about "safe, sane, and consensual." She didn't understand the first two but liked the idea of consent and tried to talk about what she'd learned with her partner, who was in such denial that she got frustrated and ended up leaving a year later. Still, they continued to get together for two more years, on and off, before he drank himself to death. "He would fly me here and there," she said. "I whipped his ass in Trump Tower. By that time I even had a little toy bag." But the real turning point came when, after she had broken up with her partner, Kris disclosed the nature of their relationship to one of her partner's friends who, in response, offered her $300 to spank him. She was broke at the time and took the money, then started really seeking people out to teach her about this line of work.

Kris's first mentor was a female former marine, who drilled her on the importance of the "head aspect"—that BDSM was about the mind, and she had to honor and respect this. Through her education, Kris also learned to believe in magic, because, she said, "what we do is magic. To manipulate the most powerful energy on the planet, sexual energy, is magic—to be able to control that, to make it ebb and flow." This was the moment she moved closer to me and suggested that she could get into my mind and have me doubt whether she would slit my throat. I think it was her way of illustrating not only her physical power but also the power of her mind. Because she respected this power, she also drew a hard limit at humiliation during play, saying, "You just don't know what landmines you're gonna step into." For this reason, humiliation likewise had no part in her relationship with the several (male, female, and trans) slaves she owns, despite popular imaginations of degradation as central to the Master/slave relationship in BDSM and chattel slavery. When I asked her about the violent racial history of this relationship, she acknowledged a historical link but also insisted on crucial differences between the two contexts. Most importantly, according to Kris, a slave ultimately has agency in a BDSM relationship—even if only the initial agency to relinquish it through a contractual agreement with a Master. In this way, a BDSM slave is both subject and object of an ownership contract that allocates the risks and obligations in a Master/slave relationship.[9] But she also argued that her slaves have a measure of agency within the vicissitudes of their long-term relationship, which is characterized not only by the slave's unmitigated commitment and submission but also by mutual trust, "because it's not a relationship you go into lightly. There's stages," she said. "The slave has taken the time to truly get to know me, to know what I would want and not want. And they can actually make decisions in my stead." This is why she claims that slaves are more proactive than submissives, for whom servitude is often a more casual affair. She knows she can always trust her slaves to have her best interest in mind.

Still, I wondered about that historical link, signified in the Master/slave relationship, that brings slavery's violent past into the present of BDSM practice. According to Kris, who always gave me the impression that she was somehow above the fray with respect to racial issues within the community, the history of slavery in the United States certainly prevents more African Americans from engaging in BDSM and leather sex. Although she had no problems with terms such as "Master" and "slave," she knew people of color for whom such terminology was sensitive enough not to use in the presence of white peers—if at all. A lot of her Black peers felt uncomfortable and alienated in majority-white public BDSM spaces, where, as she had witnessed too many times to count, Black submissives were more likely to be touched inappropriately. But she also contended that Black people were "still a little repressed, sexually. I don't think they're comfortable expressing their sexuality around white people when there aren't that many [Black peers]. They just won't come out." Moreover, in her experience Black community members tended to treat gay leather and BDSM as "more of a sexual thing," while their white peers were more committed to the cultural history, with its attendant protocols and rituals. When I asked her whether this could be explained by the fact that leather/BDSM history is so white, she hesitated for a moment but then agreed and added, "African American history, our history, is all negative on it." For Kris, however, the biggest problem with this negative positionality was not so much the erasure of Black kink's historical presence but how it resulted in Black practitioners' ignorance about harm-reducing and potentially lifesaving protocols:

> I am seeing so many new people coming into this thing, getting their heads scrambled and even being harmed physically because "I'm Black and I just wanna play with Black people, and Black people ain't been doing this necessarily all that long, so I'm gonna figure this shit out by myself, and then I'm gonna fuck up all these people, 'cause I don't know what the hell I'm doing, because I don't wanna go and even go *watch* the white people play." Talk to them. Ask them how you do this thing!

It all comes down to education, and Kris believed that the knowledge of more experienced practitioners should be respected, even when this means listening to white people who aren't always responsive to racial issues. Fortunately, more Black people who have entered the scene over the past decade have taken it upon themselves to educate their peers—Black and white— through workshops, conferences, and other events. The most prominent organization to come out of this movement is Black BEAT, mentioned earlier, with which both Kris and Monica were associated at the time. Monica was especially adamant about reaching out to new people of color, not just for educational purposes, but also because she liked having them around and wanted to make sure they stayed and felt comfortable. "It's important for white people to see them there, too," she said. "They're pretty, those big brown people walking around naked. . . . It makes me feel a little bit better when my big brown ass walks around naked, too!" Yet while she viewed the inclusion of a broader range of body types as important from a social, aesthetic, and political perspective, she was mainly concerned with numbers—or safety in numbers, to be more precise. When there are more people of color at an event, it becomes safer for all of them, because they can keep an eye on one another as long as they are playing in the public parts of a club. Monica said she repeatedly noticed a difference between being the only Black person at a party and having a few others around: "People in the community are just a cross-section of the community at large. They don't know how to talk to Black people, and they'll talk to us differently when there's eight of us. You know, people make racist jokes at play parties, shit about wanting to be with an African Queen and stuff like that." Sexist and racist stereotypes such as these put Black men and women off and cause them to leave the club-based public scene to look for more private, all-Black parties, if it does not turn them off BDSM altogether.

This is what most worried Monica, because, she said, events felt different when they were mixed, which involves not only the issue of safety but also something she referred to as a difference in "flavoring." She loved the flavor of events that had more than a few Black people in attendance; they "add their own spin" to the composition of play scenes, she said.[10] "It's almost like a very worship-centered head space. We add a flavor to the standard techniques and I've seen people start singing in the middle of their play." Yet this kind of experimentation is inhibited by racial tensions and incidents that still too often dodge a community that prides itself on its progressive politics: "Really, a lot of the most racist people I've met are kinky, like straight up and down. But they believe that because they're open about their sexuality they are open about everything else and that doesn't correlate, that's not the same thing." One of the areas in which racial tensions are most prevalent is the use of language. Monica noted that Black people were often addressed or referred to as "slaves" in situations in which it was not clear whether or how this term related to a particular relationship or play scene, leading to a number of very awkward moments and a few (near) altercations. This made the need for better cultural education painfully clear to her, in particular for those who are just entering the scene, and she and some friends had organized classes on race in the BDSM community. While the classes have helped to some extent, she said that there was only so much she could do, in terms of the number of people she is able to reach, and while she continues her efforts, she also realized that the issue of race would never really be "resolved."

Freedom in Bondage

Bracketing momentarily the question of whether the issue of race should be resolved or overcome in the first place, such an aspiration would ignore the fact that some of the community's most prevalent protocols, subject positions, and fetishes are rooted in a history of racial domination. Besides the Master/slave relationship, the term "boy" carries the legacy of (settler) colonialism,[11] while the collaring of slaves at parties invokes the history of chattel slavery that gave birth to this public display of ownership.[12] And then there's the whipping, beating, and bondage. Even though many people in the scene tried to assure me that these violent rituals are not racial, let alone racist, because they have accumulated their own, specific subcultural meanings and because the majority of slaves and boys in the community are white, I was less than convinced that these supposedly color-blind practices and subject positions could be so easily detached from America's violent past. Moreover, alongside these more-or-less implicit references to slavery, the most explicit and therefore most controversial practice on the leather and BDSM scene is known as "race play," which intentionally dramatizes and eroticizes racial domination in interracial scenes. It was controversial, at first sight, mainly among African American practitioners; most white community members I spoke with claimed to have no interest in this practice and usually attempted to avoid the subject altogether. When they did "admit" to engaging in race play, they described it in terms of enacting a fantasy and emphasized its consensual foundation and the safety measures that were carefully taken into account, including a safe word that, when uttered, would immediately stop the scene. Thus, they implicitly admitted that this type of scene was potentially high risk due to its elicitation of racialized historical trauma while at the same time downplaying this trauma and its attendant *political* affects by framing race play as a matter of consent-based (inter)personal fantasy or shared proclivity.[13]

Monica knew that a lot of her peers refused to engage in race play, which for them could not signify anything other than a painful history of systemic violence and denigration. At the same time, some of her friends and acquaintances did enjoy it and usually provided the same explanation as the white practitioners I talked to: it is just about consenting adults acting out a hot fantasy. When I pressed her about her own experience and position, Monica remained equivocal about this thoroughly troubled practice, assuming a liberal position that depended on a clear distinction between private choice and public responsibility:

> My personal thing about race play is . . . I don't have a problem with it, politically, in the context of a private relationship, because if that relationship is built on integrity, then whatever you do in there will have to be with integrity and mindfulness. I don't particularly wanna

see it, or be a part of it, but . . . if it's really important to you, then once again it's over there, and I'm not gonna go over there to tell you how you need to have your relationship. But I don't wanna be a part of it, though. Race play is one of those scenes, if it's done in public, you will probably get a lot of shit for it, so you should be aware of it and take your responsibility. But it is also my duty, as someone who is outside of this scene, if I don't like it, to walk away.

If it is a privilege to be "out there" in public as a practitioner of leather sex or BDSM, as Monica argued before, then engaging in race play (quasi-)publicly is even more of a privilege, one that will be less available to Black queer folks due to the controversy it could generate. As a result, race play is frequently consigned to the domestic sphere of the committed relationship, whose privacy protects such play from public scrutiny and social antagonism. Given Monica's politically radical stance toward many other topics we discussed, I was surprised that she seemed to so easily endorse the privatization of something as controversial as race play. Perhaps she did so because she had partially given up on the play parties at the Playhouse and other venues outside Baltimore, instead opting to be more selective about who she played with and sticking to small house parties. Or maybe the liberal "not in my backyard" position was just the easiest for her to take, allowing her to be critical of the historical violence that clearly troubles yet also eroticizes and makes possible race play while simultaneously avoiding judgment of those who engage in it for whatever personal reason. This would certainly follow Kris's moral compass: never judge others. I never pushed Monica to further explain her position, which I regret now, but she did comment on other issues that allowed me to make more sense of her understanding of the politics of race in Baltimore's leather and BDSM community.

For instance, we talked about how being kinky in public is a privilege that is unequally distributed among Black and white community members, and how this is so partly because many African Americans share an anxiety about losing their Blackness if they come out publicly as kinky. Monica related this affective inhibition to the constitutive intersectional influence of religion and slavery on Black people's racial identities:

> Even if you didn't grow up religious, religion for a lot of Black people is one of the ways in which you have a context to understand your race. Because we don't really have this strong national spirit, because we remember all that shit that happened, our home base is based

on slavery and religion. . . . So religion and slavery helped knit your family together, and those religious ideas, from Grandma to Mom to you, even if you don't really like them, have been ingrained in you for so long that what Jesus would do and what white people do are different. . . . It's kind of like, religion is almost race; they're that closely connected for Black people.[14]

In other words, the Black Church condemns leather sex and BDSM not only because these activities are kinky but also, and perhaps especially, because they are *white*. As I argue above, leather and kink histories are white histories and—to adopt Kris's phrase—"African American history is all negative on it." In this history, the notion of race is interwoven with violence and the uplifting power of religion to the point of being practically indistinguishable, which performatively produces Blackness in stark opposition to any force that could loosen this tight triangular bond in which the nuclear family functions as a sacred glue that is persistently threatened with dissolution (Collins 2004: 107–108). Growing up in an African American family and realizing that you are "kinky," or "freaky," thus presents a challenge. As Monica noted, "It takes a lot for people to break out of that enough to do something that is so counter to what they have been taught." More precisely, it takes courage and mobility to embark on what leathermen and leatherwomen like to call a "journey," and mobility is not equally available to Black queer folks, who often have to struggle to make ends meet. When you cannot afford to detach from your biological family, emotionally or financially, and they are not willing to love you for who you are, it becomes a lot harder to explore new practices of pleasure and self-transformation that potentially involve the sacrifice of what you have learned to embrace as the core of being Black in the United States. This is also why institutions such as the UFCB and the Ball community are so crucially important for queer Black people in Baltimore: they provide spaces of reprieve, reflection, and belonging that not only are geographically within reach but also closely align with African American cultural experience.

Monica did "break out" with the help of scholarships that allowed her to go to college and explore a whole new world of sexual activity. She had to find out what it means for her to be both Black *and* queer, which has also entailed a rethinking of where God fits into her life. It took her a few years, but as she slowly became more comfortable in her Black skin, as it was wrapped in and flogged with cow skin, she started to tie her spirituality more directly to her BDSM practices. "Because [BDSM] was changing me as a person, I started to connect this to my idea of God," she said, "so now I talk to God when

I do this stuff, just like I talk to God when I'm driving my car. You know, God is everywhere, so why wouldn't he be in my kink life? Why can't I be an upright, moral, spiritual person who likes some things that some people consider wrong?" This was one of the very few occasions in which I heard Monica explicitly negotiate the religious values she had been taught in her youth to reclaim her moral worth and the presence of God in her life. Usually she was less defensive about her lifestyle and was typically unconcerned about other people's judgments. Yet in moments such as this one, I realized that "breaking out" is a difficult and gradual process that may not always be fully feasible, desirable, or complete. While Monica has now integrated God into all areas of her life and has regular conversations with a divine entity, she did not envision God "as a person in the sky." Rather, she thought of "it" as an image or more like an ideal that is attainable through what she called "diligence." For Monica, becoming a diligent person—which is an objective closely associated with leather/BDSM culture's emphasis on duty and/as a readiness to serve one's community—means cultivating a persistent attentiveness and responsiveness vis-à-vis her surroundings, something with which BDSM has allowed her to experiment. At the same time, her efforts to be more diligent increased the pleasure she derived from her kink life, helping her to move closer to her ideal of God as the embodiment of "justice and honesty." Kink thus provided her with a new world, or an ethical space, in which she could work on herself in the affirmative presence of God and her peers to become a more valued and virtuous person whose strength could set an example for others in her community.

Indeed, it is this sense of duty toward the community, articulated as an "immanent obligation" (Povinelli 2011a: 33) to be responsive to the needs and desires of peers through an erotically charged care of self and others, that infuses the ethical space of kink with political pertinence and possibility. As Jafari Allen (2011: 193) has argued, the erotics of Black self-making are ultimately about "cultivating spaces of critical enunciation, transgressing the hegemonic, and transforming the standard dehumanizing practices of Black genocide" while creating counterpublics "in which new forms of art, affective and erotic relations, and rules of public and private engagement not only inform all our choices, as Audre Lorde suggests, but in fact may condition new choices and new politics." For Monica, leather/BDSM culture served as one such counterpublic, despite its white male hegemony, because as long as she persisted in her diligent efforts to assemble other Black folks, it enabled her to act on her own desire: to experiment with her erotic subjectivity, tentatively encompassing "deeper understandings and compulsions of the body and soul, simultaneously embodying and invoking sex and death" (ibid.: 192). Again, it is crucial to emphasize that such experiments are a *collective* endeavor that enunciates the potential for what Allen calls "transcendent erotics and politics," a "sensuous practice that includes the deployment of sexualities pitched and styled to play various games [including the game of truth] more effectively or to at least less painfully experience psychically or materially marginal circumstances" (ibid.: 95). Allen's concept resonates with the notion of civic intimacies developed in this book, which likewise pertains to erotically and spiritually charged modes of collective survival and flourishing that persist below the radar of civic intelligibility.[15] The affinity between our projects becomes especially clear when Allen reflects on the relationship between citizenship and freedom:

> If an individual cannot be a citizen . . . , can he or she at least be (in one form or another) *free*? I query citizenship here not only because of the barriers Black queers face when attempting to enjoy the full complement of citizenship—full "rights" within the political body of the nation—but more pointedly to ask whether the notion of citizenship, with its obvious rules of exclusion and exception, stands in for a wider range of assurances and freedoms. Is the larger freedom we seek more available outside of the purview of the state? (Ibid.: 130)

My short answer to these questions, and a synopsis of my overarching argument, is that Black queers—as the constitutive outside of immunitary civic personhood, despite inclusionary efforts that are always strategic, temporary, partial, and conditional—see themselves as forced to develop alternative practices of freedom that draw on intimate ties and build support structures that cannot afford to fail but are often on the precipice of doing so. While citizenship may inherently fail to deliver the "larger freedom" desired by those welcomed into the body politic, it thus becomes essential for political outsiders to nourish any kind of freedom at all—large or small. "How do people find freedom in bondage?" Kris asked me rhetorically as we were discussing what it means to "journey" in the world of BDSM. In her understanding, a journey was both a deeply personal experience and a collectively guided adventure, something akin to Foucault's idea of a transformative "political spirituality," addressed in the previous chapter, where she—as the dominatrix—conducts the conduct of her slave or submissive while, ideally, getting off together:

To journey is about finding out where to go. But it's your personal journey, whether it's meeting people, growing with people, expanding your "outer thing," like your wardrobe or your interactions. But it's also a journey into you: it touches places that . . . [I]t has a kind of specialness, a kind of safety; it's yours alone. There's avenues in you that you have no idea are even there! Oh my god, how is it I feel free and soaring, but I can't even move?! It's about how you end up relating to it, dealing with it, feeling about it, processing it afterwards. And who *are* you afterwards? That's a hell of a journey!

What attracted Kris most about her own journey as a dominatrix was the power—getting power, using power, giving away some power, and ultimately translating power into value: "It's about creating value according to the dictates of my spirit. Knowing that if I die right this second I will have spent every dime with passion and lived according to what I believe." This is the freedom she had created for herself, but this freedom also exceeded her and fed back into her community as value. For Kris, community was about having a "common denominator," which, in the case of her community, came down to a "shared kinkiness and oppression." It is on the cusp of these two shared experiences that she contributed her value. "I don't teach how to flog," she said. "I don't teach how to do those things. I do the basics, and for me the basics is protecting your head, your heart, and your spirit." Kris's work—one could even call it her calling—is all about getting back to the basics of looking out for one another, which, she felt, was something her peers had increasingly neglected over the years. It is also about protecting one another's health—the physical, mental, and spiritual conditions of life. "The mental has to do with your thought of yourself," Kris said, "because we're subject to so much mental oppression, especially as Black women." Pushing back against such oppression, by doing what she does best, was Kris's primary objective.

Monica's preferred method of working on her mental health and attaining her ideal of the divine was scripting BDSM scenes that featured her as a bottom getting severely battered. She loved wearing leather during these scenes, which made her feel "sexy and strong and protected," but unlike many of her peers, she did not consider herself a real leather fetishist because the material itself did not turn her on. Neither did pain, for that matter. As she told me during one particularly intimate conversation, "Some people actually do get pleasure from pain, I do not. I get pleasure from the accomplishment of enduring the pain. The pain is something I survive." She had been surviving the pain of childhood rape and abuse for many years, and the scenes she orchestrated and underwent were an important way for her to deal with persistent feelings of self-doubt and powerlessness:

> For years and years I would just feel horrible, because something happened to me that I had no control over. And then I contrast that to . . . I am the shit so much that I can willingly walk into a room and say, "I want y'all to beat the shit outta me," stand there, take it, and then walk out of that room again. It makes you realize that you do have a sense of power . . . that I'm capable of withstanding more than I thought I could.

On these occasions, doing scenes in which she was beaten by several "assailants" helped her to regain a sense of control over her life, or what could be called a measure of "practical sovereignty" that has to be negotiated in relation to social forces that can alternately augment and attenuate one's power to act. Whereas for Lauren Berlant (2011a: 98) practical sovereignty entails certain "unconscious and explicit desires not to be an inflated ego deploying power and manifesting intention," I would argue that Monica's efforts indicate how it can also function as an aspirational ideal geared precisely toward the intentional deployment of power by those who have long been deprived of it. Thought of in this way, practical sovereignty is necessarily precarious, as it is tentatively achieved in an often hostile environment that can easily overwhelm and further deflate an already damaged ego.[16] Indeed, what seems to be at stake in these scenes is the staged but very real exertion of overpowering and self-shattering violence whose force has to be endured and negotiated in a controlled space so that the "victim" can conjure the power to transfigure her violated position and thereby compose new life scenarios out of the fantasies and realism of everyday life. In other words, this is about the measured orchestration of an impersonal reparative strategy that strives for *more* ego inflation, not less, where the ego is understood to be incapable of insulating itself from what threatens to undo it. There is certainly a Christian motif of redemption at work here. As Anne McClintock (1995: 158) writes, "Like Christianity, S/M performs the paradox of redemptive suffering and like Christianity, it takes shape around the masochistic logic of transcendence through the mortification of the flesh." Yet for Monica, this was not so much a matter of redemption in a heavenly afterlife as it was about surviving and thriving in a world haunted by the afterlife of slavery and its brutal routines of racialized sexual domination. Such routines are not solely enacted by white men who feel entitled to have their way with the hypersexualized bodies of Black women. They also function as methods by which Black women are violated and held captive—psychically and physically—by Black men (Collins 2004: 225–232). In this protracted situation, redemption can only ever be provisional.

Yet her strategies did not always work out as imagined, and Monica was quick to add that there were times when there was no clear connection between her urge to do a particular scene and her experience of having been raped, because she also did the scenes "just for fun." Still, pleasure was something she in all instances would define as the feeling of being powerful and knowing that you are capable of much more than you initially thought. Surviving pain and humiliation, pushing through something traumatic and then coming out on top, was a sexual and ethical process of self-transformation, as well as self-care, that provided her with a great sense of "relief" and "triumph"—even though she was aware that such affective victories are usually fleeting. But this process also required her to open herself up to the threat and the actual infliction of violence, which meant that she had to put herself in an immensely vulnerable position that was bearable only in a space of trust and safety. This, then, is what returns us to the problematic of race. Engaging in BDSM or leather sex always entails playing with risk, and there is no such thing as an absolutely "safe" play scene, which is exactly what attracts so many people to these practices in the first place. The eroticism of playing with risk is in not knowing what will happen next and in the excitement of surrendering the imagined security of one's individual sense of control to others in an intimate scene, even when aspiring to come out of this scene more powerful than before. Still, even—or especially—in the most hard-core scenes, trust is a vital element that no participant can do without, given that violent play could otherwise result in life-threatening violence. Although violence, like risk, is an inherent element of leather sex and BDSM, and many practitioners are driven by the erotic pleasures of "self-shattering," which some psychoanalytically inclined queer theorists would identify with the death drive (Bersani 1995; Edelman 2004), these practices are nevertheless geared toward flourishing through a modulation of intensities that complicate and elaborate the self in close relationship to others, rather than snuffing it out altogether. It is precisely because partners in a scene always have to walk a tightrope between the violence of mutually scripted fantasies and actual forms of violence that figure as a set of reference points, punctuating such fantasies and loading them with substance and density, that a level of mutual trust has to be established beforehand.

However, the racial tensions and incidents that Monica, Kris, and other Black queer women have had to endure at community events have in some cases severely damaged their trust in, and comfort with, their white peers. This violation of trust is an important reason many of them started to look for alternative spaces and preferred private house parties to events at clubs whose patrons were mostly white.[17] More fundamentally, however, the issue of interracial trust points to a racial incongruity at the heart of the leather and BDSM community. As Margot Weiss (2011: 195) has argued, people of color are always already engaged in race play when they enter scenes with white people at public events, even when the scene does not explicitly draw on histories of racial oppression. This is true because, as a minority, they are the racially marked other who "cannot participate in a (or, indeed, the) 'neutral' scene, nor are they the normalized subjects of such a scene."[18] Black queer women thus find themselves in a precarious position where their sexualized racial difference is both disavowed as a political issue with a fraught history and fetishized as an attractive yet not fully intelligible force, whose alluring negativity serves as the constitutive outside of a "general" (i.e., white, unmarked) gay leather and BDSM culture in which these women nevertheless retain a conflicted investment, to the extent that its violent pleasures offer a sense of empowerment and well-being. This complex, exciting, and intensely ambiguous predicament is exemplary of what Christina Sharpe (2010: 119) has termed "the sadomasochism of everyday Black life" lived on the margins, violently positioned at once inside and outside the strategically flexible yet carefully policed normative boundaries of our immunitary citizenship regime, which both elicits and discards the "*Black* unspeakable."

The Sacred Space of Intimacy

What allows this racial incongruity to persist as a nonissue that has nevertheless shaped the historical unconscious of gay leather and BDSM? I think David Eng's notion of "queer liberalism" may help us to make sense of this situation. Eng (2010) argues that at the heart of queer liberalism one finds a color-blind assumption that the fight for racial justice has been completed and has given way to a postracial society in which the next logical step in the march for freedom is the legal recognition of the homosexual couple as a legitimate and respectable civic unit. This color-blindness enables a "racialization of intimacy," in which the private sphere is isolated as a "distinct and rarified [white, unmarked] zone outside of capitalist relations and racial exploitation" (ibid.: 10). In other words, queer liberalism desires a space for intimacy untainted by the racial tensions, violence, and injustice that nonetheless form the condition of its possibility. Weiss (2011: 199) detected this aspiration among white practitioners in her study of BDSM in the San Francisco Bay Area, writing about "a desire for unmarked sex—sex outside of politics—that relies on the universalization of whiteness." This reminds me of Lee Edelman's *No Future* (2004), in which sexuality seems to figure as an autonomous zone uncontaminated by racial or class differences (cf. Muñoz 2009: 94). Yet where Edelman sees this zone as marked by incoherence and negativity, always agitating against the political promises of futurity and collectivity, the same zone is held up as a beacon of free choice, agency, and transparency by liberal queers whose faith in the salvific power of the "intimate event" has proved contagious over the past two decades (Povinelli 2006). Indeed, it is this colorblind, postracial faith in sexual intimacy as a zone of freedom, choice, agency, and transparent relationality that informs how Baltimore's leather and BDSM community perceives itself, as well as the story it communicates to outsiders. More specifically, the scripted scene central to sexual play by and large is considered a sacred and exceptional "safe space" in which participants negotiate and enact fantasies whose social and political baggage should, it is expected, be transgressed or transcended. One "enters" this distinct immunitary zone, which McClintock (1995: 143) likens to an enchanted "magic circle," by choice and under the provision that mutual consent has been established between two or more participants who recognize each other as trustworthy, responsible people, and, once the scene has been concluded, one subsequently "leaves" the space of fantasy—usually after a moment of debriefing or "aftercare."

To be sure, this formal narrative about leather sex contrasts sharply with the many experiences narrated to me—and found in various community publications (e.g., Bean 1994; Thompson 2004)—about the permeability of boundaries between the self and the other, fantasy and reality, and control and release, as well as the space of play and any other type of space (Van Doorn 2013a, 2016). So why are these accounts so different? In my estimation, it is because the latter account destabilizes the ostensible autonomy of the play scene, as well of as the players, which in turn would compromise queer liberalism's investment in a redemptive intimate sphere free from racial antagonisms. If the space between play and politics, or between fantasy and history, is actually complex and nebulous, then it means that the gay leather and BDSM community would have to reassess its history and might find itself forced to deal with the national problems of race and anti-Blackness in ways that move beyond recognition, representation, or "racial sensitivity." If, however, this space remains solid and airtight, Black queers such as Monica will continue to be welcomed into the community on the condition that they play like responsible, consenting adults—and thus like good sexual citizens—checking at the door any chip they might have on their shoulder. But what are they asked to consent to and at what cost? And is "consent" even the right word here? After all, as Ariane Cruz (2015: 416) has argued, the "dynamics of domination and submission, particularly when stratified by the processes of racialization, disrupt understandings and enactments of already complicated sexual consent."[19]

It should be noted here that queer liberalism's (post)racial order of things informs not only white kink discourse, as demonstrated in Weiss's ethnography, but also the judgments and expectations of Black queer folks on Baltimore's scene. This is illustrated by Monica's negotiation of thresholds during play:

> Usually, when you come into a play party, you've dealt with that [racial tension] before. This is not the first time you've been in a room full of white people, so . . . [A]nd usually they're a little more like, "I can handle this, I'm coming here for a reason, and I'm not gonna let one dumbass ruin it." So, if all of us are like that a little bit, then it makes it less . . . something that happens, you know?

By being able to "handle" racist remarks or racial tensions within the intimate zone of a play party, by absorbing and defusing racial antagonism for the sake of sexual pleasure, Black practitioners such as Monica allow the racial incongruity at the heart of gay leather and BDSM to persist without critical resistance or interrogation. On the one hand, such efforts to "dedramatize" racial tensions by playing along in order to keep the space of sexual intimacy 'unsullied' and make sure everyone can enjoy themselves may be read as a mode of "lateral agency" (Berlant 2007). Lateral agency enables people to cope with, or to retain a semblance of sovereignty in the face of, the overwhelming yet mundane reality of having to reproduce life—a life whose desires often destabilize many of the anchors that ground one's existence and give it meaning and purpose. Despite the bitter taste, sometimes the measured absorption and defusing of racial antagonism may just be what it takes when what you really need from life is some sexual pleasure and decompression. Yet on the other hand, we have to ask what, exactly, is sacrificed in this recurrent sacrifice. What is the cost of consenting, or *yielding*, to not only racialized sexual harassment but also the preservation of a *cordon sanitaire* around leather sex and BDSM? One can answer this question properly only by keeping in mind that the *cordon sanitaire* functions not to keep the kink from flowing into the outside world but, rather, to keep the politics of race and racial violence from entering the sacred space of sexual play as anything other than consensually enacted fantasy—however deviant or provocative.

I believe what is sacrificed here is a capacity for "racial truth telling," a term I borrow from Jonathan Rossing (2014). I think that the project of racial truth telling, which fosters a critical pedagogy of racial literacy and justice, is at once more difficult and more indispensable in queer liberal times. The crucial goals of such a project are to dislocate the linear historical narrative of racial progress, liberation, and inclusion and to bring race squarely into the present as an urgent political problem and deep fissure that cannot be contained by racial neoliberalism (cf. Goldberg 2009). In the context of gay leather and BDSM culture, racial truth telling should be directed at bodily pleasure. As the community's "ethical substance," or its "prime material of . . . moral conduct" and reflection (Foucault 1990b: 26), bodily pleasure is the object(ive) in relation to which its members engage in the ethical work of establishing proper conduct, or protocol (see also Povinelli 2011a: 15). As I discussed in the previous chapter, this ethical work on the self and others is closely concerned with the relationship between power and truth, which also makes it a political exercise. Truth here figures as a test, rather than a target, which requires both a *commitment by* and a *transformation of* the subject, in which the latter is necessitated by the fact that truth is never given and the true life is thus always an *other* life, in an *other* world (Foucault 2011: 340). Truth telling, or *parrhesia,* as the transformative engagement with the test of truth, therefore refuses the hegemony of existing normative orders and strives for radical transformation by showing how things could be different, which is also what makes it such a risky practice. So what racial truth should be told about bodily pleasure in the gay leather and BDSM community?

The primary issue is that this ethical substance is not equally available among all community members, and this skewed distribution is most explicitly articulated at racially mixed public events. If bodily pleasure forms the material sensation around which practitioners of leather sex and BDSM coordinate their ethical conduct and vision of the good life, then the ritual forms and protocols through which this pleasure comes into being *structurally subordinate* Black queers to the extent that these rituals and protocols are rooted in a national history of racial slavery and (de)sexual(izing) violence that continues to ingress into the everyday lives of postslavery subjects—Black *and* white (Sharpe 2010). To be sure, this does not mean that Black queer practitioners are incapable of enjoying BDSM practices, that they should refrain from seeking its pleasures, or that all Black (trans) men and women relate to this history in the same way. It does imply, however, that the ethical experimentation with such ritual forms and protocols displays "an intimacy with sexual objectification that is intrinsically linked to racialized and classed narratives of the coercive deployment of power" (Rodríguez 2011: 342)—narratives that tell of Black people's violent transformation into property whose ownership provided access to the privileged sphere of liberal white humanity. As Saidiya Hartman (1997: 51) has argued, this is "the history that hurts—the still-unfolding narrative of captivity, dispossession, and domination that engenders the Black subject in the Americas." Even though contemporary scenes, norms, and protocols of staged subjection are now ostensibly "race-neutral" (save for marginal[ized] categories such as race play), they thus continue to place Black queer women in a strained position where their racial difference is at once invoked as a sexual fetish and disavowed as a political issue that critically reflects the history of this fetish. Thus, this tension constitutes a racial fissure of the community's ethical substance, whereby bodily pleasure becomes an affectively, ethically, and politically ambiguous material for Black female BDSM practitioners.

Here, the test of truth demands the community's commitment to a sustained interrogation of the racial politics of fantasy, especially with respect to the pervasive whiteness of gay leather and BDSM history, to develop a more critical racial literacy, repoliticize race, and break open the contractual *cordon sanitaire* established by queer liberalism. Again, to be clear, such an interrogation is not intended to discipline or reject fantasy as a generative space with transformative potential for Black queer women. As Juana María Rodríguez (2011: 343) has forcefully argued, "To deny our fantasies because they are too complicated, too painful, or too perverse, to erase their presence or censor their articulations in public life, constitutes a particular kind of insidious violence that threatens to undermine our ability to explore the contours of our psychic lives, and the imaginary possibilities of the social worlds in which we exist." However, it is exactly because such fantasies do not take shape in a vacuum and cannot be contained within the psychic and physical spaces of sexual intimacy, instead bleeding into and out of "the social worlds in which we exist," that the leather and BDSM community needs to learn how to speak truthfully about race as a constitutive and conflicting force in its historical formation. In the words of Ariane Cruz (in Wachter-Grene 2016): "The imagined split between fantasy and reality obscures the materialities of sexual fantasy and our own personal stakes in and responsibilities for both our sexual fantasies and practices." As long as white practitioners are not willing to acknowledge and engage with the complicated, painful, and perverse fantasies of Black queer women, or merely choose to interpret them as "private" desires, their own whiteness will remain invisible and apolitical and, with it, the privileges—such as the privilege of publicness—of belonging to the unmarked majority.

Again, what racial *parrhesia* could address are the conditions of possibility for such belonging: on what genealogy, or generational knowledge, is this particular form of belonging predicated? Certainly, the ritualized distribution of this knowledge has enabled the tightly delineated articulation of "new relational modes" (Bersani 2000), which posit sexual pleasure as the ethical locus of an intricate process of governing self and others that has yielded forms of community, kinship, heritage, and reproduction that contest the logics of deracinated subjectivity currently structuring queer liberalism (Van Doorn 2016). Yet at the same time, the leather community's affirmation of queer liberal discourse reproduces the racial blind spots in its generational knowledge and keeps it from recognizing how, despite attempts to be more "inclusive," Black queer women continue to occupy an ambiguous and vulnerable position within its project of historical (be)longing. The truth is that the risk inherent to intimacy and community is not equally distributed, as some—raced, classed, gendered—subjects are more exposed than others and will thus have less capacity to be publicly visible subjects of pleasure, especially when their historical experience is "all negative on" the symbolic history of the community they cannot fully embrace. Ultimately, if BDSM and leather sex are, or should be, about the "theatrical exercise of social contradiction" that "plays social power backward, visibly and outrageously staging hierarchy, difference and power, the irrational, ecstasy, or alienation of the body, placing these ideas at the center of Western reason" (McClintock 1995: 143), and if they are thereby supposed to convert "the scene of disavowal into the scene of theatrical display" (ibid.: 158), then the queer liberal reason that permeates Baltimore's leather and BDSM community instead restages its racial disavowal over and over again in a scene that short-circuits the "circuits of sexuality" constitutive of this very community. Rather than interrogating these circuits, which, according to Weiss (2011: 7), materialize "the complex and often contradictory social dynamics that produce and are, in turn, reproduced within particular sexual cultures, practices, and desires," many of the white practitioners I met seek to contain and thereby neutralize the violence of such contradictory dynamics by consigning them to the secured and sacred scene of play, scripted and circumscribed by intimate fantasy. Yet, as Candace Vogler and Patchen Markell (2003: 3) have asked, "How does the pursuit of redemption *from* violence relate to the pursuit of redemption *through* violence?"—in this case, the immunitary violence that attempts to suppress (anti-)Blackness as a deeply political issue that never ceases to trouble the psychic life of power (play). For reasons that I address below, I concur with their proposal to cultivate "a more modest sort of redemptive imagination"— one that does not strive for the eradication of violence as such, thereby positing violence as fundamentally antithetical to life, but one that attunes us to "those concrete acts of compensation and counterbalance that, in assigning meaning and value to violence suffered, enable agents to project possible futures (though not necessarily fundamentally transfigured ones) in its wake" (ibid.).

The Value of the Negative: A Coda and a Prelude

The discussion above points to what may ultimately be the most profound violence of liberalism, queer or otherwise: the containment and neutralization of negativity. Chapter 6 provides a more elaborate discussion of how I understand the nature and value of the negative with respect to the forces of affirmation that drive the composition of Black queer civic intimacies. I want to end this chapter with a brief reflection on these themes within the specific context of Baltimore's gay leather and BDSM community and its own racially charged civic intimacies. This will then set up a broader investigation of the political valences of queerness, Blackness, and negativity, as they inflect and inform the book's central concern with rethinking citizenship from the perspective of that which exists beyond its purview. In contrast to Edelman's white monolithic vision of a queer negativity marked by "an ongoing effort of divestiture, a practice of undoing" and a death-driven repetition of the subject's failure to repair what is constitutively broken about sex and life (Berlant and Edelman 2014: 19), Monica's story suggests a less austere, socially situated— yet no less intractable—take on negativity. This is a negativity that is inflected by contradiction, anxiety, and conflict, but also by pleasure, curiosity, and the effort to be otherwise. Like Berlant (2014: 278), I think it is more useful to understand negativity as "a scene of incompatible subjective forms to which we are attached" and that, despite efforts to neutralize or disavow them, continue to complicate our ability to retain a sovereign composure amid the push and pull of desires, norms, obligations, and aspirations that attest to the inevitable ambiguity of being in relation. In this view, negativity does not find its purest or most violent articulation in a sexual psyche ruptured by *jouissance*, and neither are sexual negativity and incoherence necessarily the main source of (anti)social conflict. Instead, the force of the negative is articulated as a multiplicity—an intricate assemblage of mobile, folded antagonisms informed by the inequities of race, class, gender, geography, religion, and other social formations.

Monica's upbringing in a deeply religious environment bestowed on her a moral compass that pointed faithfully toward sexual respectability. Her emerging desire to "break out" and forge a new sexual ethics and identity conflicted with her home church's condemnation of kink as an essentially white sin, which induced a sense of anxiety about the incommensurability of her sexuality and her Blackness. In an attempt to resolve this incongruity, she had made a concerted—and perverted—effort to bring God into her kink life by tying her spirituality more directly to her BDSM practices, which allowed her to keep working on herself and become a more community-oriented, "diligent," and strong Black queer person through the orchestration of scenes in which she subjected herself to acts of impersonal violence. This serves as a reminder that the impersonal is not the opposite of the personal but, rather, its temporary interruption, as well as one of its (underprivileged) conditions of possibility (Berlant 2011a: 125-126; Esposito 2010b). Although in Chapter 3 I (ap)praised the impersonal as an interstitial realm that facilitates an ecstatic political ethics of improper intimacies and common vulnerabilities in the face of biopolitical capture, I do not conceive of it as some kind of autonomous sphere that could by itself sustain an ego-shattering, anti-personal sexual ethics (cf. Dean 2009). The impersonal traverses the personal; it haunts the person in its ongoing effort to compose what can pass for a stable, relatable, dependable self. Sex, even violent sex or sexualized forms of violence, presents one resource for such a precarious project of (de)composition, which always requires one to reach out to an "other" who may sometimes be anyone willing and available to partake in a scene full of impersonal fears and favors. As Berlant (2009: 262) notes, "Sexualized attachment is possible precisely because desiring subjects are not only incoherent, but seek divesture of the ego at the same time as they are looking for confirming reciprocity." Again, this is a sense of reciprocity that extends beyond not only the (inter)personal but also the scene of sexual performance and fantasy, whose pleasures are peripatetic and animate a host of world-building practices that sustain marginalized kinky collectivities. Yet it should also be reiterated that the ethical work of pleasurably painful self-transformation, in which the affective negativity of abjection "can intensify the determination to survive" and enables practitioners such as Monica to find out what their female, queer, kinky Black bodies can do (Halperin 2007: 93), takes place in an environment whose pervasive whiteness and depoliticized racial tensions threaten to infringe on their attempts to flourish.[20] While she works through a confluence of tensions and ambiguities that crystallize in her sense of embodiment, Monica's body—together with the bodies of other Black queer folks who are at once in and out of the lifestyle—simultaneously comes to figure as a negative remainder that resists full incorporation into the common ethical substance of Baltimore's leather and BDSM community.

Racial negativity could drive a political problematization of the community's mode of governing self and others, including its postracial common/good life imaginary predicated on a distinction between fantasy and reality. It could illuminate which protocols, so carefully cultivated by generations of mostly white leather men and leather women, cannot fully dissimulate "racial-sexual alterity" (Cruz 2016a), and which ritual practices do not adequately account for the ambivalences of desiring membership of a cultural formation in which one's body is at once abjected and desired—indeed, desired *because of* its racialized abjection. It could, that is, fuel the radical practice of racial *parrhesia*. Yet as I discussed above, the capacity to tell the truth about race in the community is sacrificed in queer liberal efforts to immunize the sacred space of sexual intimacy, thereby positioning politics beyond the realm of—even quasi-publicly staged—sex and effectively discarding any kind of negativity that cannot be sublimated through the "safe" and consensual enactment of fantasy. As a result, Black queer women are expected to absorb this negativity or otherwise avoid it by creating their own private play spaces—their "architecture[s] of the unseen" (McClintock 1995: 149)—which protect them from racially antagonistic encounters but also deprive them of the ability to visibly take part in, and thus have some measure of control over, the historically fraught rituals constitutive of "their" community. Meanwhile, the immunitary contractual logic at the heart of this scheme is precisely what allows for the *negative preservation* of Baltimore's gay leather and BDSM community (Esposito 2010a), through the containment and compartmentalization of what threatens to disrupt its purported harmony/unity.[21] It places Black queer women at once within and beyond the pale of community life, thereby suspending the transformative potential of their pleasure-seeking bodies as they navigate a majority-white social space whose members are reluctant to trace the color line that both subtends and frays the historical ties that bind.

6

Support Structures

On Negativity and Reparativity

I ended the previous chapter by identifying a racial incongruity in queer temporal experience, when Black (queer) history is "all negative" on the historical present of white gay leather/BDSM. My aim in this closing chapter is to use this incongruity as the entry point for a sustained reflection on the role of negativity with respect to the survival and flourishing of Black queer life. In other words, I aim to "tarry with the negative," to use Hegel's well-known phrasing, to investigate the persistent ambivalence and antagonism that conditions the possibility of Black queer world making in the future, past, and present tense. In doing so, I ultimately return to the central question that provided the impetus for this research project: how can we rethink citizenship from the perspective of its outside, or that which is superfluous, excessive, or unintelligible to modern immunitary citizenship regimes? In the previous chapters, I worked through this question by examining the "durative present" (Povinelli 2011a) of Black queer life in Baltimore, whose civic intimacies are imbricated with various makeshift yet frequently persistent temporalities that point to different iterations of an "elsewhen" protruding from the present proper. One of those elsewhens materializes in the form of competitive Balls, which, as I wrote in Chapter 3, provide "a temporality that deviates from the claustrophobic time inhabited by many queer youths of color who are forced to imagine their lives under the constant threat of HIV/AIDS." By offering a reprieve from the highly regulated and often dreadful temporal framework of Test and Treat campaigns, these Balls figure as a temporary escape from captivity during which participants can perform not only their grievances, outrage, and fear, but also the optimism, hope, and joy that remain an indelible force when House children come together and take the stage. Moreover, against the post-crisis/post-AIDS climate of white queer liberal time, and against the white bureaucratic time of biomedical prevention schemes and other institutional programs that ostensibly have the best interests of House children in mind, Balls in Baltimore offer a distinctly *Black* queer temporal experience that embodies what Robyn Wiegman (2014: 15) has called "the asynchronies of an affectively vital political negativity." I am intrigued and inspired by this particular phrasing, which pushes us to query the relationships among time, affect, negativity, and the political. Likewise, and by extension, I believe it problematizes the conceptual distinction between survival and flourishing that has been pivotal to much (Black/queer) social and political theory to the extent that it acknowledges the generative force of the negative and refuses a redemptive image of the good life and what it means to flourish. While survival and flourishing are certainly not identical, both modes of social reproduction demand consistent courage and effort to work through/against/with various forms of negativity, and each therefore constitutes a thoroughly ambiguous experience. As will become evident, this ambiguity is central to my notion of civic intimacies and to the argument I develop in this chapter.

In what follows, I critically assess the extent to which radically negative ontological approaches in Black (and) queer scholarship offer conceptual frameworks, or tools, that can help us to make sense of the concrete and complex realities of Black queer survival and flourishing in Baltimore. I query the (in)ability of such approaches to highlight the inexorable negativity inherent in Black queer world making without simultaneously relinquishing its affirmative/reparative potential. To be sure, I realize that this endeavor may seem misguided or inappropriate insofar as it risks conflating the analysis of Blackness and queerness as *structural positions* with (the study of) Black and queer lives as they are lived in all their particularity, but I nevertheless want to explore the conceptual and ethico-political space that at once separates and connects the two because it provokes the question of how each speaks to the other.[1] As I mentioned at the start of this book, this is the space that mediates between Saidiya Hartman's attempt to bring into view "the position of the unthought"—that is, the position of the slave in the United States—"without making it a locus of positive value, or without trying to fill the void," and attempts at preservation and revaluation made by Cleo and his peers, which precisely aim to "fill the void" of Black queer existence in the afterlife of slavery yet do so without seeking "integration into the national project" (Hartman and Wilderson 2003: 185). Despite the different nature and purpose of each undertaking, I argue that the latter problematizes recent ontological theorizations of Blackness and queerness as negative spaces saturated by death and dereliction, not by disproving them, but by demanding that our scholarly accounts have bearing on the ordinary modes of belonging and affirmation that persist despite all the horror and the violence.

In addition to being conceptual and ethico-political, this mediating space is thus also methodological, as it contains a tension between critical and reparative approaches that each in their own way strive to deal with this horror and violence. Interrogating this tension is part of the stakes of this chapter, which draws from and builds on the ethnographic narratives presented in the four preceding chapters to engage in an empirically grounded dialogue with various queer and Afro-pessimist theorists on the topics of negativity and reparativity. This dialogue then offers an opportunity to further elaborate my conception of civic intimacies, which at the start of the book I provisionally defined as the everyday reparative work of building support structures that draw on carefully cultivated intimacies. There I suggested that the notion of civic intimacies forms the key to formulating an answer to this book's central question, insofar as this concept enables a rethinking of citizenship from the perspective of what remains excluded from and superfluous to the modern immunitary regimes that scaffold it. Civic intimacies, as an affirmative concept and practice, is grounded in this negative perspective, which is the perspective of Black queer Baltimore. While I substantiate this assertion below, I also return to the problem—at once ethical and methodological—of using the language of citizenship to describe, as well as "do justice to," practices and experiences that are not understood in this language by those included in my ethnography. The chapter closes with a reflection on this incongruity, addressing the promises and shortcomings of my efforts to develop a conceptual framework for the analysis and appreciation of Black queer world making as a practice that turns the grammar of citizenship—its terms and conditions—inside out.

Blackness, Queerness, Death

In even starker terms than those offered by Hartman, Frank Wilderson theorizes Blackness as radical negativity and negation. To grasp the severity of Wilderson's perspective and to illustrate its para-Lacanian inflection, it is worth quoting at length a passage from his agenda-setting text "The Prison Slave as Hegemony's (Silent) Scandal":[2]

> We must accept that no other body functions in the Imaginary, the Symbolic, or the Real so completely as a repository of complete disorder as the Black body. Blackness is the site of absolute dereliction at the level of the Real, for in its magnetizing of bullets the Black body functions as the map of gratuitous violence through which civil society is possible: namely those bodies for which violence is, or can be, contingent. Blackness is the site of absolute dereliction at the level of the Symbolic, for Blackness in America generates no categories for the chromosome of history, and no data for the categories of immigration or sovereignty. It is an experience without analog—a past without a heritage. Blackness is the site of absolute dereliction at the level of the Imaginary, for "whoever says 'rape' says Black" (Fanon), whoever says "prison" says Black, and whoever says "AIDS" says Black (Sexton)— the "Negro is a phobogenic object" (Fanon). (Wilderson 2003: 25)

These assertions move Wilderson (2003: 23) to the conclusion that "from the incoherence of Black death, America generates the coherence of white life." Still, as either a "prison-slave" or a "prison-slave-in-waiting," the Black body persistently threatens civil society with the "incoherence of civil war," at which point the ethical embrace of (social) death becomes the ultimate political weapon against the body politic and its dialectic of hegemonic struggles (ibid.: 26). Rather than striving for inclusion as "one of civil society's many junior partners" (ibid.: 18), which is misguided insofar as it is structurally impossible, true Black revolutionaries should pursue "an endless antagonism that cannot be satisfied (via reform or reparation), but must nonetheless be pursued to the death" (ibid.: 26). In this text and in Wilderson's subsequent work, we find perhaps the most crystallized and austere articulation of Afro-pessimist thought. Interestingly, his conception of Blackness as disorder and dereliction almost perfectly mirrors Lee Edelman's vision of queerness as a structurally impossible position whose death-driven negativity must nevertheless be embraced in a defiantly antagonistic fashion (Edelman 2004). Echoing Edelman's Lacanian insistence on the destructive force of sexual *jouissance*, Wilderson conjures the orgasm as a model for an antipolitical ethics of self-shattering, in which politics is equated with the hegemonic, future-oriented power struggles of civil society (Wilderson 2003: 26). For these authors, the reproduction of our antiqueer and anti-Black body politic, respectively, can be resisted only by delivering oneself from one's self—by becoming undone. As Wilderson (2003: 26) writes about Blackness: "One must embrace its disorder, its incoherence, and allow oneself to be elaborated by it, if indeed one's politics are to be underwritten by a desire to take down this country." Edelman (2011: 148) has repeatedly articulated such a desire, which drives his concomitant refusal of the "contemporary ideology of social and cultural survival" that grounds our political order, although it emerges from a decidedly different—white, gay—positionality, which Wilderson would surely judge to be incommensurable with his own.

I examine Edelman's particular notion of survival below, but I first want to address his concomitant assertion that queerness is nothing other than nothingness, to highlight the nihilistic impulse shared by the two authors. In Edelman's (2011: 149) words, to be queer "is not to be, except insofar as queerness serves as the name for the thing that is not, for the limit point of ontology, for the constitutive exclusion that registers the no, the not, the negation in being." The queer thus "occupies the place of the zero" (ibid.), which is the negative space that saturates and ruptures the politics of survival, as well as the survival of politics, while its erosive force remains beyond comprehension. Only in moments of traumatic *jouissance* does the zero conspicuously punctuate "the Symbolic's law of the One" (ibid.), presenting itself as a horrific encounter with the Real against which the political order must inoculate itself to survive. Thus, Edelman posits the queer nothing as the "ungrounding ground intrinsic to the formulation of any politics, as the primal negativity that shapes it, the zero that procures and undoes at once everyone and every 'One'" (ibid.). In this austere phrasing, steeped in the binary logic of a digital metaphysics,[3] Edelman's ethics of the Real is most forcefully formulated. Figured through the antisocial queer zero, or the obscene sexual void that hollows out the wholeness of any communal One, it frames "a project that's willing to forgo the privilege of social recognition and so is willing to break the compact binding the image of the human to a social order speciously conflated with kinship and collectivity," instead embracing "the foundational negativity that keeps the symbolic from achieving self-identity to the extent that the nonidentical persists within as internal antagonism" (Edelman 2007: 473). Instead of the prison slave (in waiting), Edelman thus posits the queer zero as hegemony's scandal, an apolitical nothing that negatively conditions the possibility for politics as such. If this seems like a misguided proposition at a time that white, middle-class gays and lesbians are granted "junior partnership" in civil society's institutions while a staggering number of Black (trans) men and women are locked up in prisons or killed by police and policies all across the United States, one should remember that for Edelman, as well as for Wilderson, queerness and Blackness, respectively, are structural—or, rather, *structurally impossible*—positions rather than concretely situated identities. It is in this sense that these authors share a nihilist impulse, which is to say that both totalize (queer/Black) negativity by turning it into an absolute metaphysical abyss beyond meaning, relationality, or recuperation.[4] Queerness and Blackness can then be associated only with (social) death, inimical to any positive form of life or politics. The strength of this argument lies in its unrelenting critique of conventional modes of political theory and practice, whether articulated through identity politics or more universal claims to human or civil rights, which are ultimately satisfied with some (token) measure of inclusion, acceptance, or redress. In a radical countermove, it shows how such integrationist practices are always already premised on the violent suppression of a "foundational negativity": the queer death drive for Edelman; the derelict prison slave for Wilderson. But is nihilism the only, or even the most apposite, alternative to political projects centered on inclusion and reform? Is death—social, symbolic, physical—the only possible object of desire, destination, or habitat for queer (and) Black life? And is negativity most adequately understood as an antirelational void or abyss? These are some questions I address in the following section, where I take a detour through debates on ontology and politics to develop a different, more nuanced and ambiguous perspective on negativity as it pertains to survival, relationality, and futurity.

The Structure of Survival

As stated above, I use the term "digital metaphysics" to describe Edelman's binary opposition between the Symbolic One that safeguards the coherence of the social order and the queer zero that embodies the Real as the disruption of that order. His attendant approach to politics consequently assumes that any political community, which for him means any heteronormative social order adhering to the ideology of "reproductive futurism," is inevitably marked by the desire for *fullness*. Against this ostensible desire for the whole(some) One, Edelman then posits the queer zero as a constitutive lack that at once drives this desire and makes it impossible to fulfill. Analogically, he understands survival as the reproduction of the One and the same, against which he conjures an atemporal death drive that resists the stale futurity integral to such reproductive practices. However, in response to Ernesto Laclau's similarly Lacanian adherence to an ontological lack that undercuts any radical investment in fullness—an investment that, in Laclau's view (Butler, Laclau, and Žižek 2000), nonetheless grounds all hegemonic politics—Martin Hägglund (2008: 194–195) has argued that the impossibility of a perfectly full and self-present social order is not due to any ostensible lack but, rather, should be attributed to the social's inherent temporality, which subjects it to constant transformation. Any political community is necessarily a temporal community, which means that it cannot fully coincide with itself and that its foundations are contingent and finite. Negativity is thus a *disjunctive* force inherent to time's passing rather than an atemporal limitation. There no discrete distinction between (the desire for) the zero and the One, nothing and plenitude, death and life, as the force of the negative exerts its violence in moments that are decidedly more ambiguous than any metaphysical opposition between these polar extremes could account for.

To better grasp Hägglund's argument, it is important that we understand the particular way he deploys the Derridean concepts of autoimmunity and survival, both of which are pivotal to my argument. In Hägglund's work, autoimmunity forms the fundamental and inescapable condition of life itself, whose logic "spells out that everything is threatened from within itself, since the possibility of living is inseparable from the peril of dying" (Hägglund 2008: 9). This condition is, in turn, predicated on what Jacques Derrida calls the "structure of the trace," which Hägglund explains this way:

> The structure of the trace follows from the constitution of time, which makes it impossible for anything to be present in itself. Every now passes away as soon as it comes to be and must therefore be inscribed as a trace in order to be at all. The trace enables the past to be retained, since it is characterized by the ability to remain in spite of temporal succession. The trace is thus the minimal condition for life to resist death in a movement of survival. The trace can only live on, however, by being left for a future that may erase it. (Hägglund 2008: 1)

As Hägglund emphasizes, this radical finitude and precariousness of survival is not a lack of being. Instead, it should be understood as opening at once "the chance for everything that is desired and the threat of everything that is feared" (ibid.: 2). To survive therefore means to be subject to continuous alteration without guarantees, given the undecidability of the future. Furthermore, one has no option other than to affirm survival *unconditionally*, because without this affirmation, one could not live on, as life is finite and essentially structured by the autoimmune logic of survival. To be exonerated from this logic, to have absolute immunity with respect to the perils of survival, would be "to close all openness to the other, all openness to the unpredictable coming of time, and thereby close the opening of life itself" (ibid.: 43). Here we should compare Hägglund's take on survival with that of Edelman, who likewise draws on Derrida's work to formulate his argument against the reproductive futurism he believes is embodied in this very concept. Whereas Hägglund finds in Derrida a notion of survival that is inherently equivocal, Edelman conjures a different Derrida, for whom survival is a conservative force that strives for wholeness as it is besieged by the attrition and loss induced by the queer nothing.

Accepting Derrida's assertion that survival is a structural and originary given that precedes life and death, thus making it difficult—if not impossible—to distinguish between the two, Edelman oddly follows up on this idea by arguing that survival nonetheless precipitates what he calls the Symbolic "*or*der" that enforces a binary distinction between being and nonbeing, the one and the zero: "It occasions and requires a conceptual geography of places in which everything 'must be *or* not be,' such that even non-being would inhabit a place, would assume the signifiable form that turns it into a one. In short, survival determines the Symbolic as the *or*der *of* survival, giving rise, at the moment when immortality and 'a sense of posterity' conjoin, . . . to what I've called reproductive futurism" (Edelman 2011: 152). In Edelman's reading, survival is "something inherently resistant to, or in conflict with, the death drive" (ibid.: 154), something that affirms life by suturing the past to the future. Paradoxically, however, to affirm this *or*der of survival in which life and death are diametrically opposed, and to guarantee the future of the One that is also the same, the Symbolic mobilizes "a self-negating impulse" that Edelman associates—or, rather, conflates—at once with the death drive and the process of autoimmunity (ibid.: 149).

I think there are two problems with this reading. First, Edelman projects his own digital metaphysics on Derrida, excising all negativity from survival only to then have it "haunt" the social order from beyond the grave. It is, in fact, Edelman's conception of the Lacanian Symbolic order that conjures a dichotomy in which the queer zero fractures the "ceaseless attempt to make oneself One" and thereby induces a lack, or an absence—something that is "missing" from an order that would otherwise fully coincide with itself (Edelman 2011: 150). In contrast, as Hägglund has demonstrated in much detail, Derrida's notion of survival is fundamentally antithetical to such digital thought because it cannot help but to carry the negative within itself as its very condition of possibility. In other words, a fundamental ambiguity, not a binary "*order*," lies at the heart of survival. This brings me to the second problem of Edelman's reading: his misinterpretation of the concept of autoimmunity. As noted above, for Derrida—at least, according to Hägglund's sophisticated and convincing reading, which I follow here—the logic of autoimmunity that structures survival indicates that there can be no living on without the threat of dying and that therefore the future is undecidable. This is why we have to affirm survival unconditionally, but this is also exactly what necessitates the making of decisions about what should be protected and how—decisions that are always provisional, finite, and thus *political* (Hägglund 2008: 40). In Edelman's hands, however, autoimmunity becomes the drive toward absolute immunity and self-enclosure, which would eventually result in suicide.[5] Yet this take on autoimmunity presumes a set of binary distinctions between defense/security and threat, inside and outside, fullness and emptiness, and life and death, which are incommensurable to Derrida's mobilization of this concept as a means to account for and radically affirm the uncertainty and ambiguity constitutive of life, politics, and justice. Rather, they are more amendable to Edelman's own paranoid vision of reproductive futurism, in which "the event to come will always have taken place even before its arrival and the death drive will always be sublimated into a principle of conservation" (Edelman 2011: 169).

As established thus far, Edelman's escape plan—his "antisocial thesis" that rejects futurity *tout court*—is predicated on his conception of queer negativity as a radically antirelational force, or void, which would delimit and erode the drive toward fullness that structures the politics of survival and the survival of politics. Having addressed his problematic interpretation of Derridean survival and autoimmunity, I now turn to his equally questionable ontology of negativity as antirelational. Here I draw on Roberto Esposito's remarks on the relationship between community and nihilism, which offer an account of negativity that turns Edelman's notion inside out. In one of his most succinct statements, Esposito (2009: 41) channels Martin Heidegger when he asserts that "community is not proscribed, obscured, or veiled by the nothing: it is constituted by it." Consequently, rather than treating community and nihilism as mutually exclusive projects, where the former has to defend itself against the latter in a perennial conflict, it is precisely this "nothing" that community and nihilism have in common. Indeed, the expropriating relationality at the heart of *communitas*, embodied in the *munus* as the gift that cannot be received but only creates the perpetual obligation to give, or to share, realizes a "subtraction of subjectivity" in which members of a community are "constitutively exposed to a propensity that forces them to open up their own individual boundaries in order to appear as what is 'outside' themselves" (Esposito 2010a: 138). In other words, against Edelman's vision of an antirelational queer death drive that fissures the formation of political collectivity, Esposito's political ontology posits a *relational negativity* as the essence of such collectivity: its "no-thing-in-common" (ibid.). It is the relation, the openness to alterity and the risk of attachment, that threatens to undo the political subject, *not the absence of relation*. Moreover, as Hägglund has argued with respect to the negativity inherent to survival, this "no-thing" is nothing like a lack, because this would imply that there is something missing from a political community, as if it is incomplete and would strive in vain for a fullness or closure that is barred by this "no-thing." Such an interpretation disavows the thought that community is nothing other than an interval, a threshold, or "the spacing that brings us into relation with others in a common non-belonging, in this loss of what is proper that never adds up to a common 'good'" (ibid.: 139). Hence a political community does not lack anything, but it exposes its members to a loss of sovereign personhood and incapacitates the formation of a unified "general will." As Esposito writes, "It doesn't keep us warm, and it doesn't protect us" (ibid.: 140).

Esposito attributes such an intentional misreading of the "no-thing" as lack to the paranoid vision inherent to the modern immunitary paradigm, which has given birth to political nihilism. Starting with Thomas Hobbes, who initiated this "completely negative and indeed catastrophic interpretation of the principle of sharing with" at the core of *communitas,* the excessive element of this principle was reconfigured into not just a defect but also a crime, "indeed an unstoppable series of potential crimes" (ibid.: 141). In an attempt to immunize against this criminal loss of what is proper and secure, Hobbesian political nihilism has consistently pursued the negation of the relational negativity that disjoin(t)s community, or that indeed *is* community. To neutralize or rise above the volatility and antagonism inherent to the relational "no-thing," it substitutes for this "no-thing" the absolute nothing devoid of any relation except for the artificially enforced vertical one between the citizen-subject and the state. From this perspective, then, the reproductive futurism Edelman inveighs against is actually propelled by this nihilist drive to negate the "no-thing-in-common," insofar as it perpetuates the consolidation of an immunitary body politic that privileges a socially and politically deracinated (queer) citizen-subject who aspires to live a constitutionally protected life of privatized domesticity. Put differently, the wholesomeness Edelman associates with the survival of the Child and its community of parents is the product of a *suppression* of the relational "no-thing," which is nothing other than the perilous negative space of queerness. Far from being an antirelational zero, I would argue, the negativity inherent to queerness stems from its structural incapacity to avoid being touched and transmogrified by its environment. This means that, far from being condemned a priori to the absence of a future, the future becomes a difficult question, or a problematic horizon, for queers to negotiate. While this more than likely will involve encounters with various forms of violence, "such threats of violence cannot be eliminated—since they are concomitant with the very possibility of relations—but can only be mitigated in essentially precarious processes of negotiation" (Hägglund 2008: 100; see also Ruti 2008: 115). Despite, or rather *because of* the fact that the negative space of queer relationality "doesn't keep us warm, and it doesn't protect us," it will constantly have to be defended against inevitable violence and in this sense it is less anti-immune than autoimmune.[6] Queerness is the radical absence not of the future but of all and any guarantees. Following the imperative that subtends the logic of autoimmunity, queers will have to affirm survival without guarantees, and with it the coming of an undecidable future, essentially because they have no other choice: the future will arrive anyway.[7]

The Problem of Futurity

That is, of course, except when queers are killed and the very notion of futurity is complicit in their murder or slow death. Here we get to the problem with Hägglund's Derridean take on survival and futurity, which is ultimately based on the presumption that we desire life in its—indeed *because of its*—temporal finitude, given that this finitude is what generates any kind of desire in the first place (Hägglund 2009: 159–161). The problem with this onto-"logic" is that it does not differentiate its "we," simply because it claims universality and such differentiation therefore is neither necessary nor possible. In short, it claims to describe existence as such, or human life itself, not its (bio)political organization. Yet, as I argued in Chapter 2, the conditions of possibility for survival—let alone flourishing, to which I return below—are unevenly distributed among Baltimore's segregated population, so while I think Hägglund's take on autoimmunity offers valuable insight into the ambiguous persistence of negativity in everyday life, I also question his color-blind ontology of everyday death. For Hägglund, death is not just part of life; it is more precisely understood as fundamentally contingent on the (f)act of living, of being alive as a human being. But as Wilderson has noted, the contingency of death, or of deadly violence, is a privilege of civil society that is secured only at the expense of the gratuitous—that is, *noncontingent—*

violence that kills Black people every day. It is this discrepancy that Wilderson and other Afro-pessimist scholars understand as at once a symptom and the transhistorical premise of the ontological distinction between the Human and the slave, where the destitution of the latter enables the conditions for flourishing of the former (Douglass and Wilderson 2013; Warren 2015; Wilderson 2003, 2010). From the perspective of Afro-pessimism, then, the category of Humanity still includes the non-Black queer who can find a place at the table as one of civil society's "junior partners," notwithstanding Edelman's injunction that his queer readers should embrace the death drive without reserve. For Black queers, in contrast, to exist in proximity to death, or to exist in a state of superfluity beyond the purview of civil society and its humanist universalism, is a condition inherent to the afterlife of slavery where Black people are consigned to an "existence without standing in the modern world system" (Wagner 2009: 1).

So we have to ask, with the Afro-pessimists: for whom will the future arrive anyway? For whom is the future held open as a promise? How can Black queer folks be expected to affirm the future unconditionally when the past's dehumanizing violence never ceases to haunt it, in an equally unconditional fashion? As Stephen Dillon (2013: 42) notes, time does not pass but accumulates and captures. Following Ian Baucom and Hortense Spillers, he imagines the past not as a separate temporal space but as something that is continually amplified, modified, and protracted into the present and future. As I noted earlier, Black Baltimoreans know this phenomenon all too well with respect to AIDS—that disease from "the past" whose relevance and urgency has come to pass in the daily experience of many white queers who prefer to ignore how it continues to destroy Black communities in amplified, modified, and protracted form. The time of AIDS has not passed; it has merely accumulated on the Black side of the color line. But I have also shown how Ballroom culture presents Black queer youth with a reprieve from their captivity in white, state-enforced temporal frameworks whose disciplinary regimes of surveillance threaten to constrict the life they are ostensibly trying to save. Balls heed José Muñoz's (2009) much discussed call for the proliferation of future-oriented practices and imaginaries to the extent that they conjure alternative prospects and project feelings of hope, thus sketching a potential for things to be otherwise than the dominant anti-Black and antiqueer forms of temporal accumulation and captivity. Nevertheless, I think Dillon raises an important issue when he questions whether such projects should be (seen as) oriented toward the future, given that "the future is a time those without a future cannot risk" (ibid.: 47). I do not take this statement as implying that Black queer folks lack a future a priori, only that they should not and cannot invest in a future that does not include them or includes them only as biomedical input for new public health statistics. It is the difference between the two interpretations—or, perhaps, the lack thereof—that is at stake in this debate.

This is to say that the debate over Black queer futurity is about the degree of temporal autonomy that can be forged through Black queer world making, as well as the political implications of such efforts. Like Muñoz, I firmly believe in the critical power of relatively autonomous temporal practices and imaginaries, even while acknowledging their often provisional and fragile composition. As I argue above, Balls, like Sunday services at the Unity Fellowship Church of Baltimore (UFCB) or BDSM scenes at a play party, are imbued by what Wiegman has called "the asynchronies of an affectively vital political negativity," when Black queer folks build pedagogical timespaces that are warped, kinked, and pulled out of sync with the anti-Black/queer infrastructures that threaten to pull them under or, eventually, pull them apart. I see great value in such interstitial zones of social reproduction dedicated to reprieve and recomposition, in which minoritarian memories, genealogies, and legacies can accumulate and thrive. It meant a great deal to people in the Ballroom scene when Deon became Legendary, a status whose indigenous history presents a politically capacious counternarrative to the world-narrowing captivity of the "treatment and linkage to care" scenario attached to HIV-positive status.[8] Yet unlike Muñoz, I am questioning whether these temporal practices are best understood in the register of futurity, as the preoccupation with an imaginary "then and there" at the potential expense of the "here and now." As indicated by Dillon's question, another dimension of the debate over Black futurity concerns temporal "direction": should experimentations with temporal autonomy be future-oriented or rather be directed solely at the present conditions that infringe on Black queer life? Dillon (2013: 48) advocates the latter approach, which he envisions as a "confrontation with the future as a horizon of death through a politics of urgency and presentism" where the only temporal space available to Black queers is located squarely in the "now." When time does not pass but accumulates, when the future thus inevitably reproduces the violence of the past and thereby foreshadows imminent death, this future must be avoided at all cost. It is indeed the urge to destroy *this* future that aligns Afro-pessimism with Edelman's antifuturistic polemic, insofar as each apprehends "the future" as an absolute and undifferentiated horizon identified fully with the political order's temporal regime. Only the destruction of *this* future can bring about the dissolution of civil society.

Yet where Edelman posits an atemporal death drive as the universal queer's sole escape route away from state-mandated reproductive futurism, Black queer scholarship pushes us to conceive of an alternative temporal ethics that may be able to negotiate futurity in a more politically enabling way. As Kara Keeling (2009: 579) asks, "Undisciplined and vulnerable, firmly rooted in our time, might we nevertheless feel, even without recognition, the rhythms of the poetry from a future . . . ? Might we allow those rhythms to move us to repel the quotidian violence through which we currently are defined without demanding of the future from which they come that it redeem our movement now or then?"[9] Keeling's questions remind me of my experiences at the UFCB, whose "undisciplined and vulnerable" congregation learns how to resist the immunitary temporal logic of sacrifice and sacrificial love that promises redemption as reward for a life of fearful submission and disavowal. Passing up on such a redemptive future, the UFCB nevertheless fervently experiments with divinely inspired rhythms, musical as well as sermonic, that articulate the poetry from a future that faith in the abiding presence of a loving God makes available in the here and now. As I argued in Chapter 4, it is these poetic rhythms that—if expressed in the right tonality—move Black queers of faith to repel the quotidian violence through which they are currently defined and encourage them to redefine themselves in more affirmative terms. Likewise, the rhythms associated with a distinctly Black queer "flavoring" of BDSM scenes are, for Monica, the lifegiving poetry that discloses a future that does not redeem her from the trauma with which she is still learning to cope but, rather, provides an environment that is more conducive to her flourishing in all of its ambivalence and aspiration. It is precisely this ambivalence that makes it at once so tempting and so difficult to completely reject the aspirational impulse of affirmative thought. As I discuss in the next section, there is a vital space between negation and affirmation, or between the desire for the nothing and the need for something, in which the ambiguity of survival and flourishing comes into focus as the most pertinent problem for our thinking about Black queer collective life today.

The Ambiguities of Nothingness

In "The Case of Blackness" (2008), Fred Moten offers a critical and detailed examination of the particular way Afro-pessimist scholars have mobilized

Frantz Fanon's work to tie Blackness exclusively to decay and pathology while accounting for Black life as only an "object in the midst of other objects" on the threshold between life and death (Fanon, quoted in Sexton and Copeland 2003).[10] Moten's response likewise draws on Fanon but excavates what he terms "a kind of pre-op(tical) optimism" from his texts, made possible by a conceptual slippage that is left unattended by his interlocutors (Moten 2008: 182). This slippage in Fanon's *Black Skins, White Masks,* according to Moten, can sensitize us to a "gap" or a "troubled, illicit commerce" between the "fact" of Blackness and lived Black experience (ibid.: 180). Rather than focusing on "the fall from prospective subject to object that Fanon recites" (ibid.: 181), he inquires into the text's concurrent oscillation between the object and the thing. Building on Heidegger's reflections on *das Ding*, he develops a case for the "thing" of Blackness as the gathering *of* and *as* contested matter—a form of fugitive or rogue collectivity that finds ways to evade the incessant disciplinary and biopolitical efforts to frame Black life as an object of capture, detainment, and extermination. Or, as he puts it in his own poetic language, "Some/thing escapes in or through the object's vestibule; the object vibrates against its frame like a resonator, and troubled air gets out. The air of the thing that escapes enframing is what I'm interested in—an often unattended movement that accompanies largely unthought positions and appositions" (ibid.: 182).

For Moten (2008: 187), anti-Black violence cannot fully destroy Black life, which exists "in the break" as much as in the hold and therefore is shaped by an "irremediable homelessness" that is also an "undercommon disorder" whose precariousness and ambivalence need to be embraced, not as social death or absolute dereliction, but as a site for the production of subterranean forms of love and life. Indeed, it is the defiant/deviant fugitivity of Black life, or of Black lived experience, that refuses an ontology of Blackness as pathological and death-driven just as much as the daily annihilation of Black life has verified and reified this ontology. Because of this tension, Moten argues, "Blackness needs to be understood as operating at the nexus of the social and the ontological, the historical and the essential" (ibid.). His argument resonates with my experiences in Baltimore, where public health policy generates an ontology of Blackness as a pathological object of surveillance and capture in terms of "community viral loads" that measure the extent to which captive Black populations in the eastern and western districts of the city have been infected with the virus that has come to define them. Still, as I have shown, this ontology not only is carried as a burden by Black queer youth but is also actively refused and reconfigured through the celebration of a form of life that exceeds calculation and containment. Ball culture, among other world-making efforts, proves that ontology is not a metaphysical destiny and *can be built from the ground up*. But can such efforts really (afford to) transcend, even partly, the death and pathology that haunts their survival and deeply informs their affirmative drive? As Moten himself asks, echoing Povinelli's question addressed in Chapter 4, "What survives the kind of escape that ought never leave the survivor intact? If and when some thing emerges from such a place, can it be anything other than pathological?" (ibid.: 208–209).

In response to Moten's reflections, Jared Sexton (2012: n.p.) acknowledges the "intimacy" between social death and social life, in which each conditions the other's "impossible possibility." However, he argues that, despite the undeniable perseverance and occasional flourishing of Black social life, its various articulations do not erase or make any less urgent the fact of Black social death. Building on Fanon's and Wilderson's insights, Sexton asks us to consider whether any affirmation of Black social life can survive without also truly embracing its negation in the form of social death, as that corrosive reality is intimately constitutive of Blackness in the afterlife of slavery. According to Sexton, Moten implicitly underwrites such a consideration to the extent that he associates Black life with terms such as "disorder," "derangement," and the "uninhabitable." While recognizing the critical value of Moten's subtle distinction between Blackness and Black experience, he ultimately favors Wilderson's political ontology because it focuses on the more pertinent distinction between Blackness and anti-Blackness, or "the gap between the place of slaves and the places of all others" (Wilderson 2010: 120). Instead of insisting that Black experience does not coincide with the ontology of Blackness that has congealed (in) an anti-Black world, one would do better to fully accept this pathological position:

> Though it may appear counter-intuitive, or rather because it is counter-intuitive, this acceptance or affirmation is active; it is a willing or willingness, in other words, to pay whatever social costs accrue to being Black, to inhabiting Blackness, to living a Black social life under the shadow of social death. This is not an accommodation to the dictates of the anti-Black world. The affirmation of Blackness, which is to say an affirmation of pathological being, is a refusal to distance oneself from Blackness in a valorization of minor differences that bring one closer to health, life, or sociality. (Sexton 2012: n.p.)

But as I asked in Chapter 1 with regard to political theories that exalt the political as the site of endless antagonism, who will be able to answer the injunction at the center of such austere imaginaries? None of the Black queer Baltimoreans I met could afford the social costs that accrued to their Black being. And none of them felt—or felt that they should feel—any less Black for refusing to affirm their Blackness as pathological being, whether in church, at the Playhouse, or at a Ball sponsored by the city's Health Department. Why should their aspirations to achieve better health, life, or sociality distance them from Blackness, or, more important, why should this be any of their concern?[11] Again, Blackness may be ontologically saturated by dereliction and nothingness, but a truly *political* ontology does not simply manifest destiny and can be challenged and reworked in historically situated social projects. Ultimately, Sexton's "transvaluation of pathology" forms an attempt to identify Black social life with social death and thereby bring Moten's Black optimism closer to his own position. Yet what this unifying move obscures is that, despite their many agreements, there remains a crucial difference in their respective understandings of the relationship between negation and affirmation. Whereas Sexton and Wilderson start from the paradigmatic nature of anti-Black violence that produces Blackness as a void, or abyss, for Moten Blackness is the originary movement of affirmation punctuated (punctured) by anti-Black negation. In the tradition of Michel Foucault and Gilles Deleuze, resistance comes first, and every striated space can barely contain its lines of flight.

This becomes particularly clear in Moten's ruminations on nothingness, which form a response to his Afro-pessimist interlocutors. While in "The Case of Blackness" Moten focused on the improper "thing" of the "no-thing," his aim in two subsequent texts is to linger on the "no-": "We come from nothing, which is something misunderstood. It's not that Blackness is not statelessness; it's just that statelessness is an open set of social lives whose ani*mater*ialized exhaustion remains as irreducible chance" (Moten 2013a: 239). In another text, published the same year, he again takes exhaustion as his site of departure for thinking the social life that animates Blackness and that exists/persists not in social death but in "*political* death" (Moten 2013b: 739).[12] Proceeding analogically to Wilderson's analysis without accepting his totalization of anti-Black political violence, Moten envisions Black nothingness as the place of exhausting and exhaustive improvisation that operates with a measure of stolen temporal autonomy and harbors "the promise of another world, or of the end of this one" (ibid.: 752). I think that here, at the juncture where Moten's optimism most intimately touches Wilderson's pessimism, we witness the ambivalence that marks the work of both authors. Each remains in the hold of the ship, circling around each other in this deeply ambiguous space whose nothingness cannot completely void its flights of fantasy and permanently dislocated potentiality. While Moten is committed to an affirmative notion of Blackness, he nevertheless realizes that the true flourishing of Black life would necessitate the negation of the world as we know it. Yet if "negation is the captive's central possibility for action," as Hartman has stated (Hartman and Wilderson 2003: 187), Moten refuses to theorize this possibility as an antirelational being toward death. Thus, for him the most pertinent question is how to destroy the world without also destroying the precarious Black "things" in it. Wilderson has often expressed his desire for the end of this world, which he imagines as a revolutionary death-driven act, but his radical affirmation of negation also betrays his willingness to, as Moten (2013b: 746) puts it, "reside in an unlivability, an exhaustion that is always already given as foreshadowing afterlife." Indeed, he has never stopped believing in the "tremendous life" of Black communities, and there is a strange kind of "terribly beautiful vitality" in his unrelenting interrogation of our anti-Black world, which enacts the kind of experimentation Moten finds at the heart of Black cultural production (Moten 2008: 188). So for Wilderson, Moten's question pertains with equal force and urgency. Both desire the end of this world and the destruction of its deadly political order, together with its attendant ontology, epistemology, and value system, yet neither wants to relinquish the (ap)positionality of an unstable outside as a site of improvisation and ethical critique, even as each is cognizant of the paradoxical fact that it is precisely this outside—however dynamic—that sustains the political order's expansionist anti-Black drive.[13] It may be true that, as Sexton (2012) phrases it, "Black life is not lived in the world that the world lives in," but both worlds nevertheless continue to be intricately connected in a unilaterally abusive and perversely codependent relationship.

While I am moved by Moten's lavishly poetic articulation of Blackness as residing in the space between the "no" and the "thing," which turns nothing into something without ever losing sight of the negativity that permeates Black life, I wonder how his radical vision accounts for the survival, let alone the flourishing, of this life in and through its exhaustion. If the celebration and improvisation central to Black sociality are premised on—at best—precarious foundations, as indicated by his invocations of homelessness, dislocation, disorder, and fugitivity, and if this dynamic insecurity is, in turn, exactly what should be celebrated over and against modes of (bio)political capture and captivity, then what is it that capacitates and sustains the "informal, informing, insolvent insovereignty" of a Black undercommons (Moten 2013b: 774; cf. Harney and Moten 2013)? As Esposito reminds us, the "nothing" of *communitas* doesn't keep us warm and it doesn't protect us against expropriating violence, which is something Moten seems to acknowledge when he asks, "What survives the kind of escape that ought to never leave the survivor intact?" Yet Moten's Fanonian predilections, which tie him so closely to his Afro-pessimist interlocutors, lead him to embrace such expropriating violence as a radical kind of shattering that forms the condition of possibility for the constitution of this Black undercommons that resists being framed in/ by the political order. Like Esposito, Moten identifies personhood fully with the realm of immunitary biopolitics, against which he posits the impersonal, improper fugitivity of Black life as a disorderly "break" or cut. As discussed in Chapter 3, I, too, recognize the force of impersonality and impropriety as modes of being in common that escape and resist the modern paradigm of immunization and its stifling nexus of sovereign personhood, propriety, and property. But subsequent chapters have also shown that there is a vital space between sovereign personhood and disordered, dislocated, and disheveled existence, in which Black queers—with and without their non-Black peers— struggle for more power, more home, more world, and even some measure of sovereignty and personhood. This, in my view, is the ambiguous space between survival and flourishing, which does not allow for easy dichotomies. While Moten concurs with the Afro-pessimist assertion that Black people cannot desire such impossibilities, I have argued that these aspirations are exactly what can turn mere life into more life, survival into flourishing—not in the yet to come but in the here and now.

Moreover, I contend that these aspirations, together with the infrastructures they help to create and that in turn scaffold new aspirational thoughts and affects, are *political* rather than "just" social. My biggest problem with respect to the terms of the debate sketched above is how they consistently tie the "necro" to the political, which thereby figures as nothing other than a system that reproduces white supremacy by capturing and destroying Black life. This kind of absolute thought cannot imagine or account for articulations of the political, or ways of being and thinking and acting in a political manner, that are "constitutive" (Negri 1991) or "compositional" (Latour 2010a), in the sense that they build, sustain, and hold things together in the face of perpetual antagonism. It is precisely such articulations that I have attempted to examine and appreciate through the notion of "civic intimacies" as a Black queer practice of composition that is politically capacitating in its refusal to relinquish its claim *to* the city by way of its improper inhabitation *of* the city, which remains a hostile polity for many fugitive outsiders. In Baltimore, as elsewhere, Black queer residents are engaged in the fragmented and precarious constitution of "another way of living in the world, a Black way of living together in the other world we are constantly making in and out of this world" (Moten 2013b: 778), which points us to the fact that Black life is lived in different worlds at the same time while it conjures different temporalities in the same world. As C. Riley Snorton (2014) has recently suggested, "The survival of Black life (and Black thought) is a queer proposition." Furthermore, scholars such as Roderick Ferguson (2004), Kathryn Bond Stockton (2006), Kara Keeling (2007, 2009), E. Patrick Johnson (2008), Jafari Allen (2011), and Marlon Bailey (2013) have each offered distinct accounts of the mutual imbrications of Blackness and queerness in terms of their social, aesthetic, erotic, and political composition, encouraging us to think these categories through one another and to realize that there is no one "Black way of living together." Collectively, this work attunes our critical imagination to the intersectional precariousness and exuberance of Black queer life by continuing to prompt the politically urgent question of what holds up/open the often narrow spaces between death, survival, and flourishing that mark its trajectories. Over the course of this book, I have offered one answer to this question by identifying civic intimacies, or the ongoing maintenance and repair of intimate support structures, as a vital resource for Black queer world making. As Allen (2012: 217) has argued, "For Black queers, survival has always been about finding ways to connect some of what is disconnected, to embody and re-member." Yet as I discuss in the next, penultimate section, this "reparative impulse" has been the subject of critical debate within queer theory as the field reassesses its own—often color-blind—investments in optimism and pessimism.

Negativity and Reparativity

How would we benefit from a return to queer theory's engagement with negativity, which would also lead us back to Edelman? According to Amy Villarejo (2005: 75), "Queer theory can offer . . . a way to grapple with feeling and with response (affect), a way to work in the interstices of contacts, affiliations, relations." That is, it can focus attention on our attachments to a variety of objects that are at once psychic, social, political, and material. Since Eve Kosofsky Sedgwick's work has cultivated an increasingly rich understanding of such attachments, I want to examine how her reparative thought has been taken up in the wake of her death to further elaborate my conception of civic intimacies as the production of intimate and material support structures able to generate the conditions of felicity for forms of Black queer survival to edge toward flourishing. Drawing on the narratives of Black queer experience presented in earlier chapters, I thus want to take reparativity beyond the affective economy of individual psyches and its methodological association with literary criticism, instead conceiving it as the arduous ethico-political work of composing collectivity, or the desire for a sense of being in common that is also permanently undermined.

Many queer critics have been inspired by, and have critically elaborated on, Sedgwick's endeavor to compose an alternative mode of analysis that relinquishes its critical sovereignty in favor of a reparative reading practice in which "the critical act is reconfigured to value, sustain, and privilege the object's worldly inhabitations and needs" (Wiegman 2014: 7). In Sedgwick's treatment of Kleinian object relations theory, the critic assumes the "depressive position," which for Melanie Klein is characterized by a longing to restore and nourish the broken or fragmented object of attachment, to make it whole again and thereby ward off the threat it poses to the self. In the context of scholarly criticism, this translates into a rejection of critical distance and a desire for intimacy and generosity toward one's object of study, which one neither masters nor holds in contempt but instead attempts to affirm, despite the risk inherent to such affirmation. One of the main points of critique leveled at Sedgwick's reparative project is that it ostensibly approximates a mode of optimism that cultural criticism, dedicated to the labor of the negative, cannot afford and should not desire. From this perspective, an investment in reparativity is closely associated with an investment in redemption, where to repair would be tantamount to restoring some originary plenitude that is currently lacking. Lauren Berlant, for example, is perhaps one of Sedgwick's most prominent champions, yet she is hesitant to fully embrace Sedgwick's longing for the reparative to the extent that "the overvaluation of reparative thought is both an occupational hazard and part of a larger overvaluation of a certain mode of virtuously intentional, self-reflective personhood" (Berlant 2011a: 124). Here Berlant fears that the problems Sedgwick identified with paranoid forms of criticism have the potential to return in projects that too eagerly—and optimistically—invest in the autonomy of the reparative reader. Elsewhere, Berlant (2011b: 117) expresses similar concerns while taking the notion of reparativity beyond the context of scholarship toward the work of getting through the day: "Activity toward reproducing life is neither identical to making it or oneself *better* nor a mimetic response to the structural conditions of a collective failure to thrive . . . —such activity is also directed toward making a less-bad experience. It's a relief, a reprieve, not a repair." Relief and reprieve, in their tentativeness and transience, are here clearly distinguished from what Berlant takes to be constitutive of repair: completion, mastery, and permanence. But is this an apt description of reparativity? Is reparativity able to negate the persistence of the negative by turning it into a positive? Berlant's hesitations are understandable, given the language Sedgwick at times used to phrase her project: she writes about the desire to "confer plenitude" on an object and emphasizes Klein's association of the reparative process with love and nourishment—phenomena typically suspect among paranoid readers (Sedgwick 2003: 149). Jackie Stacey (2014: 43) has expressed similar worries about "the loss of ambivalence enacted by the desire for the reparative" when this psychoanalytical concept is translated into an idiom of cultural criticism. What gets lost in translation, more precisely, is the conflicted nature of our attachments to the (part) objects we attempt to love, since love is never unambiguously triumphant and cannot be completely dissociated from hate—Klein, after all, coined this position "depressive" for a reason. As Stacey argues, "Extracting and privileging love's place in the reparative position has somehow been read as an invitation to amplify love, leaving behind the less appealing dynamics of these object relations" (ibid.: 46). These "less appealing dynamics" are also addressed by Wiegman (2014: 17), who notes that "both the paranoid and the reparative positions are responses to the same environmental conditions of ambivalence, risk, and dependence." Indeed, such dependence is "necessary for survival but also its greatest threat" (ibid.) and, as Sedgwick (2003: 150) already observed, a reparative position is "no less attached to a project of survival" than a paranoid one. While they mobilize different survival strategies, both positions are equally invested in defense and self-preservation, and they are similarly permeated by anxiety and contradictory desires.

But as Sedgwick also knew, these different strategies of survival matter a great deal. Whereas the paranoid position enacts self-preservation through the immunitary mechanisms of dissociation, negation, and neutralization, cutting the self off from the "outside" world and rejecting any threatening "external" object that cannot be neutralized as unambiguously good, the reparative or depressive position acknowledges the impossibility of upholding binary oppositions such as "inside-outside" or "good-bad." Facing up to the intransigence of ambivalence and relationality, it attempts to protect the self not just by opening it up to the world whose objects are both potential threats and sources of nourishment, but also by offering protection *to these objects* that may very well be threatened by the violence of the self's defensive impulses.

Obviously, this is a more difficult and precarious mode of defense, but it is one that ultimately can offer more viable chances of survival and even of flourishing to the extent that it refuses to give up on the world—even when this world is "inadequate or inimical to its nurture" (Sedgwick 2003: 149)— or on collective world making. Moreover, it refuses to give up on love as at once an intimate, spiritual, and political force that assembles and sustains even as it continues to disappoint and hurt. Love—God's love, as well as worldly love—was a recurring motif throughout my fieldwork in Baltimore and has featured prominently in the previous chapters: the love Anthony, Deon, and Marlon have for their outreach work and their community; the love of God that capacitates the UFCB congregation and allows its members to walk in their truth; a divinely inspired love shared by Monica, which mediates her conflicted love for BDSM and for the sense of self she is trying to cultivate; a self-love and a love of Blackness and SGL people that is so crucial to Cleo's pedagogical project. For so many of the people I met in Baltimore, love was akin to a reparative support structure that provided an invaluable resource for psychic as well as social and material sustenance. Yet again, this isn't to say that love's reparative impulse was experienced as unambiguous or unproblematic. I have also shown how the love that propels the lifesaving aspirations of Deon, Anthony, and Marlon was frequently unrequited and disappointed by the very institutions that had managed to magnetize their hope for a better future. And Monica's experiences perhaps most poignantly attest to the gendered and racialized ambivalences that pervade a reparative investment in self-love, safety, and a sense of communal belonging that would capacitate such aspirational fantasies. In all of these situations, the impulse and effort to repair was imperfect and unfinished, and despite the structural optimism of their attachments it certainly didn't always feel good.

Even though her readers recognize that Sedgwick was careful to account for the fundamental ambivalence inherent to the reparative project she developed and promoted, this recognition apparently does not prevent the recurrent charge that her position embraces an unwarranted optimism that "avoids grappling at length with the less salvific implications of reparation" (Wiegman 2014: 17). The optimism of her project is once again the topic of debate in a recent conversation between Berlant and Edelman, which reflects on Sedgwick's reparative thought in light of her life's work, as well as her premature death.[14] According to Edelman, Sedgwick's notion of reparativity "grounds itself in a notion of aesthetic coherence that opposes the incompletion, division and defectiveness of failure" (Berlant and Edelman 2014: 42). By holding on to such an opposition, Sedgwick's reparative project is said to exhibit the paranoia she criticizes as self-defeating. Only by disavowing the intractability of negativity and splitting off reparativity from paranoia can she sustain a mode of optimism that nevertheless, despite its best intentions, continues to be mired in dread. It is this persistent sense of dread in Sedgwick's work that Edelman finds most theoretically valuable, as it attends us to "the rupture to which repair is bound, the persistent place of the 'no'" (ibid.: 45). In response, Berlant identifies dread as the primary affective state of the depressive position, given that one is forced to acknowledge the potential violence accompanying any act of repair. Elaborating on the value of rupture emphasized by Edelman, she links this position of depressed ambivalence in Sedgwick's writing to "the relief that acknowledgment, detachment, and even dissociation can provide, suggesting that a mode of existence can be forged in which the subject lives with an open vulnerability without compulsively inducing a saturating defense that attempts to disavow the noise of abandonment and dread" (ibid.: 46–47). But here we have to once again stop and ask: who is this subject that "lives with an open vulnerability" to violence and loss "without inducing a saturating defense"?[15] And does defense necessarily entail a disavowal of negativity? I think the ethical position Berlant suggests here moves too closely toward the color-blind ethics of self-shattering promoted by Edelman, which atomizes the affective economy of an abstract queer subject and hence ignores what it takes for Black queer folks, socially as well as psychically, to survive and to flourish. While antagonism, detachment, and dissociation were certainly omnipresent in Baltimore's fractured LGBT community, traceable along racial and (trans)gender lines, this continued to generate new attachments that answered to the widespread need for protection and belonging. In Monica's case, for instance, her experimentation with self-abandonment and her pursuit of physical and emotional vulnerability were intricately tied to her concomitant desire to become a more "diligent" and stronger person who could likewise make her community stronger, just as her efforts to detach from predominantly white BDSM club life coincided with the parallel creation of a new network of pleasure and belonging located in Black practitioner's homes. The same motif of detachment and reattachment structured the journeys of Black queer Baltimoreans who joined the UFCB or sought refuge with one of the city's Houses—two vital support structures in both the psychic and material sense.

Berlant's comment also reminds me of a more general ethical embrace of vulnerability in feminist and queer social theory, exemplified by work of Judith Butler. In different publications, Butler (2006, 2010) has reflected on our current geopolitical condition in which vulnerability is unequally imposed on particular groups—that is, immigrants and refugees—whose lives are marked by precarity while their deaths are to a large extent ungrievable. Like Esposito, Butler attributes much of today's violence and precarity to the desire for immunization that has intensified since the 9/11 attacks, which has resulted in a paranoid, defensive, and volatile state of affairs in which life is preserved only by sacrificing it through increasingly constricting and ultimately lethal security strategies. Her response to this situation, equally reminiscent of Esposito's analysis, is to propose "reimagining the possibility of community on the basis of vulnerability and loss" (Butler 2006: 20). Where Esposito's *communitas* constitutes an expropriating void that neither keeps us warm nor protects us, Butler's imagined community is likewise marked by a foundational negativity and a concomitant realization that "we are not only constituted by our relations but also dispossessed by them as well" (ibid.: 24). This ethical acknowledgment of a shared existential precariousness would then provide an antidote to the violence of immunitary forces that disavow their own vulnerability, thereby enabling a more capacious collective process of mourning lost life (cf. Watson 2012). While I am sympathetic to the notion of a shared sense of vulnerability, I have serious doubts about the extent to which such an ethics of loss and becoming undone can actually empower people to turn survival into flourishing. First of all, as Julian Reid (2011: 773) has argued, it is not at all certain whether an ethics of corporeal vulnerability will lead to a dismantling of the immunitary paradigm that governs our current geopolitical climate or whether this realization of one's own precariousness will instead instantiate "the very demand for protection on which liberal governance depends for its legitimation in relation to the subject." Second, and more important here, this ethics is essentially docile in that it doesn't provide any conceptual or practical resources for making a vulnerable existence less vulnerable. Even though precariousness, like survival, may be a common ontological given, this does not discount the political fact that some lives, such as Black queer lives, are more exposed to violence and loss than others and will therefore require certain protective infrastructures that prevent them from being killed, violated, or slowly left to die. As noted above, even Esposito acknowledges that no life can persevere without access to at least some measure of immunization. The ethico-political question is how to conceive of immunity in a way that does not reproduce the paranoid antirelationality that has thus far dominated modern political theory and practice.

This returns us to the political potential of reparativity—and to love. As depressed as the subject inhabiting the ambivalence of the reparative position may be, s/he refuses to give up on the optimism of her/his attachments to what might offer a more viable and even pleasurable life. In other words, s/he does not settle for vulnerability just like that. In response to Moten's question about "what survives the kind of escape that ought to never leave the survivor intact?" which is a deeply *political* question repeated by Berlant and Edelman in a different context, the reparative answer is that what survives is not only loss, as Edelman would have it, but also love.[16] Here I am referring not to the romantic and domestic kind of love that grounds the intimate event between two partners but, rather, to a political kind of love that I just likened to a reparative support structure. Here I again follow Berlant (2011b: 690), who has argued that a "properly transformational political concept [of love] would provide the courage to take the leap into a project of better relationality that would give us patience with the 'without guarantees' part of love's various temporalities." Like survival, love offers no guarantees that the sustenance we strive for will be achieved, but attempting the leap from enduring life's vicissitudes to a life punctuated by recurring moments of collective flourishing is a radically political gesture. In her conversation with Edelman, Berlant even suggests that the lack of guarantees may be constitutive of flourishing itself: "Without allowing for ambivalence, there is no flourishing. It therefore entails a complex navigation of life and noise, and the will to achieve it calls for practices and tendencies beyond mere accommodation to the world's and our own negativity" (Berlant and Edelman 2014: 12).

This is certainly a far cry from her proposal for a life lived with an open vulnerability, which would precisely amount to a "mere accommodation to the world's and our own negativity." In contrast, the "practices and tendencies" I have narrated and analyzed in this book under the rubric of civic intimacies have attested to the fact that Black queer collectives need and build support structures rooted in carefully cultivated forms of love that generate the courage and patience to navigate life as well as its noise, with the intention to celebrate rather than to merely endure being alive. At the UFCB, God's love made available the courage to walk in one's truth, which subsequently encouraged the members of its congregation to commit to an analysis of the various sources of noise in their lives, as well as pointing them to potential resources that could resist or alter this negativity. And it was the love for one another and for their communities, including but not limited to the Ball community, that pushed Anthony and his friends to persist and retain their patience despite the lack of funding, misguided policies, and all the infighting that was fracturing the Ballroom scene. This points to how the impulse to repair, immanent to civic intimacies and their support structures, not only aims to protect marginalized and dispossessed communities from what threatens them from the "outside" but also pushes them to deal with the "intramural" frictions and fissures that may undo these communities from within (Spillers 2003; see also Muñoz 2006). While such disjunctions are inevitable and constitutive of community, the work of reparative support structures is nevertheless vital to maintaining and creating anew a provisional sense of cohesion that capacitates concerted efforts to resist or, at the very least, to bear more vigorously the violent and often unbearable forces of negation, exhaustion, and attrition—wherever they may originate.

Support Structures

Passing up on the high demands of radical democratic theory, with its revolutionary politics of rupture and dissent, while refusing to withdraw from the political through nihilist apostasy or an ethics of vulnerability and ego shattering, the political import of civic intimacies instead emerges from the support structures they compose and that in turn lift up and hold together lives that otherwise would be unlikely to survive. But what exactly makes a support structure, and how does this device, which is at once conceptual and material in nature, allow us to rethink citizenship through the lens of that which is superfluous, excessive, or unintelligible to modern immunitary citizenship regimes? That is, how can it make citizenship a *sensible*—both meaningful and viscerally pertinent—category for understanding the ongoing struggles of Black queer collectivities? According to Céline Condorelli (2014), from whom I borrow the concept, support structures can be characterized by four features, which she terms "proximity," "against," "supplementarity," and "temporary."[17] I closely attend to each, because this affords a firmer conceptual grasp of the chronically undervalued civic potential I see embodied in (the work of building) support structures for Black queer forms of life. In contrast to the legal, moral, and political fable of the autonomous liberal citizen who enjoys his freedom as sufficient distance from institutions that could impose binding forms of obligation, the civic imaginary that subtends the work of building and maintaining support structures firstly demands a commitment to proximity and intimacy in all their ambivalence. As Condorelli (2014: 15) asserts: "No support can take place outside a close encounter, getting entangled in a situation and becoming implicated in it." Yet, as she notes, this intimacy also entails violence—"the violence of support" (ibid.)—because close encounters often generate friction and, as thinkers of community from Esposito to Jean-Luc Nancy have insisted, being in common entails having nothing positive in common at all.[18] The proximity that is part and parcel of providing and receiving support, then, offers no guarantees of redemption or even improvement, but this does not make the work of support melancholic—perhaps just politically depressed. Like the depressed position in Klein and Sedgwick, the position of support has to accommodate ambivalence because it is committed to the immanent obligation of being proximate: "embracing or at least being actively interested in, and concerned for, the success of a particular project, undertaking, or venture" (ibid.: 16).

Being in close proximity to the object of support, the object of one's reparative impulse, can thus mean occupying "a position of active antagonism" (Condorelli 2014: 17). The closeness that marks (the building of) support structures is not so much a matter of juxtaposition, of being next to one's object or objective, as of being positioned "right against them" (ibid.). Support structures push against their objects as they scaffold them, holding them up often in spite of themselves. Nowhere was this more visible than at the UFCB, where the clergy struggled not only *with* the members of the congregation but also *against* them, pushing them to thoroughly examine not only their lives, routines and assumptions, and fears and anxieties, but also their hopes and dreams. This was an emotionally intense and difficult process in which the truth telling that happened during Spiritual Development classes would confront those involved as much as it eventually helped them. It is only in their very "againstness" that the UFCB's support structures could achieve some form of transformation by operating on the volatile threshold of cultivation and critique.[19] This liminal operation is intrinsic to the work that support does as it takes place "on a permeable edge working within from without" (ibid.: 17), which is a place of experiment, impropriety, and—as Moten would have it—fugitivity.[20] As Condorelli (2014: 18) puts it, "This taking place is perennially peripheral, relational; it is difficult in it being laborious and intractable. Part of its awkwardness lies in it not being an affirmation in itself, but constantly defined in negation: it must not become the object, is not inside nor outside, not autonomous, nor object-bound, not fixed, not closed, un-limited, and never finished." Built to affirm and repair, support structures are nevertheless marked by ambiguity, which give them their "awkward" shape and operative location within larger institutional frameworks. This is to say, they are structured by the logic of supplementarity: a support structure appears to be added to the object as an external means to augment a perceived need or incapacity thought to be located in the object itself, yet what initially seemed to be merely supplemental turns out to have intimate commerce with what it was supposed to supplement and for which it now forms the condition of possibility. Suddenly civil society's trusted spatial and social binaries—such as inside-outside, open-closed, cause-effect, dependent-independent—become confused.

Such confusion and ambiguity was prevalent among many of the support structures I witnessed in Baltimore, where it was often not entirely clear who depended on whom for care and support. Everyone I met seemed to be involved and invested in several ongoing—yet intermittent and chronically underfunded—projects that at times crossed paths and from which they could not fully extricate themselves, given that their work of support worked to support them at least as much as it supported their intended objects and objectives. This was true for the people I met at the UFCB, but it pertained equally to the peer outreach workers at the Baltimore City Health Department, who had to deal with the ambivalence of aspiring to an institutional position that could provide them with financial and social security while doing very little to support their peers in the Ball community. Moreover, House fathers such as Deon continually navigated that "permeable edge working within from without," being an integral part of the Ball scene and yet also hovering over it as a Legend, deeply aware of the pastoral power attached to this status and attempting to exploit it in his outreach work—which was always a work of improvisation and making do. When his community thrives, he thrives, as he repeatedly made clear, which signals a deep interdependence that keeps him going and strengthens his commitment to the ambivalent institutional structures he cannot afford to abandon because they have far exceeded their supplementary status. I witnessed the same dynamic in my interactions with Carlton, whose community status, livelihood, and sense of self coincided almost completely with his HIV-prevention work. Meanwhile, Monica was dealing with her own, ambivalent relationship to the institutional setting of her support structures, as her desire to be a solid anchor for Black novices in the leather and BDSM community barely trumped the racial tension and harassment that had pushed her away from the public, racially mixed events. This other-directed project of care and education not only created new mutual dependencies and obligations but also contributed to her flourishing because of its vitalizing presence *as a project*. This project forced her to balance Baltimore's queer kink color line, which was a difficult process of being at once included and excluded while staking out ground on the periphery, welcomed in part while other parts remained unintelligible. Her support was as much *of* and *for* "the community" as it was actively working *against* it: object, objective, and objection converged.

It was also a protracted process, like all of the other processes and projects I could only glimpse during the time of my fieldwork. This brings me to the last common feature of support structures: their temporality. As Condorelli (2014: 21) writes, "The irresolvable paradox of support is that it relies on appearing temporary in order to sustain and perpetuate the inherent, naïve hope or belief that what is being supported will eventually be able to support itself; support is geared towards the independence of the object of concern, and is a process toward its own obsolescence and disappearance." Thus, the affective and material architecture that constitutes a support structure is inherently utopian and invested in emancipation in the sense that what holds it up and holds it together is the faith that its use will expire at one point in time, after which the object of concern will flourish autonomously. The "naïve" reparative impulse is to repair the object for good, to make it whole again. But as previously discussed, this impulse is constantly thwarted by the realization that negativity is immanent to survival as well as flourishing and that this is exactly what necessitates the ongoing work of repair and support. Besides their essential incompleteness, what further subtends the ambivalent nature of support structures is the possibility that "the presence of support also prolongs the moment of crisis, and carries it through time" (ibid.), which is something I witnessed frequently in Baltimore, where so many underfunded and fledgling community-based organizations are working to keep their heads above water while achieving few noticeable gains in their communities. In other words, rather than solely creating an inhabitable environment for the object of care and nourishment, a support structure may also inadvertently extend this object's exhausting struggles and protract its suffering, even when this suffering is (temporarily) alleviated. None of the support structures I have examined in this book were exempt from this double logic, or dual movement, as they each in their own way carried the crisis-turned-impasse of Black queer survival through time without an escape route. Here we return to the violence of support, which is due to not only its proximity but also the difficult, antagonistic, and indefinite nature of the edgework without any guarantees—and often with few resources. In their open-ended and precarious experimentality, support structures resist the closure of easy, neatly formulated "solutions" to the complex and entangled issues that pervade Black queer life in Baltimore, whether they are proposed by heteronormative public institutions or well-meaning but ill-advised white queer liberals who have now found a seat at the table as "one of civil society's junior partners."

So what about those who will never be seated at this table? Many refuse such a seat, knowing that its legs, like the legs of the table, are resting on the necks and throats of their peers, whose suffocation remains disavowed and is once again swept under the rug where those at the table, *those who made that table*, stow away all that is superfluous, excessive, and unintelligible to our modern immunitary citizenship regime. For the Black, queer, and dispossessed, the notion of citizenship as it has been imagined and drawn up on this table certainly is nonsensical and quite literally offensive. Yet, as I argued in Chapter 1, instead of rejecting citizenship wholesale, I believe it is more fruitful to inquire into how we can harness the critical potential of this concept, which has been obfuscated by (neo)liberal and juridical discourses. There I also cited Linda Bosniak's (2006: 12) assertion that "describing aspects of the world in the language of citizenship is a legitimizing political act." Again, and to be sure, this act of legitimation is not intended to capture Black queerness by bringing it into the fold of civil society and its immunitary terms and conditions. Instead, it serves to radically problematize these terms and conditions by asking how the notion of citizenship has to be reconfigured—or disfigured—and pushed beyond its limits so that it may begin to speak to, and become a legitimate matter of concern for, Black queer folks. But what has the language of citizenship, as expressed through my concept of civic intimacies, accomplished here? This central question can be answered on two levels. First, on a conceptual level, it has highlighted how the composition of support structures for Black queer life forms an intimate, ambiguous, and ongoing edgework that requires commitment without offering any guarantees. Thus, it is a risky, courageous, and profoundly political articulation of citizenship as being *of* the city and claiming a non-juridical right *to* the city. This "right" consists of an ongoing improper imposition: a blatant reparative refusal to cave in or to fade away, arising from a concerted effort to preserve what is joyful, exuberant, and aberrant about Black queer collective experience, while knowing very well that "proper" citizenship—that place at the table—will never be an option. It is not only that the promise of citizenship means nothing to the terminally superfluous, the Black and queer, but that this promise can exist only at their immeasurable expense. However, as Fred Moten has so eloquently argued and as my study, I hope, made visible, those relegated to nothingness still gather their scarce yet indelible resources to make something from this nothing, as they hold up the ambivalent support structures that tentatively hold together a Black queer sense of the world. This sense is deeply marked by negativity without being reducible to it, for there continues to be a surplus of collective joy and love that cannot be contained or eradicated.[21]

In *The Sense of the World*, Jean-Luc Nancy (1997: 111) writes about common sense, or a sense of the common that is also a sense that is common, as being essentially excessive and located on the threshold of interiority and exteriority. He suggests the figure of the "(k)not" to attune his readers to a political imaginary of "the in-common *through which there is sense* that circulates and that ties and enchains itself . . . without having any 'sense' other than tying itself" (ibid.: 113). The sense of the (k)not exists only in the recurrent temporal space of the interval, where "the tie is taken up again, recast, and retied without end, nowhere purely tied or untied," which makes it a profoundly ambiguous sense whose politics "would henceforth be neither a substance nor a form but, first of all, a gesture: the very gesture of tying and enchainment of each to each" (ibid.: 112). Rejecting both the substantial interiority of the modern subject and the formalist exteriority of the modern citizen, Nancy instead finds the locus of political action in what I have called the practice of composition—the practice of composing collectivities through variegated, provisional, and necessarily incomplete gestures of connection, of tying and retying the (k)not that is also a (w)hole.[22] In this way, he helps me to move from a notion of citizenship as autarchic substance or form to a more sensible and sensual conception of citizenship as anti/ante-archic *consistency*, which is viscerally pertinent to a Black queer sense of the world because it pertains to the composition of support structures. If we think of the work of citizenship in terms of consistency, which is to think civic intimacies, this allows us to ask two questions: (1) what does it consist of? and (2) how consistent is it? Whereas the first question considers how the gathering of resources and their particular configuration hold together a support structure, the second question is interested in matters of durability, cohesion, and texture. In other words, if the first question asks "how is a support structure composed?" the second asks "how *well* is it composed?" (Latour 2010a). To think of citizenship in terms of consistency thus opens up the political imagination to its articulation in an architectural register, where building, composing, and supporting are some of the main idioms that can be used to express the spatiotemporal practices of Black queer world making that oscillate between survival and flourishing. Here, support structures form experimental architectures of the good life, where this notion regains its improper sense through the radical revision and revaluation of what good can be distilled from life lived in, or in proximity to, social death.

The work of revaluation is crucial here, especially with respect to the question of how well a support structure is composed. Revaluation, as the cultivation of a love of self and others, as praise and appraisal, as the making of worth and a "changing of the currency," is what makes Black queer collectivities not only more durable, by enforcing their textural density, but also more forceful and able to resist what diminishes their power to act (see Chapter 4). Responding critically to Butler's ethics of vulnerability, Reid (2011: 778) argues that "political subjects do not merely depend on their milieus or desire the sustainability of the conditions for living the lives they do; rather, they resist those conditions and at times overcome them and transform them into what they were not, thereby establishing new conditions for life." I agree, except for the opposition his argument creates between practices of political freedom and/as resistance and practices that "merely depend on their milieus" or attempt to sustain existing conditions for living. As discussed in Chapter 1, my problem with such an imagination of political subjectivity or citizenship, which adheres to the tenets of radical democratic theory and its exaltation of the autonomy of the political, is that it still thinks citizenship as autarchic substance and consequently posits a self-sufficient, inexhaustible citizen-warrior who transcends his conditions through the waging of battles and the staging of claims.[23] While I am not arguing against the value of waging battles or staging claims per se, I have shown in this book that resisting one's conditions and creating new ones is an often exhausting, incremental, and makeshift process whose temporalities are far from spectacular and that requires the composition and maintenance of intimate support structures that keep these efforts from collapsing on themselves.

Resistance and sustenance are two sides of the same coin, and both are fundamentally collective endeavors consisting of rituals and routines as much as improvisation—indeed, depending on routine improvisations—to create more consistent architectures of solidarity and *obstinacy*. Black queer collectivities are obstinate in their ongoing improper imposition: their blatant reparative refusal to cave in or to fade away and withdraw from the life of the city. This is their sense of citizenship, their con-*sensual* and sexual civic intimacies that form "the affirmative force of ruthless negation, the out and rooted critical lyricism of screams, prayers, curses, gestures, steps (to and away)" (Moten 2003: 255). The affirmative force of these gestures, these screams and prayers that pervade the UFCB and the Ball scene, as well as the play scene, gives Black queers the courage and energy to negate—or, at least, to negotiate—what consistently attempts to negate them, conjuring a push to become more "diligent," as Monica would have it. Antonio Negri's question is pertinent here: how are we to "comprehend the nature and position of the negative in a way that leaves it open, without resolution but without rendering it merely formal—without throwing us onto the mystical, and so opportunism, or back into the arms of the dialectic?" (Negri, in Mandarini 2009: 74). I believe that Monica and other Black queer Baltimoreans offer one possible practical, if not pragmatic, answer: by diligently, obstinately, and incessantly working through negativity and thereby refusing to equate survival with the void of social death; by consistently insisting on "mak[ing] a way out of no way" and "tak[ing] the tragedy and mak[ing] the magic."[24] I believe that this is perhaps the only way negativity can be said to have political value—when it is not rendered "merely formal" through its identification with either a mystical abyss or a transhistorical dialectic but is affirmed in concrete daily practices "without resolution."[25] These daily practices are the very stuff of citizenship as they "reinvent, from the scene of survival, new idioms of the political, and of belonging itself, which requires debating what the baselines of survival should be in the near future, which is, now, the future we are making" (Berlant 2011a: 262).

Finally, the question of what is accomplished by using the language of citizenship to describe Black queer architectures of the good life can and should also be answered on the level of methodology and its ethics. In essence, this is a reparative move, even though I am well aware that my work ultimately does very little to actually improve the lives of the people featured in this book. They also did not ask for their lives to be scrutinized, let alone in the language of citizenship. As mentioned in Chapter 1, the category of citizenship did not make much sense to many of my interlocutors, and its juxtaposition with the notion of intimacy only caused additional confusion. Still, as I was trying to make sense of their routines, rituals, reflections, and intimate world-making practices, I came to understand them as alternative civic formations. While my interlocutors did not describe their activities in the language of citizenship, they *did* readily acknowledge them as crucial to the survival and flourishing of their communities, and I therefore wanted to value them accordingly. In other words, I have intended to do justice to the life-affirming practices I encountered in Baltimore. But what does it mean to "do justice" to such practices? Does it require taking the accounts of my interlocutors at face value and thus giving up on the notion of citizenship because they had? Or is it more "just," in contrast, to augment their accounts with my own conceptual frameworks (cf. Fassin 2014)? And how relevant is the notion of "doing justice" to those I have studied, given that the resulting work can do very little, if anything, to support the survival—let alone the flourishing—of

Black queer collectivities? The only thing I could do is convey their stories and world-making practices in a way that highlights how these collectivities persistently turn nothing into something that is immensely valuable but also too often glossed over in critical accounts of anti-Black and antiqueer violence.

Still, I also wanted my study to have some kind of value for those it studied and to have it contribute to their own studies.[26] This objective formed the reparative impulse that energized my project, which, like every reparative project, was marked by failure. In a certain way, this failure was built into the project to the extent that its funding scheme restricted the time I could devote to fieldwork; Baltimore demanded more sustained scrutiny than I could afford. But I also failed on various occasions during my research and, despite my many inspiring conversations and experiences with participants who allowed me to share my study and to partake in theirs, I feel like I eventually came up short. I could have done more to communicate my findings to the communities I studied (with). I should have done a better job of translating my understanding of their civic intimacies into a public format that would have been able to manifest, celebrate, and question their enduring forms of life, opening up my ideas to a process of collective reflection and debate. Why did I procrastinate, repeatedly telling myself that I would materialize my good intentions in a few weeks, after this paper or that interview was completed? If only I had pushed myself more to actually plan that event, invite community members, pick a date and location. Looking back, I have plenty of regrets. These regrets have waxed and waned as I have lost touch with most of my friends and acquaintances in Baltimore since moving back to Amsterdam in September 2012, where my new position has provided me with a steady stream of teaching and research obligations. In the face of time constraints, geographical distance, and an ever thinning social thread connecting me to my "field," I have had to come to terms with the fact that my reparative project has not been realized in the way that I had imagined it, which continues to evoke disappointment and unease. Nevertheless, I also retain a modest degree of optimism—or, perhaps, it is stubbornness—because I still believe in the basic tenets and arguments of this project. As Jafari Allen (2012: 221) writes, "Scholarly work does not create everyday resistance within and survival by the most multiply vulnerable among us, but it can give light to it—helping expand recognition of those sites as legitimate political expression." I can only hope that this book has provided such light.

This brings me back, one last time, to the antirelational ontological approaches to Black and queer negativity I have investigated in this chapter. I argue that it matters greatly whether the political imaginaries invoked in these approaches, and in the debates that have ensued around them, are able to account for actual world-making *and ontology-building* practices that persist despite the violence and attrition informing so many Black queer realities. Rather than positing an alternative ontology, my ethnographic project has aimed to show how people are intimately implicated in the constitution of their realities, enacting and studying their being/becoming in all its fleshy, messy concreteness. Indeed, as I argued above, a truly *political* ontology can be nothing other than the outcome of this collective enactment and study, and here the political contribution of ethnography is to make such world-making and lifegiving activity sensible to a public through the work of mediation, by navigating or "passing through" the field's unstable boundaries between inside and outside. As Martin Holbraad, Morten Axel Pedersen, and Eduardo Viveiros de Castro (2014) have argued, "The politics of ontologically inclined anthropological analysis is not merely logically contingent on, but internally constituted by and morally imbricated with, the political dynamics in which the people anthropologists study are embroiled, including the political stances those people might themselves take, not least on the question of what politics itself 'could be.'" The reparative value of ethnography, then, is to affirm—to nourish and show the worth of—the often slight, tentative ways people give shape to the political as the potential for things to be otherwise. Here, the otherwise is the "could be" that persists despite the recurrent proliferation of impossibilities and interdictions that have absorbed so much critical academic energy that it has become difficult to imagine any ontological determination—any form of tenacity or force—that is not systemic, structural, metaphysical, or lethal.

This obviously is not to say that my research participants could determine their being or becoming, or that their study of what conditions their existence was successful or "accurate." But it does counter the ontological pessimism of current Black and queer critical approaches to the extent that it has elucidated how Black queer life is not fully determined by the death-driven interiority of a queer psyche nor by anti-Black violence perpetuated in the afterlife of slavery. Ultimately, this study has much more affinity with the reparative projects of love and obstinate imposition undertaken by Deon, Shawn, and Monica than the critical endeavors of Edelman or Wilderson, because it demonstrates that Black queerness is not reducible to nothingness or to structural conditions of impossibility but is also something—something at stake; a project to be projected, built, nourished, supported, sheltered, celebrated, and rethought. This difficult work needs to be taken into account so it can be rightfully valued, and I have opted to take on this challenge by adopting, while also thoroughly revising, the language of citizenship. As I argued before, this is a political move because it highlights that citizenship is not given, as a clearly delineated institution with a concomitant set of rights and obligations, but is *taken* as something that will have to be composed and recomposed indefinitely. Civic intimacies have nothing to do with civil society or a seat at its table. Their grassroots ontology is deeply improper, fugitive, and experimental, while their practical aim is to create support structures at the peripheries of our immunitary citizenship regime.

Notes

Chapter 1

1. In her chapter on intimate citizenship in the *Handbook of Citizenship Studies,* which represents a commonly held position in the field (cf. Plummer 2003), Ruth Lister (2002: 199) writes:

> Intimate citizenship is not to be confused with intimacy itself: it concerns public talk and action about the intimate. This supports my argument that "intimate citizenship only constitutes a sphere of citizenship *practice* when its claims are made in the public sphere" (Lister 1997: 128). In other words, "the intimate" represents a proper object of citizenship struggles, but it is not the site of these struggles, which is not to deny the potential political nature of conflict within the intimate sphere.

By arguing for a distinction between "intimacy itself" and the intimate as "a proper object of citizenship struggles," Lister effectively reinstates the much contested liberal dichotomy between the private and the public, where the denuded life of intimacy in itself is withdrawn from the political life of civic deliberation *about* intimacy. Apparently "the intimate sphere," which seems to be mute and has to be spoken for in public, can by itself have political potential only if it is in some way disrupted by conflict and does not have the capacity to be conducive to citizenship in a more affirmative sense. And how could it when citizenship is limited to "public talk and action"? Meanwhile, by implicitly equating the intimate with the private, she relinquishes the possibility of (semi-)public intimacies and the political forces they might engender.

2. This psychoanalytic strand of queer theory, most prominently advanced by Leo Bersani (1995, 2009) and Lee Edelman (2004), has inaugurated a conceptual perspective on queer psychic life as affectively negative, dissociative, and essentially self-destructive. I engage with Edelman's work in Chapter 6.

3. As Ellis Hanson (2011: 106), with tongue in cheek, has noted: "Most queer theory about affect is really about trauma. For example, how many feelings need to be bypassed in the archive in order for Ann Cvetkovich's book *An Archive of Feelings* to arrive at its subtitle *Trauma, Sexuality, and Lesbian Public Cultures?* Or a more recent example, how many feelings have to be tossed overboard for Heather Love's book *Feeling Backward* to arrive at its subtitle *Loss and the Politics of Queer History?* Note to self: if it's not broken, don't write about it."

4. I elaborate on the notion of immunization in Esposito's work in Chapters 3 and 6.

5. This schism has been addressed by scholars in the fields of critical race studies and queer of color critique, who have examined how the acquired privileges and immunities of some queer citizen-subjects in the United States are structurally predicated on the subordination and abandonment of other queer lives (see, e.g., Puar 2007; Reddy 2011). In his particular contribution to this literature, David Eng (2010: xi) theorizes the concept of "queer liberalism" in an effort to think (queer) family and kinship beyond the purview of liberal idea(l)s concerning freedom and intimacy. According to Eng, much recent LGBT activism in the United States is founded on the color-blind belief that the project of racial justice and equality was completed by the Civil Rights Movement of the 1950s and 1960s, which has paved the way for gays and lesbians to finally achieve full and universal citizenship in "a contemporary post-racial new world order of freedom." Such an assumption not only disconnects race from sexuality in severely problematic ways, ignoring how struggles for sexual freedom and justice continue to be deeply permeated and complicated by race, gender, class, and nationality; it also enables the emergence of a political project whose stakes are based on narrowly defined aspirations of market-regulated freedom, privacy, and equality before the law while denying the long history of racialized oppression that forms its condition of possibility. For Eng, such color-blind obfuscation of white queer privilege is predicated on queer liberalism's "racialization of intimacy," which is accomplished through "efforts to isolate and manage the private as a distinct and rarified zone outside of capitalist relations and racial exploitation, as well as dissociated from its domestic and global genealogies" (ibid.: 10). This is to say that liberal norms concerning familial privacy are rooted in the legacy of racial slavery and anti-Black violence that has structurally suppressed alternative configurations of intimacy and kinship over the past four centuries, both globally and domestically. However, this is not what Eng says—at least, not explicitly. At the very moment he warns against the disappearance of race and writes people of color into queer liberalism's color-blind narrative of homosexuals' steady ascent to universal emancipation, he also obscures the distinct nature of Black suffering that has made this narrative possible. Thus, Eng's analysis is afflicted by a condition Jared Sexton has termed "people-of-color-blindness": "a form of colorblindness inherent to the concept of 'people of color' to the precise extent that it misunderstands the specificity of antiblackness and presumes or insists upon the monolithic character of victimization

under white supremacy—thinking (the afterlife of) slavery as a form of exploitation or colonization or a species of racial oppression among others" (Sexton 2010: 48). According to Sexton, this conceptual misunderstanding can produce only deficient accounts of modern power, since it misses how Black existence, as opposed to other, nonwhite modes of being, cannot be integrated into civil society's subject categories, given that it has historically been subjected to a *"singular commodification"* whose gratuitous violence continues to mark and maim Black bodies (ibid.: 38; cf. Woods 2013).

6. This study received IRB approval from Johns Hopkins University prior to its execution (Protocol #2010106). All personal names that appear in this book are pseudonyms, except when research participants either preferred that I use their real names or were so publicly visible and prominent—within their communities and beyond— that pseudonyms were not feasible. In cases in which tension arose between the aims of providing ethnographically rich descriptions and ensuring the confidentiality of the information gathered, I requested participants' informed consent to use their real first names. To obtain informed consent, I invited these participants to read the manuscript chapter(s) in which they were featured so they knew how they would be portrayed and the kinds of personal and professional information would be made public. In all four cases, consent was granted on the condition that I made a few minor corrections and adjustments (which I implemented).

7. As the chief executive and founder of the African American Advocacy, Support-Services and Survival Institutes (also known as the AmASSI Health and Cultural Centers), Cleo has developed his Critical Thinking and Cultural Affirmation (CTCA) methodology, which is both rooted in and focused on the daily experiences of Black homosexual and bisexual men. The CTCA methodology "builds the competence of participants to think critically, reason and discern race-based self-concept dilemmas, self-defeating mythologies, un-constructive peer pressures and negative societal influences, to value their community, themselves and family, and to commit themselves to constructive and risk-reducing behavior as a way of life and being" (Manago 1996). As a community-centric and evidence-based approach, CTCA has been positively evaluated by the Centers for Disease Control and Prevention (CDC), which deemed it a "successful intervention" whose "cultural and historical congruence" helps to reduce the risk of HIV in homosexual and bisexual Black men (Williams et al. 2009). As I show in Chapter 3, however, interventions such as CTCA have come to play an increasingly marginal role in the CDC's biomedicalized approach to HIV prevention.

8. For further details on IDEHA and its position within Baltimore's HIV-prevention system, see Chapter 3.

9. Despite their Eurocentric blind spots (Weheliye 2014; see also my discussion in Chapter 3), Michel Foucault's notions of modern "state racism" and race war usefully—if implicitly—suggests the extent to which white supremacy has operated historically through a bellicose, zero-sum imaginary: "The fact that the [Black] other dies does not mean simply that I live in the sense that his death guarantees my safety; the death of the bad [Black] race, of the inferior race (or the degenerate, or the abnormal) is something that will make life in general healthier: healthier and purer" (Foucault 2003: 255). Here Foucault, without mentioning him explicitly, is clearly taking Carl Schmitt's political thought to its logical extreme by showing how its antagonistic ratio-

nale facilitated and, indeed, promoted the kind of state racism that would be developed and intensified by the National Socialist Party, which Schmitt publicly endorsed and served during its reign. In other words, he shows us how Schmitt's politics evolved—or, rather, devolved—into biopolitics and how his notion of war developed into race war. Here's how Foucault invokes Schmitt's legacy, by using his precise terminology: "This is not, then, a military, warlike, or political relationship, but a biological relationship. And the reason this mechanism can come into play is that the enemies who have to be done away with are not adversaries in the political sense of the term; they are threats, either external or internal, to the population and for the population. In the biopower system, in other words, killing or the imperative to kill is acceptable only if it results not in a victory over political adversaries [as Schmitt would have it], but in the elimination of the biological threat to and the improvement of the species or race" (ibid.: 255–256).

10. I use the slash here to denote both how anti-Black violence is always already antiqueer violence and how antiqueer violence is exacerbated and intensified by anti-Blackness. I return to this relationship in Chapter 6.

11. The term "social death" is central to the Afro-pessimist argument I take up in Chapter 6. It is adopted from Orlando Patterson's highly influential comparative study *Slavery and Social Death*, in which he provides a transhistorical definition of slavery as "the permanent, violent domination of natally alienated and generally dishonored persons" (Patterson 1982: 13). As Patterson insists, natal alienation produces social death: "Alienated from all 'rights' or claims of birth, [the slave] ceased to belong in his own right to any legitimate social order. All slaves experienced, at the very least, a secular excommunication"—an event that also isolated them from the social heritage of their ancestors (ibid.: 5). In his insightful analysis, Vincent Brown (2009: 1233) has pointed out the limitations of this category with respect to its genesis: "It is often forgotten that the concept of social death is a distillation from Patterson's breathtaking survey—a theoretical abstraction that is meant not to describe the lived experiences of the enslaved so much as to reduce them to a least common denominator that could reveal the essence of slavery in an ideal-type slave." This tension, or discrepancy, between "theoretical abstraction" and "lived experiences" runs through my project and is addressed most explicitly in Chapter 6.

12. In their willingness to theorize this "break," which is at once epistemic and affective, each is also indebted to Fred Moten's (2003) lyrical ruminations on the phonohistorical break constitutive of the Black radical tradition and of Blackness as a queer and recalcitrant "case" navigating the space between subordination's violent reality and the lines of flight that emerge from the vicissitudes of lived experience. I engage with Moten's work in Chapter 6.

13. I return to Crawley's work in Chapter 4, where I narrate my encounter with Black queer Pentecostalism in Baltimore.

14. While Sharpe (2016: 22) asserts that "if we are lucky, we live in the knowledge that the wake has positioned us as no-citizen," Crawley (2017: 239) advocates a Black-pentecostal glossolalia that is "not interested in the production of citizenship and statehood." In other words, both authors conceive of citizenship as a zero-sum relationship between what is inside and outside the civic realm; accordingly, they see no value in using it as an analytical lens with which to study Black/queer possibility.

15. As Jafari Allen (2011: 14) notes, "Ethnography complicates the elegant and useful contending formulations of Black agency and resistance . . . , which seem to be at odds with one another but are revealed on the ground—even complexly, messily, inelegantly—to be facets of a process of (or at least potentiality for) 'radical becoming.' Small practices of self-making through erotic subjectivity . . . are political, in the sense that these actions challenge the allocation of social and material capital, and look toward improving the individual's felt and lived experience."

16. As "a form of relationality that one finds oneself drawn to and finds oneself nurturing, or caring for in the midst of critical reflexivity" (Povinelli 2011a: 33), the force of such a mode of obligation is not so much based on an individual "decision" to act or care for others as cultivated in the proximity of particular scenes that demand one's attention, which over time can develop into enduring affiliations.

17. Baltimore also had its own ACT UP chapter, founded by John Stuban in 1990 and disbanded not long after Stuban's death in 1994 (Selby 1994). Baltimore historically has been at the center of the HIV/AIDS crisis, not only because of the many AIDS deaths in the city, but also because Johns Hopkins University and the National Institutes of Health (NIH), two of the country's most renowned medical research institutions and key actors during the early development of the epidemic, are located in or near the city. Both institutions were engaged in early clinical trials of potential drug treatments and, when bigotry and bureaucracy blocked or delayed the desperately needed results, provoked the ire of ACT UP and other AIDS activists around the United States. For more on the evolution of HIV/AIDS prevention work in Baltimore, see Chapters 2–3.

18. My smartphone often mediated such challenges, making them intelligible in a specific way by assembling and juxtaposing their respective articulations and frames of reference in one device. As I have written elsewhere, it shaped how I oriented myself in the field I was producing as I traversed the social and geographical margins of the city and its LGBT landscape, collecting materials in different digital formats, all recorded, stored, and organized by a technology that informed the uncertain and flexible parameters of my fieldwork (Van Doorn 2013b). To be sure, Baltimore was not my "field," although it certainly formed some of the conditions of possibility that enabled something like a "field" to emerge. Here I follow the argument in Isin (2002: 49) that a city is a "difference machine" to the extent that it cannot be contained within the parameters of physical urban limits and instead functions as an assemblage of sites that cluster and intensify, but also modulate and resist, geo- and biopolitical power relations. During my research, I processed a number of these sites, with varying degrees of success, by repeatedly navigating their socio-material and affective infrastructures and thereby assembling, or composing, what slowly congealed into a recognizable yet indeterminate field I could work with.

19. I also had to pass up several events simply because they took place outside the city and I could not find a ride or because they happened late at night in an area with limited public transit. I experienced similar practical setbacks during my fieldwork in the HIV-prevention community—most notably, when the Baltimore City Health Department rejected my repeated requests to accompany peer prevention specialists on their outreach work in clubs such as the Paradox, where a lot of Black queer young

adults gather. In this case, my request for access was declined not because I was a male researcher but simply because it was feared that my presence *as a researcher* would disturb the atmosphere of trust and safety during these nights. At least this was the official explanation I received. I also suspect that some individuals at the Health Department didn't want me to ask patrons potentially difficult or controversial questions about the goals and effectiveness of this form of outreach and its associated campaigns (see Chapter 3).

20. Fassin (2014: 47) continues: "Taking the liberty to explore beyond what the subjects of their research know and tell, they [anthropologists] bring together biographies and history, storytelling and political economy, the text of the narratives they collect and the context in which they are inserted, the empirical facts they observe and the theoretical frames with which they interpret them." I return to my decision to reclaim and reconfigure the language of citizenship to describe Black queer world making at the end of Chapter 6.

Chapter 2

1. Some of these strange juxtapositions scattered through Baltimore's urban landscape include the city's oldest gay leather bar being located next to a store selling halal meat; a block of strip joints and sex shops well known for its prostitution, panhandling, and drug crime that also features Baltimore's Police Headquarters and Central Police District House; the Johns Hopkins hospital and medical campus built in the middle of a poverty-stricken and underserved area in East Baltimore; the experimental music venue Red Room operating across the street from the Northside bar, known for rough clientele and early morning drinking; and the much hyped Station North Arts District incorporating a number of blocks on North Avenue, which has long been an area marked by disinvestment and dilapidation. I further discuss a number of these examples below. While some of them are delightful and may give one the impression that Baltimore is indeed the quirky and permissive melting pot it promotes itself to be, they are overshadowed by the more pernicious incongruities that display the city's historical organization of race and capital.

2. This interview was part of my research to understand how the city was responding to the rapid increase in HIV infections among Black queer youth. The next chapter discusses my findings and analyzes how race, sexuality, and conceptions of life and health converge in Baltimore's fight against this epidemic.

3. Johns Hopkins received its nickname "the plantation" among African Americans sometime after its move in 1915 from its Mount Vernon location to the old Homewood estate a couple of miles north, in the Charles Village neighborhood and then known as Peabody Heights. Although Homewood was not a full-fledged plantation like those found in the South, about twenty slaves were kept on the old estate grounds, and their duties and hardships closely resembled those of southern plantation life (Arthur and Kelly 2004: 97; see also "From Fells Point to Homewood Farm: Perspectives on Slavery in Baltimore," symposium presented by Homewood Museum of Johns Hopkins University, https://www.youtube.com/watch?v=dobQZ6wjMOQ.

4. This has been accomplished mainly through a public financing method known as tax increment financing (TIF). Rachel Weber (2002: 534) explains this method this way: "TIF creates a special taxing jurisdiction around an area targeted for redevelopment and earmarks future property tax revenues to pay for the up-front costs of redevelopment. The area in question must meet the definition of 'blight' found in the state enabling legislation. However, the existence of blight is most frequently demonstrated by the presence of obsolete structures and land uses and by property values that have not grown as quickly as some benchmark (usually the average growth rate of the municipality as a whole)." This growth is crucial because "TIF depends, not on absolute levels of property taxes, but on the 'increment' or difference between property taxes in the year of designation and the subsequent years. . . . In other words, surplus value only accrues to the local state and, by extension, the market when assets are repriced upwards."

5. This figure is from 2010. In that year, 49 percent of all revenues came from patient care and clinical services, while grants and contracts accounted for 31 percent, tuition and fees accounted for 2 percent, investment income accounted for 2 percent, and contributions and gifts accounted for about 1 percent (Appleseed 2011).

6. To be sure, this was the second wave of suburbanization to hit Baltimore after an initial wave was set in motion near the end of the nineteenth century, instigated first by horse-drawn trolleys and then by the introduction of an elaborate network of streetcars that stretched into the newly developing suburbs just beyond the edges of the city (see Pietila 2010: 9).

7. I take the phrase "arsenal of exclusion" from *The Arsenal of Exclusion/Inclusion*, a blog and book project by the architecture and urban design firm Interboro Partners (see http://arsenalofexclusion.blogspot.com). It details the "101 weapons that architects, planners, policy makers, developers, real estate brokers, community activists, and individuals use to open and close the city." For other commentary on MLK Boulevard, see Harvey 2001; Silk 2010.

8. Both Schindler (2015) and the popular architecture and design-centered radio show 99 Percent Invisible have attended to this form of architectural exclusion (see http://99percentinvisible.org/episode/episode-51-the-arsenal-of-exclusion). It may be redundant to add that no public transit line runs from Greenmount Avenue into Guilford—or vice versa.

9. As Phillips (1997: 118) writes, "Once established, Black churches quickly became the social, political, economic, educational, and even cultural centers of the Baltimore Black community. Black Baltimoreans' earliest organized efforts at economic self-help, education, and political organization revolved around Black churches." (For a detailed account of the history of African American religious organizing and the quest for Black spiritual autonomy in Baltimore, see ibid: chap. 5.)

10. Writing about Baltimore in the early 1990s, McDougall (1993: 104) notes: "Redlining today had become more subtle and sophisticated, part of the corporate and institutional culture. Loans for improvement, renovation, or repairs are barred, inner-city homes under-appraised, and exorbitant down-payments demanded to discourage borrowers." As I discuss below, during the 1990s and 2000s this denial of credit to

Black residents was augmented by a different trend known as "reverse redlining," or the practice of predatory lending that targets Black customers to overcharge them for financial services otherwise provided at a lower rate to non-Black customers.

11. Although the research by McRoberts and Hyra was conducted in other U.S. cities—Boston, Chicago, and New York—which in many ways are very different from Baltimore, their findings nonetheless resonate with Baltimore's urban development trajectory over the past two decades (see Philipsen 2015).

12. Wyly (2010: 512, 523) continues: "Over time, loan officers and brokers had fewer incentives to find and serve well-qualified, low-risk borrowers with good loan products. New incentives made it more lucrative to pursue consumers who could be tricked into abusive, risky mortgages packed with usurious interest charges, confusing and hidden fees, and various other provisions designed to ensure maximum risk-adjusted yield for investors. . . . In this new regime, home 'owners' still had to pay the rent collector. Wall Street finance capital became the new slum landlord."

13. It should be noted here that both Harold McDougall (1993) and Patricia Fernández-Kelly (2015), in their otherwise very different book-length studies of West Baltimore's Black communities, are more sanguine about the proliferation of entrepreneurialism and grassroots economic initiatives in impoverished neighborhoods. Although they each argue that such economic development can be successful only when accompanied by sustained public investments and policies that enable a redistribution of wealth, Fernández-Kelly especially seems unwilling or unable to think of modes of Black collective flourishing that are not predicated on liberal-democratic market principles. This is a critical blind spot, given that she thereby neglects how capitalist markets are historically imbricated with anti-Black regimes of slavery and colonial exploitation and how they continue to depend on the subordination and regulated superfluity of Black life.

14. Quoted in Berger 2007: 36. In an insightful and detailed study, Jane Berger contends that the macroeconomic policies of the Nixon, Carter, and Reagan administrations fueled Baltimore's decline and took a particularly devastating toll on African American women who were employed by the city but lost their jobs due to federal-level spending cuts on antipoverty measures, especially in the 1980s. Alongside the gendered and racialized dimensions of these policy outcomes, the study highlights how the devastation experienced by Baltimore's poor Black populations were not just the result of deindustrialization and economic depression but also followed from political decisions taken at the highest level of national government—"decisions not typically associated with urban policymaking" (ibid.: 44).

15. Martin O'Malley coined the "Greatest City in America" slogan in 2000, the first of three slogans he added to an extensive list of nicknames and catchphrases intended to promote Baltimore to both residents and visitors (Wenger 2015).

16. Maryland incarcerated just over 22,000 people in 2010, of whom 7,795 were from the City of Baltimore. Most were Black men from West Baltimore neighborhoods such as Sandtown-Winchester, where Freddie Gray grew up, and neighborhoods in the east located next to the Johns Hopkins Medical Campus, such as Middle East and Dunbar Broadway (Justice Policy Institute and Prison Policy Initiative 2015; V. Smith 2015). In his historical study of the various architectures of confinement that shape Black Chicago, Rashad Shabazz (2015) brings to light the racializing and gendering

forces of carceral power, which "spatialize Blackness" by means of urban planning, policing, and surveillance. (On Blackness and surveillance, see Browne 2015.) As Shabazz argues, such practices contain, mold, and in many cases destroy the lives of African American urban communities, particularly—or most directly—through the mass incarceration of Black men. Linking mass incarceration to the HIV/AIDS epidemic that disproportionately affects Black Chicagoans, Shabazz notes how the former creates an enforced and uneven geography of risk: "Prisons did not create HIV/AIDS; instead, they exacerbated the epidemic by providing a safe space for the disease to incubate, to remain untreated, and in some cases to spread among the prison population. Indeed, carceral power was the glue that held the geography of risk together" (Shabazz 2015: 99). While not specifically focusing on the role of incarceration in Baltimore's HIV/AIDS epidemic, the next chapter is likewise concerned with the racializing forces of immunization, capture, and containment that have shaped the geography of the disease, as well as the city's institutional response to it. Like Shabazz, I situate the carceral power that drives these forces within slavery's history and afterlife, which have forged "an entirely new ontology of space" (ibid.: 6)

17. As Mbembe (2004: 380–381) writes, "In the calculus of superfluity . . . racism's function was to institute a contradictory relationship between the instrumentality of Black life in the market sphere, on the one hand, and the constant depreciation of its value and its quality by the forces of commercialism and bigotry, on the other. Here, superfluity was akin to the dissipation of value and its reorganization in the realm of the biopolitical." Mbembe's account suggests how the entanglement of necropolitics and biopolitics is mediated by the market as a technology whose "calculus of superfluity" is rooted in the capture, commodification, and making Black life fungible as raw material in the economics of chattel slavery—constituting the disavowed imperial *nomos* of neoliberal capitalism. I return to this *nomos* in Chapter 3. On necropolitics, see Mbembe 2003.

18. For an early account of the link between a newfound notion of gay sexual citizenship and consumption, see Evans 1993.

19. It took until 2013 for the City of Baltimore's Police Department to form an LGBT advisory council, after the severe beating of a gay man in East Baltimore. The council featured a personal aide to Mayor Rawlings-Blake, who also functioned as one of the first LGBT liaisons to the Mayor's Office.

20. I learned about this in conversations with local gay residents who had lived in Mount Vernon since the 1980s and 1990s. The MVBA's website boasts how it "prevented the State from locating a prison facility in the middle of a residential block" and "formed a coalition with downtown community and homelessness advocacy groups to oppose plans by downtown businesses to shift the homeless population into the surrounding neighborhoods, including Mount Vernon" (see http://www.mvba.org/page-1734472).

21. This rebranding has recently yielded modest results, as a study by the San Francisco–based financial advice website NerdWallet named Baltimore the fifth most LGBT-friendly city in the United States, unsurprisingly naming Mount Vernon and Hampden as its most LGBT-friendly neighborhoods (C. Miller 2015). Hampden mainly scores points with its annual Honfest, a purported celebration of white, working-

class femininity and southern charm embodied by beehive-sporting "Hons" whose mannerisms have been spectacularized and turned into a kitsch object of drag adulation among gay men.

22. Many of these survival sex workers recurrently face homelessness and physical violence, as do Black transgender women in general. In the summer of 2014, two Black transgender women, both of them with a history of prostitution, were found murdered within the span of six weeks, totaling four murders in as many years (Pilkington 2014). Yet it should be noted that each of these murders formed the horrific end to a life marked by the constant abrasion of less spectacular forms of violence, from having nothing to eat to being harassed by the police, that mostly go unreported.

23. The ongoing "It Gets Better" project was institutionalized as an Internet-based 501(c)3 nonprofit by the gay author and activist Dan Savage and his husband, Terry Miller, in September 2010 to launch a YouTube-centric media campaign in which gay adults—frequently celebrities—promote the affirmative and comforting message that the future will be a less menacing place for LGBT teens. Critics have accused the project of "highlighting an exceptional class of aspirational gay citizens at the expense of others" (Puar 2010), pointing to the exclusion of queer of color narratives whose negativity may impede on the upbeat white, middle-class message that emphasizes optimism and eventual inclusion. See also Puar 2012 and, for a different perspective, Goltz 2013. The following chapter details how the Baltimore City Health Department opted for a strategy of containment and responsibilization in its fight against the HIV/AIDS epidemic among Black queer youth.

24. With reference to Grindr hookups and cruising, I should add that Baltimore still harbors a great variety of cruising spots. Although my research didn't focus on this aspect of gay life, I learned that there are several popular cruising websites where men share, rate, and review spots in and around Baltimore. Some of the favorite destinations are Druid Hill Park and Mondawmin Mall, two predominantly Black spaces, but also the JCPenney in Owings Mills and the second-floor bathroom of Gillman Hall, the main building on Johns Hopkins's Homewood Campus (see, e.g., http://www.cruisinggays.com/baltimore/c/areas). These spaces form a circuit of illicit shadow geographies that are simultaneously navigated and disavowed by Baltimore's respectable gay establishment.

25. The abbreviated historical account that follows is necessarily partial and incomplete, based on some archival research but mostly on interviews with community members, who would occasionally provide me with further documentation. I ultimately focus on Baltimore's Black queer history here, but for a more comprehensive and abundantly illustrated history of the community as a whole, see Parker Kelley 2015.

26. Despite the predominantly white, middle-class identity of this community, it did develop strong ties to the People's Free Community Health Clinic on Greenmount Avenue, which was the joint project of a left-wing group of white doctors and nurses affiliated with Johns Hopkins and the local chapter of the Black Panther Party. Laurel A. Clark (2007: 6) offers the following account:

> The clinic hosted feminist events such as a weekly women's night and, between 1969 and 1980, shared its space with women's liberation rap groups,

the Lesbian Community Center, and the journal [*Women: A Journal of Liberation*]. During the 1970s, the area surrounding the clinic also housed a variety of communes, nonprofit offices, the Women's Growth Center, a bookstore for women and children, a coffee house, and a food cooperative. These and other institutions and organizations lasted anywhere from several months to many years. Lesbians in search of support and community joined other feminists and New Left progressives who were living and working in Waverly and Charles Village.

As Judson L. Jeffries (2010) notes, the Black Panther Party in Baltimore was under heavy surveillance at the time and frequently found itself the target of police harassment and repression, which contributed to its eventual demise in 1972. This carefully orchestrated federal and local crackdown on the Black Panthers destabilized or halted the various community-based programs and projects initiated by the party and thereby indirectly sabotaged the efforts of affiliated radical collectives such as the socialist feminist lesbians in Waverly and Charles Village, effectively stifling a burgeoning atmosphere of grassroots coalitional activism focused on social justice and anticapitalist forms of life. Meanwhile, the political activities of the BGA—and later, the GCCB—in Mount Vernon were more concerned with establishing a sense of sexual community and ensuring gay visibility and safety, which may have seemed less threatening to local and federal authorities at the time. This is thus another way the uneven distribution of racialized violence and protection formed a condition of possibility for Mount Vernon's ascent as the city's "gayborhood."

27. In hindsight, the split between the GLCCB and Chase-Brexton Health Services marked the beginning of a long history of problems and controversies that damaged the center and led to its increasing isolation, given that the clinic's independence entailed the loss of a major stream of public and private funding for the battle against HIV/AIDS in the 1990s. This lack of funding, which resulted in chronic understaffing and a dearth of public programming, converged with the previously discussed advent of a conservative national agenda based on rights-based inclusion, entrepreneurialism, and consumption, to the extent that the activities of GLCCB's leadership started to prioritize the promotion of gay cultural events and the solicitation of corporate sponsors for their annual Pride festivities at the expense of projects and programs that served the various needs of the community it was supposed to represent. Indeed, perhaps the primary source of antagonism over the past two decades has been the deep racial, class, and gender divide between the GLCCB, which has been governed mostly by white, middle-class gay men, and the community at large, which, like Baltimore itself, is majority-Black and composed of a great variety of gender and sexual identities/practices that in turn are inflected by class differences. The center's failure to accommodate such diversity—or, at least, to recognize the various needs and agendas of its many stakeholders—has resulted in the proliferation of various factions that represent the interests and cater to the needs of their particular segment of the community, all vying for the same scarce funding.

28. The final objective listed in the NCBG's brochure from the early 1980s was "to maintain and stress the beauty of Black culture and lesbian/gay culture, thereby projecting our motto: 'As Proud Of Our Gayness As We Are of our Blackness'" (see

http://ufdc.ufl.edu/AA00001470/00001/pdf). Cathy Cohen (1999: 98) has noted how the response of the NCBG and other organizations initiated by Black gay men during the early days of the AIDS epidemic "concentrated on educational activities and service provision. This is not surprising, since the predominant activities during this first stage were increasing recognition and acceptance of AIDS as a disease affecting Black communities and obtaining basic services for those in need."

29. Peay mentions two other causes for the decline of Black gay bars and clubs during the 1980s: poor management and owners who gave nothing back to the community.

30. BUGLE, which was co-founded by Louis, was engaged in several projects during the late 1980s, such as co-organizing the city's AIDS Walk, supporting HERO's Buddy Program, and helping to increase the enrollment of men of color in a large HIV/AIDS study conducted by Johns Hopkins.

31. With respect to the gradual disintegration of the NCBLG, Louis explained: "We never recovered from AIDS. . . . We lost the political activists because they died of AIDS. You know, I have whole address books of people I lost. It drained you emotionally and spiritually. It drained, especially among the men early on, everything." Writing about "the structural vulnerabilities that limited the preservation of a Black LGBT past in postwar decades," with a specific focus on Washington, DC, Kwame Holmes (2015: 67) concludes: "Tragically, then, as the HIV-AIDS epidemic robbed Black gay communities of invaluable intergenerational cultural memory, it produced a critical mass of politically and historically legible Black gay subjects in Washington, and around the country, for the first time." Despite its geographical contiguity to Washington, however, Baltimore did not see the same emergence of such a "critical mass." As I discuss here and in the next chapter, the city's fight against HIV/AIDS has predominantly been led and shaped by its medical "anchor institutions"—most notably, Johns Hopkins University—which has resulted in the biomedicalization and consequent depoliticization of the ongoing epidemic. In this context, Black queer Baltimoreans have had to struggle to achieve and maintain their legibility as political and historical subjects by resisting their recurrent instrumentalization in "evidence-based" prevention schemes.

32. Holmes makes a similar observation with respect to the situation in Washington, DC: "It is in response to the epidemic that DC's Black gay social clubs banded together to organize an education forum on HIV-AIDS in the Black community, even as they began to lose members at an alarming rate" (Holmes 2015: 67; cf. C. Cohen 1999: 98). As noted above, such an educational community forum had already been organized in Baltimore two years earlier, in 1984, enabled by the sponsorship of HERO.

33. In his case study of the early impact of HIV/AIDS on Black gay populations in Washington, DC, particularly the local community response to the emerging epidemic, Darius Bost (2015: 2) presents a similar finding regarding the importance of Black gay clubs: "The ClubHouse—DC's most famous Black gay and lesbian nightclub—became a key site of AIDS activism because of its prior visibility as the center of African American lesbian and gay nightlife and as a local venue for Black lesbian and gay activist efforts. . . . [T]he ClubHouse emerged as a local site where the devastating impact of the virus on Black same-sex-desiring men was both recognized and felt."

34. MOCAPP organized various events, such as safe sex workshops, community conversations on identity and self-love, a stage play, a tea dance, and the unveiling of the Men of Color AIDS Quilt.

Chapter 3

1. House families are not the only alternative kinship structures available to Black queer youth, who often have extensive "gay families" with many different cousins, uncles, and aunts, as well as "gay parents" who function as mentors outside of the House/Ball context. House families and gay families are thus parallel—and sometimes overlapping—kinship structures that replace or augment these youths' relationships with their biological families, producing a hybrid socio-familial environment in which the traditional connections among biology, filiation, and kinship are complicated and reinterpreted (see M. Bailey 2013: chap. 3).

2. For a discussion of these performance categories within the larger social framework of Ball culture, especially in relation to its gender system, see M. Bailey 2013: chaps. 2, 4.

3. Marlon Bailey (2013: 184) asks similar questions, which express his doubts about the intentions of a CDC-funded Black gay HIV/AIDS organization in Detroit, where he worked as a consultant. In the final section of this chapter I return to Bailey's argument about Ballroom culture's potential to generate more creative and empowering prevention initiatives.

4. During my fieldwork, case managers working at a primary health-care provider in Baltimore informed me about the excessive caseloads they had to deal with. One case manager lamented that once he reached 160 cases, he realized that he was no more than a "paper processor." He also indicated that this work pressure contributed to a process of triage, in which case managers are indirectly encouraged to spend most of their time helping clients who are eligible for insurance recertification while disregarding "those who are pretty much lost causes" (by which he meant the homeless and drug-addicted).

5. TLC+ is a program recommendation that resulted from a think tank convened in Washington, DC, in December 2009, where a multidisciplinary group of HIV/AIDS experts met to consider whether a Test and Treat strategy should be integrated into the NHAS (Project Inform 2010). The name Testing and Linkage to Care Plus explicitly does not use the term "treatment" to avoid the negative connotations that a Test and Treat program evokes within some communities. Yet as the authors of the document admit, this is largely a cosmetic measure to make the strategy more appealing to HIV-positive people, and treatment figures as a crucial element in HIV care and prevention.

6. I use quotation marks for the term "care" here, both to indicate its frequent vernacular use among service providers and outreach workers and to point to its inadequacies. While "care" sounds generous and assuring, it mainly denotes the clinical monitoring of a patient's viral load and T cell count, as well as referrals to other services, such as housing, which usually have extended waiting lists. As I argue, this clinical form of care, tightly associated with disciplinary surveillance, stands in stark contrast to the forms of care that the Ballroom community makes available.

7. For an application that lets users navigate a map of Baltimore, which contains information about the number of HIV infections in different areas of the city, see the website at http://ideha.dhmh.maryland.gov/apps/HIV.

8. The 2005 Behavioral Surveillance Research (BESURE) study—conducted as a joint effort of Maryland's Department of Health and Mental Hygiene and the Johns Hopkins Bloomberg School of Public Health—found that 58 percent of HIV-positive MSM were unaware of their status. The percentage was higher among young men (89 percent for those age eighteen to twenty-four) and Black men (64 percent). Three years later, the 2008 wave of the study showed that the proportion of unrecognized HIV infection had risen to 74 percent among all HIV-positive participants and 77 percent among infected Black men. Interestingly, this sharp increase was largely driven by white men in the study, whose proportion of unrecognized infection rose by 32 percent, compared with the smaller increase of 13 percent among Black men. This difference, however, did not evoke any response. According to the authors of the study, the results confirm "the disproportionate HIV burden borne by Black and other minority MSMs [sic] in Baltimore" and "expand on prior reports of pronounced racial disparity in HIV among young Baltimore MSMs [sic]" (German et al. 2011: 84). They conclude with a warning that testing activities are not adequately reaching young MSM of color in Baltimore, which limits this group's access to treatment.

9. On sexual citizenship within the specific context of HIV prevention, see M. Brown 2006; Davis 2008. On sexual citizenship more generally, see Bell and Binnie 2000; Cossman 2007; Weeks 1998.

10. Esposito identifies Thomas Hobbes's political philosophy as inaugurating this preoccupation with the negative preservation of life, to the extent that his conception of the Leviathan posited a prototypically modern "state against nature," an apparatus that defends its citizen-subjects against bodily harm while simultaneously subjecting them to the violent threat of sovereign power. In the Hobbesian immunitary state, rooted in fear and (in)security, modern citizenship is grounded in a vertical contractual relationship of "protection-obedience" that "coincides with the breaking of every communitarian bond, with the squelching of every social relation" (Esposito 2010a: 14).

11. Esposito derives his argument about the fundamental ambivalence of immunization from his etymological tracing of two terms that function as pivotal interpretative keys in his work: *communitas* and *immunitas*. Both terms have their root in the Latin word *munus*, which denotes at once a gift and an obligation. *Communitas*, according to Esposito (2010a: 6), should be understood as an expropriating configuration in which "the totality of persons [are] united not by a 'property' but precisely by an obligation or a debt"—a debt embedded in the *cum* of *communitas*. In contrast, *immunitas* is the condition that defends the individual from this expropriating nature of the *cum*, by way of a dispensation from the obligation of the *munus*, insulating her or him against the risks that come with the gift and the relations of indebtedness it generates. I return to these terms in Chapter 6.

12. The Testing Makes Us Stronger campaign, which targets Black MSM, is part of the Act against AIDS Program initiated by the White House in 2009. A five-year, $45 million investment, it is a forerunner of the president's 2010 National HIV/AIDS Strategy (see www.ACTagainstAIDS.org).

13. Didier Fassin (2009) uses the term "biolegitimacy" to conceptualize the moral and epistemological foundation of this humanitarian trend, which indicates "a shift in the sort of life politics is interested in. To the life of the refugee, with its painful past and its political meaning, is henceforth preferred the life of the sick, with its present suffering and its physical evidence." Whereas Arendt ([1951] 1979: 296) could still argue with respect to those "outside the pale of the law" that the "prolongation of their lives is due to charity and not to right," these two liberal institutions have converged in contemporary human rights discourse that adjudicates whose life, and what kind of life, is to be protected and preserved. As Fassin (2009: 51–52) writes, "Talking of biolegitimacy rather than biopower is thus to emphasize the construction of the meaning and values of life instead of the exercise of forces and strategies to control it." In this chapter I map and attempt to come to terms with both aspects.

14. I use the adjective "biological" here, rather than "sexual" or "intimate," to suggest that the governmental interest in these youths' sexual intimacies is, within this context, primarily motivated by the epidemiological risk of viral transmission.

15. For a recent study on the expected growth rate of the HIV testing/diagnostics market, see http://www.grandviewresearch.com/industry-analysis/hiv-diagnostics-market. Hortense Spillers's assessment of the dehumanizing economics of chattel slavery feels eerily resonant in the present context: "The procedures adopted for the captive flesh demarcate a total objectification, as the entire captive community becomes a living laboratory" (Spillers 1987: 68). On the relationship between superfluity and fungibility, Susan Marks (2011: 3–4) writes:

> Something is superfluous when it is expendable, disposable, useless, unwanted, undesirable, worthless, senseless, or supernumerary. That may be because it is unneeded or ineffectual, or because it is needed and useful but readily replaceable. With the idea of superfluity often comes this sense of fungibility, as though the excess were a matter not just of over-abundance but of inexhaustible supply, so that each instance can always be substituted by another. At the same time, what is fungible is relatively indistinguishable; put together, it forms a mass, the components of which have few individual features.

16. In Bailey's argument, the notion of intravention "captures what so-called communities of risk already do, based on their own knowledge and ingenuity, to contest, reduce, and survive the impact of HIV on their own terms" (M. Bailey 2013: 204).

17. On the impersonal as an affective, aesthetic, and political realm that may harbor alternative forms of justice, pleasure, and relationality that deviate from modern (neo)liberal conceptions of subjectivity and action, see Bersani and Phillips 2008; Esposito 2010b; Lim 2010; Sharp 2009. It is noteworthy how these authors, while sharing a commitment to the impersonal, draw from often diverging theoretical lineages, ranging from psychoanalysis (Bersani and Phillips) to Spinozist feminist theory (Sharp), Deleuzian-inspired affect theory (Lim), and the writings of Simone Weil (Esposito). Obviously, thinking the impersonal as an affective sphere—and as something related yet irreducible to the interpersonal—has a much longer history, which could be traced back to Émile Durkheim's notion of "collective effervescence" or James's notion of "pure

experience," as well as the crowd psychology of Gustav Le Bon. A discussion of this history is, however, beyond the scope of this book. I return to the conceptually and politically ambiguous relationship between the impersonal and personhood in Chapter 6.

18. Here my argument again closely resonates with Bailey's, who writes, "Over the long haul, Ballroom members perform the labor of caring for and the valuing of lives that is integral to building and sustaining a community in the midst of crisis" (M. Bailey 2013: 215).

19. See Donà 2006: 62–67; Esposito 2011: 165–177. See also the concluding chapter in E. Cohen 2009. As Esposito (2011: 165) writes, "Can we imagine a philosophy of immunity that, without denying its inherent contradiction, even deepening it further, reverses the semantics in the direction of community?" Donna Haraway (1991: 225) is also instructive here: "Immunity can also be conceived in terms of shared specificities; of the semi-permeable self able to engage with others (human and non-human, inner and outer), but always with finite consequences; of situated possibilities and impossibilities of individuation and identification; and of partial fusions and dangers."

20. Here I am inspired by Bruno Latour's discussion of the work of Étienne Souriau on the different modes of existence, as well as his earlier meditations on the intellectually lazy and potentially harmful practice of reducing things to a particular substrate, often using the vernacular terminology belonging to the mode of existence of another thing (see Latour 1993, 2011).

21. For a different and early take on the creative potential of queer promiscuity in the battle against HIV/AIDS, see Crimp 1988.

22. See http://en.wiktionary.org/wiki/promiscuous.

Chapter 4

1. Of course, many young Black queer men do not have any affinity with the Ballroom scene, but I am referring here to the context of Chapter 3, which addresses those who do.

2. E. Patrick Johnson (1998) and Jafari Allen (2009) have eloquently written about the club as an alternative environment for the embodied experience of religious spirituality and belonging. Johnson's essay in particular posits the club as a space that capacitates a more "fleshly" communal experience for Black gay men who have been told by their church to save their souls by denying the pleasures of their profane bodies. Thus, the dance floor offers these men an opportunity to be intimate at once with the Holy Spirit and the flesh of other men. While taking these insights to heart, I dedicate this chapter to examining the queer-affirming church as an alternative religious space for truth telling and the articulation of a being-in-common that is divinely inspired.

3. As Ann Pellegrini (2005: 94) has argued, religion "remains a vital site of collective belonging and meaning-making life practices" for queers of faith, many of whom are queers of color, whose relationship to religious practices and doctrines frequently involves a complex mixture of discomfort, disavowal, and negotiation. For two powerful meditations on the marginalized and ambivalent position of Black queers in the institutional setting of the Black Church, where the queer body takes shape as both

an abject and a generative locus of discursive, performative, and sonic circulations, see Crawley 2008, 2013a. As Crawley (2013a: 28) writes: "The Black queer subject is thrown in a narrative as irreducible incoherence while he concurrently grounds a narrative of Black, Christian normativity."

4. In many of these studies, the term "spiritual" is used loosely to refer to a wide variety of "circum-religious" practices, attachments, and feelings that cannot be contained within the space of the "religious." For more on the circum-religious, see Crawley 2008. For an incisive ethnographic study of the complex relationship between "religion" and "spirituality" in the U.S. context, see Bender 2010.

5. Studies that have examined the connections between Black queer life/experience and religion, religious faith, or spirituality, both in fiction and "in real life," include Allen 2009; Cobb 2001; Crawley 2008, 2013a, 2013b, 2017; Johnson 1998; Moore 2008; Sneed 2008.

6. See Cobb 2001: 286. For instance, neither the field-defining *Black Queer Studies* anthology (Johnson and Henderson 2005) nor its sequel (Johnson 2016) includes a single contribution on religion or religious spirituality. As I noted in Chapter 1, Blackness has always been rendered queer by the institutions, norms, and values of heteronormative white supremacy. In this sense, queer Blackness is a tautology. Still, I use this term in tandem with the notion of Black queerness to point to the precarious nexus in which Black queers at once Blacken queerness and queer Blackness. For more on this nexus, see Chapters 5–6.

7. The Yoruba religion is the indigenous religion of the Yoruba people, whose homeland comprises southwestern Nigeria and the adjacent parts of Togo and Benin. As Shawn Copeland (2013: 632) notes, "The term Black in Black religion cannot but insinuate rupture—a fragmenting of the sacred cosmos mediated by the traditional religions of West Africa; yet, it also implies contact and cross-fertilization, creativity, and reconfiguration."

8. I owe this phrasing in part to Elizabeth Povinelli (2011b), whose work aims to develop an "anthropology of the otherwise." The other part is obviously a nod to Paulo Freire's classic *Pedagogy of the Oppressed* ([1970] 2000). Freire's pedagogy proposes the idea and practice of a "problem-posing education" where "people develop their power to perceive critically *the way they exist* in the world *with which* and *in which* they find themselves; they come to see the world not as a static reality, but as a reality in process, in transformation" (ibid.: 83).

9. Ashon Crawley (2013b: 51) writes: "The aesthetics of BlackPentecostalism operate through irreducible openness—never adhering to containment. . . . This irreducible openness is toward a 'movement of the Spirit,' or what we might simply call 'change.'" See also Crawley 2017.

10. For his discussion of divine existence in relation to utility and morality, see James 2004: 288–291. For James's conception of the "pluriverse," or "multi-verse," see James 1996.

11. While Latour shares Foucault's concern with establishing a comparative account of different "regimes of truth," Foucault's conception of *parrhesia* as a direct and unmediated mode of generating truth is diametrically opposed to Latour's emphasis on mediations and detours as crucial to any regime of truth. For Latour, the produc-

tion of truth necessarily entails the artificial deployment of technique and rhetoric, two regimes that Foucault separates from the regime of *parrhesia*. With Latour, we may question whether *parrhesia* can ever be truly enacted without any form of mediation, a possibility Foucault seems unable or unwilling to foreclose. For instance, after his discussion of five different "modes of veridiction," which he initially is at pains to distinguish from one another, he adds, "It sometimes happens, and it will happen more often than not, that these modes of veridiction are combined with each other" (Foucault 2011: 26). A year earlier, he even went as far as to identify philosophical *parrhesia* as "the *etumos tekhnê* (the genuine technique)," suggesting a coincidence of two modes of veridiction previously held to be distinct (Foucault 2010: 336). This convergence of *tekhnê* and *parrhesia* provides us with an opening to reconceptualize *parrhesia* as an experimental truth-producing procedure that is realized through the mediations, detours, and translations native to the realm of *tekhnê,* which Latour identifies as a mode of experimentation with "being-as-another" (Latour 2002: 250). It is this very "other-directedness" of *tekhnê,* or the technical mode of producing truth that always involves some kind of curve or transformation, that makes it so congenial to *parrhesia* as a practice that necessarily implicates at least one other person and whose aim is to move the parrhesiast away from her current conditions and toward another, true life—a "spiritual" transformation, in Foucault's sense.

12. The argument I develop here is inspired by the recent work of Elizabeth Povinelli and Lauren Berlant, who have both so eloquently shown that "amidst the exhausting pragmatics of the everyday" there are minoritarian forms of life that still manage to work through the current impasse by forging new ethical attachments and spaces which are affectively charged with political potential (Berlant 2011a: 262; see also Povinelli 2011a). Their work also makes clear that, for many people, political agency is often more about maintenance and repair than radical change. For more on these matters, see Chapter 6.

13. Sianne Ngai (2005: 95) provides an insightful discussion of "the ideologeme of racialized animatedness" as a discursive space in which "emotional qualities seem especially prone to sliding into corporeal qualities where the African American subject is concerned, reinforcing the notion of race as a truth located, quite naturally, in the always obvious, highly visible body." Moreover, animatedness constructs the purportedly excessive emotionality and bodily expressiveness of African Americans as the result of their animation by a third party who is *actually* in control and who *makes* these Black bodies act, often in a highly routinized manner. Any agency the subject of animatedness might appear to have therefore always comes from elsewhere; it is spurious. For an account of how performative and aesthetic exuberance is treated with suspicion in the Black Church insofar as it threatens to feminize the services and, by proxy, the men of the congregation, see Crawley 2013a. For a more general discussion of the relationship between "the letter and the spirit," or between "the intellect and the emotions" in the neo-Pentecostal movement (in which the UFCB participates), see Lincoln and Mamiya 1990: 386–387.

14. Consider, in contrast, Ashon Crawley's conception of "whooping" and its importance for Black communal life: "Rather than sacrificing imagination through the serrational edge of understanding—a project and process of rationality, of enlightened thought . . . [what] whooping relinquishes is containment, the ruse of continuity, of un-

interrupted flow. Whooping, in other words, is the *instantiation* of imaginative leap and flight, it sacrifices the concept of the enclosed liberal subject" (Crawley 2013b: 56). A bit later, he continues: "With BlackPentecostal whooping, a narrative is generated about the intentioned forms Black life took, and takes, to contend with and against a history of violent eclipses of breath—drownings overboard, whippings, lynchings, incarceration—and how those forms of life are the instantiation of life and love in the face of the plentitude of gratuitous violence and violation. It is to remember the balance between the individual and the social, to generate variations around the theme of discontinuity and openness as a way, as a form, as a politics against violent silences and enclosures, mutilations and deaths. BlackPentecostal whooping, in other words, is the care of flesh" (ibid.: 57–58). I quote Crawley at length here because he beautifully expresses a number of central concerns I am attempting to work through in this book, such as the crucial political importance of anti-immunitary architectures that offer alternative conceptions of life, love, and survival. As I address below, Shawn and the UFCB may be critical of excitable gesticulations such as whooping but they nevertheless continue to draw on its assembling power to build an affective commons that nourishes those who partake in it.

15. As Pastor phrased it, "I believe you have to show me God, as opposed to talk to me about God. If you show me the love of God in all you do, if you show that to me, then I can see God." This can be read as a variation on Latour's distinction between talking about religion and truly talking *religiously*, whereby one enunciates a divine presence. For the UFCB's clergy, actions enunciate louder than words alone.

16. At the UFCB, the divine was virtually always referred to using a masculine pronoun. This does not necessarily mean, however, that either the UFCB's clergy or its congregation actually conceived of God as a masculine entity. When asked whether they thought God has a gender, most people answered that they thought gender does not apply to the divine, although there were a few exceptions in which God was believed to be female or male. During my time at the church, God's gender never came up as an explicit concern.

17. See http://www.etymonline.com/index.php?term=inspiration.

18. In the words of Crawley (2013a: 54), who has greatly inspired my thinking of the interconnections among Black Pentecostalism, queerness, and performance and/as breath/life:

> The fact of breathing in figurations of Blackness-as-death would submit this double-gesture to the merely biological, and those relegated to the zone of breathing's 'fact' would be said to have no lived experience because we are likewise, and as an *a priori* principle, said to lack the capacity for experience. But the case of breathing, the double-gesture of respiration as *Black pneuma* rises to, while it emerges from, its specific occasion. . . . The zone of the purportedly merely breathing, those whom are 'living death,' must be rethought and this mode of thought must be an other-than-theological, other-than-philosophical project.

I develop my own critical-*cum*-reparative engagement with the notion of Blackness as death in Chapter 6.

19. Foucault's manuscript, dated 1984, ends with the following note: "But what I would like to stress in conclusion is this: there is no establishment of the truth without an essential position of otherness; the truth is never the same; there can be truth only in the form of the other world and the other life (*l'autre monde et de la vie autre*)" (Foucault 2011: 340). Here it once again becomes clear that Latour and Foucault share a mutual concern with the relationship between truth and transformation. More precisely, both agree that there can be no truth without transformation.

20. Birgit Meyer defines sensational forms as "relatively fixed, authorized modes of invoking and organizing access to the transcendental, thereby creating and sustaining links between religious practitioners in the context of particular religious organizations" (Meyer 2008: 707). On the basis of my fieldwork, I would argue that they also include less authorized modes that attune religious practitioners to a divine immanence whose presence needs to be continuously renewed through enunciations of confidence and faith.

21. In *The Courage of Truth*, Foucault on several occasions returns to the significance of the principle of "changing the value of the currency" in the Cynic tradition, pointing to the philological connection between currency and convention, rule, or law. To "change the value of the currency" is to radically alter existing conventions, rules, or laws, not by opposing them but by taking their logic to their extreme consequences and thereby exposing them as radically different from the *true* life. As Foucault asks, "For life truly to be the life of truth, must it not be an *other* life, a life which is radically and paradoxically other?" (Foucault 2011: 245; see also ibid., 226–228, 239–247).

22. See, e.g., Chen 2012; Chen and Luciano 2015; Giffney and Hird 2008.

23. On the problematic assumptions underlying modern explanations of religion and faith in terms of "belief," see Latour 2010b.

24. On the Judeo-Christian logic of sacrificial love and its incarnations in late liberal regimes, see Povinelli 2011a: 163–186.

Chapter 5

1. The compound acronym BDSM comprises bondage and discipline, dominance and submission, and sadism and masochism, and it includes a wide array of intimate relationships, sexual practices, and subcultures, which generally share a proclivity for experimenting with interpersonal power relations. While certainly not identical, BDSM and the more colloquial "leather sex" share this sexualization of power relations, as well as a concern with protocols, techniques, and the proper use of artifacts such as whips, masks, or straps. Yet whereas BDSM, as a much broader spectrum of practices and relationships, does not necessarily incorporate leather items, these obviously form the main locus of attraction and play in the case of leather sex—which, in turn, is at the heart of the highly ritualized leather community. For detailed accounts of leather sex and BDSM as sexual practices and forms of life, see Bean 1994; Lenius 2010; Thompson 2004.

2. Leather contests form a central aspect of the leather community and present the foremost occasion for leather men and leather women from around the region to come together and socialize, play, enjoy entertainment, and usually raise funds. Originat-

ing from the male beauty contests that were a staple of leather bars in the 1970s, the contests have evolved into large institutionalized and ritualistic events featuring various categories and titles for which to compete.

3. Officially the Baltimore/Washington, DC, area is served by the Mid-Atlantic chapter of ONYX, a "Leather Fraternity for Gay and Bisexual Men of Color" founded in 1995 (http://www.onyxma.com). However, this DC-based chapter, founded in 2007, had very few members who lived in Baltimore City. It should be mentioned here that my assertion concerning a lack of Black visibility in Baltimore's gay leather/BDSM community must also, at least in part, be attributed to my own positionality as a white male researcher whose first forays into the scene were facilitated by white male community contacts (Van Doorn 2013a, 2016). From there, my network quickly grew but it also remained largely white until I actively started to look for non-white, non-male connections who could offer me their perspectives on leather/BDSM as a life-sustaining practice and support structure. See also my methodological reflections in Chapter 1.

4. Black BEAT ceased operations in 2015, when its organizers went on an indefinite hiatus. Its website is also no longer available. During my fieldwork I unfortunately was not able to meet with any of the founding members.

5. One important exception is the library's inclusion of the complete collection (eight issues and a special issue) of Black Leather in Color, a magazine dedicated to "Leather on the Cutting Edge for People of Color and Their Friends" (as proclaimed by its subtitle). For a brief history of how the magazine, whose first issue was published in 1994, came into existence, see https://leatherati.com/from-the-la-m-archives-Black-leather-in-color-27596709955a.

6. For Christina Sharpe (2012: 834; see also Sharpe 2010), who follows in the footsteps of Hortense Spillers's (1987) pioneering work, "the queerness of Blackness" is characterized by a "lack of 'proper' signifying power in terms of sex and gender, monstrosity, malleability, and possibility." Likewise, Darieck Scott (2010: 8) offers a powerful complementary reflection on the concept of queerness in relation to Black history, which is worth quoting at length here:

> Its usefulness and its complications both stem from the way that the representation of queerness in an African American or Black Atlantic context, by drawing attention to nonnormative sexuality and sexual practices—again, an arena already obsessively linked in Western culture with the figures of Blackness and the imago of the Black body—might be said to create a vertiginous double queer register that matches, reflects, and helps constitute the well-known double-consciousness of Blackness. Examining queer Blackness provides opportunities to consider how the history that produces Blackness is a sexual history, that is, a history of state-sanctioned, population-level manipulation of sex's reproductive and pleasure-producing capacities. [. . .T]he queerness of Blackness entails a confrontation with the likelihood that a historical context that provided for the defiance of conventions of sexual propriety and for the relatively unpoliced expression of sexual variation—racialized slavery in the Americas—was a practice of physical and psychic domination, meant to enslave rather than liberate, to fix the human beings whose racialized

bodies made the enjoyment of a certain kind of queer freedom possible in a particularly bound identity rather than release the fluid potentialities of that identity formation.

Following this argument, we should also remember Fred Moten's contribution to the rethinking of the sexual history (productive) of Blackness, in his *In the Break* (2003)—a virtuoso sounding of the dissonant sonic aesthetics that constitute the Black radical tradition. In dialogue with Hartman's (1997) work on slavery's dehumanizing scenes of subjection, Moten asks us to consider the queerness of Blackness as its generative and improvisational phonic inheritance, the violence of which is not merely destructive but also produces a break, or cut, that harbors a radical potentiality for new scenes of performative dissent and objection. As I discuss, BDSM offers Black queer women a space in which to, tentatively but passionately, create such scenes.

7. The Playhouse in Mount Vernon folded some months after I left the city and a new, much larger Playhouse located in Southwest Baltimore opened its doors in October 2014. The new place has no connection with the original Playhouse and its owners apparently bought the name. Moreover, whereas the former Playhouse primarily catered to lesbian (trans) women, the new facility is open to people of all genders and sexual orientations—much like the newly refurbished Baltimore Eagle.

8. Monica plays with women as well as men, yet she prefers staging scenes with women. The public all-male and mixed-gender play parties that I attended during my fieldwork were largely white, with a few Black and Asian people usually in attendance. Everyone played together and socialized afterwards, and on these occasions nobody I talked to mentioned racial tensions or discomfort. This may have had to do with the setting, however, which was served as a space for convivial fun and play rather than critical reflection or complaints. In my informal conversations with some of the Black practitioners on different occasions, they did tell me that race had sometimes been an issue for them, mainly at first. Some mentioned that they had learned how to ignore or address it, while others said that education in the scene had improved the situation. This "dedramatization" of the racial tension in the leather and BDSM scene is something I return to momentarily.

9. As Cruz (2016a: 54) quips: "It is the contract that binds, not the collars, cuffs, or chains of BDSM." For a thorough critique of how gender and race complicate/unsettle liberal contract theory, see Pateman and Mills 2007.

10. A core element of BDSM is the staging of "scenes" in which participants enact a particular sexual fantasy, often employing a selection of toys such as whips, ropes, chains and cuffs, as well as uniforms and other leather or latex paraphernalia. A scene is usually scripted in advance and then played out within the context of events called "play parties," but only after mutual consent is given and a safe word has been determined. For more on the staging of BDSM scenes, see Weiss 2011.

11. A boy is a submissive male who serves his Sir—the dominant position in the relationship. These roles are not contingent on age, as the names would suggest, but depend primarily on the protocol-governed D/s (dominant/submissive) power dynamic between a boy and his Sir. While a boy belongs to only one Sir, a Sir can have multiple boys. Furthermore, Sir/boys relationships are often nonmonogamous and both Sirs

and their boys can have husbands or boyfriends outside of the S/b relationship. For more on Sirs and their boys, see Bean 1994; Thompson 2004; Lenius 2010. Historically, the figure of the boy is ostensibly modeled on the medieval page, yet this position has been distinctly racialized since the Renaissance, when it became fashionable for wealthy families to have young, mostly enslaved African men serve as decorative pages at parties and other social events—as depicted in paintings of old masters such as Titian (Bestor 2003).

12. We have to ask what has to be forgotten, or willfully un-remembered, to transform the slave collar into a symbol of love and dedication that no longer "embodies a contradiction between the extravagant display of Black slaves for their exhibition value and the total denial of the value of their lives and work" (McClintock 1995: 155)?

13. Cruz (2016a: 48) writes: "Race play reveals the profound paradox of this enduring fantasy/reality dialectic: even as these practices recite, indeed require 'real, shared world' historical and political references, such play can be imagined, enacted, and narrated as pure fantasy. This is a profound tension at the heart of race play." However, by revealing this paradox integral to BDSM's fantasy/reality dialectic, race play, "as a performative enactment and affective engagement with the history of racial domination, signals an acknowledgment of that history" and even a "rapture" in it, rather than staging its disavowal (ibid.: 55–56). While I am attracted to Cruz's theorization of race play's subversive and empowering potential, my own research nevertheless hinted at the limits of race play's capacity to "fuck and fuck with racism" (ibid.: 56), to the extent that this fucking (with) is contained within BDSM's sacred space of consensually scripted intimacy—a space that allows for an engagement with the history of gendered racial domination yet keeps its affective negativity from spilling over and becoming a political issue that exceeds its sublimation through sexual play. Although this chapter does not focus on the category of race play, I elaborate on the racial dynamics of BDSM's circumscription of play below.

14. For a discussion of the intersections of slavery, racial consciousness, and the creation of a "Black sacred cosmos," see Lincoln and Mamiya 2003: chap. 1.

15. Both concepts are, I believe, also akin to Cruz's (2016b: 380–381) "politics of perversion," which serves as "a critical, theoretical framework and a praxis of Black female sexuality" that takes seriously "the unspeakable and the perverse, as not merely modes of producing pleasure but as Black queer world-making." However, where both Allen's "transcendent erotics and politics" and Cruz's "politics of perversion" highlight how counternormative sexual pleasures harbor inchoate modes of agency and resistance to white heterosexist culture, civic intimacies do not necessarily pertain directly to sexual practices and encompass a broader range of intimate support structures—as shown in the previous two chapters.

16. Here my understanding of civic intimacies departs from Allen's (2011: 95) "transcendent erotics and politics," which assumes a more coherent, willful subject and is "grounded in a principle of a universal human endowment of positive rights and a set of human intentions to exercise those rights to things like bodily integrity, freedom from harm, freedom to fantasize, and so on." I remain skeptical about the value of political projects predicated on human universality for Black queer noncitizens who are regularly subjected to dehumanizing violence, and I am likewise unsure about a politics

grounded in intentionality. Instead, the notion of civic intimacies suggests a reparative politics of ambiguity, which accommodates for the violence, negativity, and incoherence that mark Black queer existence while investing in practices of composition and affirmation that nevertheless materialize—intentionally or otherwise.

17. This search for alternative social spaces and the consequent turn to the familiarity of Black domestic settings reminds me of Kenten's stories about the centrality of people's homes in the development of Black queer social life in 1980s and -90s Baltimore, discussed in Chapter 2. This is where he and his friends would frequently convene for card parties and other informal gatherings, in the absence of a robust Black queer public sphere—save for a decreasing number of Black gay bars and clubs.

18. Weiss's *Techniques of Pleasure* (2011) offers a very thorough and engaging ethnographic account of the BDSM lifestyle and its various ritual practices, norms, and values. While it has been an extremely useful resource for my own research into these topics, two important differences should be mentioned here. First, her study is set in San Francisco, whose urban history, social fabric, and material landscape differs significantly from that of Baltimore. Second, her fieldwork focuses on a group of predominantly heterosexual (and some bisexual) middle-class white men and women with considerable expendable income, while the interlocutors in my research were working-class LGBT practitioners, white and of color, who frequently could not afford the toys and gear that were so important to the participants Weiss studied. As such, I cannot subscribe to the part of her argument that characterizes BDSM as integrated into a late capitalist "marketplace of desire" rooted in commodity consumption. While she makes a convincing case, I did not find such emphasis on consumption and the commodification of desire in the community I have studied. In contrast, Baltimore's gay leather and BDSM community is deeply engaged in alternative economic initiatives that provided monetary support for various lifesaving support structures and projects (Van Doorn 2016).

19. Cruz also points us to Sharpe's effort to problematize "the fraught site of sexual consent for post-slavery subjects" (Cruz 2015: 417; see also Cruz 2016a: 47–49). In her *Monstrous Intimacies,* Sharpe (2010: 4) aims to "examine and account for a series of repetitions of master narratives of violence and forced submission that are read or reinscribed as consent and affection: intimacies that involve shame and trauma and their transgenerational transmission." Likewise, Jared Sexton (2008: 84), in his scathing critique of multiracialist discourse, makes the following observation: "The contest over contemporary representations of interracial intimacy and multiracial identity is bound up with discrepancies regarding the relations between power and pleasure, agency and affect, subjugation and sexuality in the past. Most pointedly, it is a dispute over what constitutes consent in the field of racialized sexuality . . . and under what conditions consent might be said to exist properly, to be thrown into crisis, or to be rendered virtually ineffective. As such, it is also a commentary on the nature of coercion and the scale at which its consideration will finally be posed." I bring these reflections on racialized sexual consent together here because they point to the inadequacies and obfuscating nature of this notion, to the extent that it isolates and (inter)personalizes a moment of decision, thereby reducing it to the liberal tenet of "choice," while such a moment is severely overdetermined and informed by forces that exceed the spatial and temporal

confines of the BDSM scene as well as the contractual imaginary that scaffolds it. I elaborate in this below.

20. Halperin (2007: 94) asks us to think about abjection "not as the symptom of an unconscious drive to self-annihilation, but as *a strategic response to a specific social predicament*—as a socially constituted affect that can intensify the determination to survive, can conduce to sexual inventiveness, and can lead to the creation of various devices for extracting heightened pleasure and even love, from experiences of pain, fear, rejection, humiliation, contempt, shame, brutality, disgust, or condemnation." His approach is Foucauldian and restages the notion of abjection as an ascetic/aesthetic practice of freedom, which locates it in the register of tactical, if not purely volitional, composure and subjectivation. This way of thinking about abjection certainly resonates with Monica's strategic response to her "specific social predicament" after having been raped. Yet if we shift registers, or broaden/deepen our analysis, we may also associate her predicament with the afterlife of slavery in which racialized sexual violence against Black women—both structural and physical—continues to be rampant. In this respect it is useful to compare Halperin's account, which posits HIV/AIDS as the paradigmatic predicament in the lives of (white) gay men, to Darieck Scott's approach to abjection, which, despite the fact that his work centers on the lives of fictional Black men, gives us an analytic lens with which to think abjection in relation to the violence experienced by Black queer women like Monica. Positioning his project as a study of "the ways that Blackness is rendered by the various cultural, social, and economic processes of white supremacist domination as the exemplar of nonnormative genders and sexualities," Scott uses the notion of abjection as "a way of describing an experience, an inherited (psychically introjected) historical legacy, and a social condition defined and underlined by a defeat" (Scott 2010: 10, 17). But rather than attempting to overcome such defeat, he is more interested in exploring strategies of survival that work *with* the experience of abjection in order to cultivate capacities "*through* the unflinching investigation, depiction, and manipulation of an originary history of violation" (ibid.: 9). His project, which is informed by Frantz Fanon as well as Black feminist engagements with psychoanalysis and Black queer studies, not only points to the value of BDSM as a practice that allows Black queer women to investigate, depict, and manipulate a painful history of racialized sexual violence and violation but also presents us with a "more modest sort of redemptive imagination" that Vogler and Markell (2003: 5) suggest we require in order to learn how to navigate "freedom with violence"—not the liberal immunitary state violence Chandan Reddy (2011) has in mind when deploying this figure, but instead denoting a political ethics that embraces a certain *generative negativity* immanent to and necessary to survival and flourishing. It is this approach to negativity, more reparative than redemptive, that I develop in the next chapter, where I further investigate the relationship between queerness, Blackness, and negativity. Darieck Scott's work exists in close proximity to the debates I address and work through there.

21. In this sense Baltimore's leather/BDSM community can be understood as a synecdoche of the city itself: each is an architecture attempting to immunize itself against the racial antagonism that forms at once its core and its constitutive (abjected) outside. The social contradiction that the community cannot stage without a concomitant disavowal is in fact the "inclusive exclusion" of Blackness in U.S. civil society,

which has created a situation in which Black life, as Sexton (2011: 28) puts it, "is not lived in the world that the world lives in." I return to his remark, and the fundamental ambiguity it represents, in the following chapter.

Chapter 6

1. As Wilderson (2010: 58–59) writes in *Red, White and Black:* "Afro-pessimism explores the meaning of Blackness not—in the first instance—as a variously and unconsciously interpellated identity or as a conscious social actor, but as a structural position of noncommunicability in the face of all other positions; this meaning is noncommunicable because, again, as a position, Blackness is predicated on modalities of accumulation and fungibility, not exploitation and alienation." On the logic of fungibility with respect to HIV prevention strategies targeting Black queer youths, see Chapter 3.

2. I use the term "para-Lacanian" in reference to how Wilderson's work both adopts and attempts to transcend Lacanian (film) theory. See chapter 2 of his *Red, White and Black: Cinema and the Structure of U.S. Antagonisms* (Wilderson 2010: 67–68).

3. On the "cybernetic unconscious" of Lacanian psychoanalysis, and on the influence of post-war American cybernetics, game theory, and information theory on French (post-)structuralist theory more generally, see Geoghegan 2011; Lafontaine 2007; Liu 2010. Like the discrete logic and operational circuits of cybernetics, Edelman's own digital metaphysics is a closed loop that feeds back on itself, abstracting the ambiguity of analog forms of life into his binary imaginary of One and zero. I return to the problematic of ambiguity below.

4. To be sure, Edelman rejects the characterization of his work as nihilist: "This [the elimination of any possibility of dissent], however, is reproductive futurism's goal, one it pursues by assigning those who challenge its supremacy to a space outside the social, outside the political as such, thus silencing any resistance in advance by dismissing it as nihilistic. Against so frivolous and feckless a charge, recall the words of Adorno: 'The true nihilists are the ones who oppose nihilism with their more faded positivities, the ones who are thus conspiring with all extant malice, and eventually with the destructive principle itself. Thought honors itself by defending what is damned as nihilism'" (Edelman 2007: 474). However, whereas Adorno's negative dialectics sought to preserve the immanent force of negativity as the non-identical and irrecuperable remainder in a world dominated by positivist science and liberal democratic values, Edelman's queer zero comes to figure as an *absolute negativity* (i.e., the Real) that at once conditions, ruptures, and transcends all positively recognizable social/political values and aspirations. In other words, what I identify as Edelman's nihilism is not the nihilism Adorno seeks to defend in the name of critical thought (Adorno [1973] 2007).

5. This is actually more akin to Roberto Esposito's use of this term to signify the ultimate disastrous outcome, or sacrifice, of modernity's paradigm of immunization as the concurrent protection and negation of life (see Deutscher 2013; Esposito 2011: 164–165).

6. Moreover, such defensive practices require a new immunitary imagination that reconfigures the status of negativity and/as the violence of alterity. As discussed in

Chapter 3, Esposito begins to sketch such an imagination through his notion of "common immunity," which tentatively signifies an architecture that refuses binary distinctions between self-other, inside-outside, or healthy-hazardous, instead embracing "a shared individuality or a sharing of individuality" that embodies "a contraction by which identity is simultaneously affirmed and altered at the same time: it is established in the form of its own alteration" (Esposito 2011: 177).

7. For two queer claims about the future's inevitability, see de Lauretis 2011; Ruti 2008.

8. I see a productive analogy between my argument here and Vincent Brown's critical assessment of the relationship between social death and political life in the study of slavery. As Brown notes, "Orlando Patterson described social death in its broadest sense as the absence of meaningful links to the past." However, while acknowledging that "Patterson was certainly correct to argue that the enslaved 'were not allowed freely to integrate the experience of their ancestors into their lives, to inform their understanding of social reality with the inherited meanings of their natural forebears, or to anchor the living present in any conscious community of memory,'" he argues that "everything in this assertion hangs on the word 'freely,' a fatal qualification for a theory of the social relations of slavery. As the Haitian Declaration of Independence teaches us, social connections and communities of memory had to be created in struggle, and alienation had to be overcome by political action" (V. Brown 2009: 1248; the emphasis in the Patterson quote is Brown's).

9. See also the virtual roundtable discussion on "theorizing queer temporalities," convened by Elizabeth Freeman in 2006 and subsequently published as part of a special issue on this theme in *GLQ* (Dinshaw et al. 2007).

10. The full sentence in *Black Skin, White Masks* that forms the hinge of Moten's disagreement with Sexton and Copeland reads as follows: "I came into the world imbued with the will to find meaning in things, my spirit filled with the desire to attain to the source of the world, and then I found that I was an object in the midst of other objects" (Fanon [1967] 2008: 82).

11. To be sure, Black queer folks do worry about losing their claim to—or sense of—Blackness, as discussed in Chapter 5 with respect to kink and its association with Whiteness. However, such apprehension stems from an identification of Blackness with religiously informed family values rather than pathological existence.

12. For Moten (2013b: 742), whose argument brings to mind Esposito's analysis of the Hobbesian immunitary legacy at the heart of political modernity, the antirelationality of our political order is deeply inimical to the relational nothing of Black fugitivity—so much so that there can be no such "thing" as Black sovereign personhood. This is to say that, in his view, Black personhood or political subjectivity not only is made impossible by anti-Black violence; it is also antithetical to Blackness as the celebration of an "undercommon, underground, submarine sociality." Or, phrased differently, civic personhood is what Black *communitas* cannot afford, should not want, and does not need. Blackness expropriates.

13. It should be noted here that Moten's conception of being "in the break" as a mode of fugitivity entails that Blackness is never located solely on the "outside" or

"inside" of civil society. As he remarks, "I am totally with him [Sexton] in locating my optimism in appositional proximity to his pessimism even if I would tend not to talk about the inside/outside relationality of social death and social life while speaking in terms of apposition and permeation rather than in terms of opposition and surrounding" (Moten 2013b: 773).

14. Edelman's paranoid mode of inquiry initially seems antithetical to Sedgwick's project. However, as Ellis Hanson (2011: 106) has noted, "*No Future* turns out to be a paranoid book with reparative effects, and Sedgwick's essay on the reparative is a remarkably paranoid reading of paranoid reading." Likewise, in a thoughtful essay that considers the turn to Adorno in the work of Edelman and Muñoz, Kevin Floyd (2010: 3) argues, "*No future* remains an indispensable volume, in my view, because it turns out to be a crypto-utopian polemic, a secretly utopian polemic, dressed up in the Lacanian drag of an anti-utopian polemic." Edelman, in his conversation with Berlant, contests such a reading while nevertheless acknowledging that his position is more ambiguous than is commonly asserted: "I am not a utopian, though I too cast my vote for flourishing. But then I don't see 'flourishing' as radically distinct from the experience of 'lives that don't work'; negativity, in my view, speaks to the fact that life, in some sense, *doesn't* 'work,' is structurally inimical to happiness, stability, or regulated functioning, and that only the repetitive working through of what still doesn't work in the end—or works only until the radically nonrelational erupts from within it once more—constitutes the condition in which something like flourishing could ever happen" (Berlant and Edelman 2014: 11). This conception of flourishing is in fact remarkably close to one that Sedgwick developed in her later work. Here I address the ambiguity that marks both projects because it highlights the persistence of the negative in any reparative endeavor, while allowing me to stress the importance of building support structures that enable Black queer life to survive such negativity.

15. Berlant's question echoes Donna Haraway's oft-cited statement, lifted from her critical account of the immunitary paradigm and its reinvention in biomedicine: "Life is a window of vulnerability. It seems a mistake to close it" (Haraway 1991: 224). However, as I argued in Chapter 3, "life" is not an undifferentiated substance or phenomenon, let alone one that is merely biological, and, as I go on to argue here, life's vulnerabilities are likewise unequally distributed among the living, who continue to survive and flourish in (bio)politically regulated environments where some bodies attract more attritional violence than others. Without advocating the closure of any windows per se, it is my contention that exactly those forms of life that are most vulnerable require efforts to generate collective architectures that provide a measure of security and immunity, where these two terms have to be disentangled from the modern triadic *dispositifs* of political sovereignty, individual property, and negative liberty.

16. As Muñoz (2006: 683) writes: "Love for Klein is thus not just a romantic abstraction; it is indeed a kind of striving for belonging that does not ignore the various obstacles that the subject must overcome to achieve the most provisional belonging."

17. As Condorelli (2014: 14) specifies: "These are not to be understood as features in a formal sense, and do not have a common external appearance; they do not trace a silhouette or any possible portrait. They are to be taken in the machinic sense (literally, like a feature in technological equipment) as distinctive characteristics of operation,

particular modalities that serve to distinguish them from others of similar types both in activity and tactic: they feature in the work of support."

It should be noted that in her groundbreaking essay "Mama's Baby, Papa's Maybe: An American Grammar Book," Hortense Spillers also uses the term "support structure," almost as an aside, to indicate "that the captive person developed, time and again, certain ethical and sentimental features that tied her and him, *across* the landscape to others, often sold from hand to hand, of the same and different blood in a common fabric of memory and inspiration" (Spillers 1987: 75). It is the composition of this common fabric that interests me here.

18. Or, as Annamarie Jagose (in Dinshaw et al. 2007: 189) suggests in the aforementioned roundtable on queer temporalities: "If our working through time and history keeps delivering us to community, perhaps that is because community, together with history, might usefully be thought 'along the seam of its becoming'; thought about, that is, as holding open a queer (because radically impersonal) promise."

19. Moreover, the support structures I have examined in this book—the Ballroom community, UFCB, and Black BDSM practices—also work against, or maintain an ambiguous relationship with, the larger institutional frameworks in which they exist/persist. As noted in Chapter 1, these institutional frameworks are Baltimore's HIV prevention system, the Black Church, and the white gay leather and BDSM community, respectively.

20. To be clear, I do not consider support structures to be antimonial to fugitivity. On the contrary, I believe one needs support structures in order to sustain fugitive modes of experimentation, improvisation and collectivity. While support structures are in essence "conservative," in that they strive for maintenance and perpetuation, they are not—or at least are not intended to be, not initially—about capture or constraint. What they attempt to conserve and nurture is precisely the progressive movement toward a collective sense of thriving in spaces and times hitherto unaccommodating to such efforts.

21. As Huey Copeland and Naomi Beckwith write in their introduction to a special issue of the *Nka Journal of Contemporary African Art* dedicated to the theme of Black collectivities, these form "a means of protection and defense that allows its participants to refuse capture by the market and the state, those white supremacist formations that have together marked Blackness as a site of value productive of both radical dereliction and tremendous wealth. As such, Black collectivity now is not so much a static formation as a state of being, a mode of becoming-together whose temporal unfolding is contingent, provisional, and always under threat of erasure but not without voice" (Copeland and Beckwith 2014: 7).

22. On the generative ambiguity of the (w)hole, see Moten's critique of Edelman's text "The Part for the (W)hole," which, according to Moten (2003: 173–174), "threatens to become an ocularcentric textualism that is not but nothing other than Eurocentric." Like the (w)hole, the (k)not is an interstitial and vibrant entity, located in the interval of nothing and something, attachment and detachment, at once indefinite and incomplete. Yet this is an ambiguity Edelman's digital metaphysics cannot capture.

23. Lois McNay develops a similar argument against what she terms the "social weightlessness" of radical democratic theory. She examines the blind spots of ontologi-

cal approaches that conceive of essence of the political as an autonomous realm, arguing that they neglect and actively withdraw from the messiness and hierarchies of the social realm. As she writes: "The routinized, inert and experientially negative quality of subordination within these hierarchical social relations is too easily passed over by a radical democratic emphasis on the political as the site of indeterminacy, contestation, and becoming" (McNay 2014: 15). Furthermore, McNay's analytical emphasis on the "experientially negative quality of subordination" aims to counter the "abstract negativism" of current radical democratic theory and its ontologies of lack and nonbeing, and she argues that such abstract negativism "needs to be bound more closely to a social theoretical negativism that places emphasis on the lived reality of oppression and domination" (ibid.: 23). While I subscribe to the core of her argument, and indeed this chapter is committed to connecting different theories of negativity to the lived reality of Black queer survival in Baltimore, I wonder to what extent her reification of the social as the site of structural oppression and suffering can contribute to an understanding of how the oppressed and superfluous actually survive and manage to flourish. In other words, I remain skeptical about her claim that "despite the undoubted importance of attesting to counter-hegemonic agency, it is not the particular concern of this book, but, nonetheless, the emphasis here on social suffering is envisaged as a complement to this constructive project rather than a negation of it" (ibid.: 22). McNay's negative approach, based on a "disclosing critique" that unmasks the suffering and injustice permeating the fabric of "the social," tends to turn into a *memento mori* of sorts, perpetually reminding political theorists to take heed of suffering's unbearable weight which they refuse to factor into their weightless theories. While this is an important contribution in itself, her promise that the approach she adopts also offers a "constructive element," central to my own project, unfortunately remains unfulfilled.

24. "Make a Way Out of No Way" was the title of a three-day symposium held at Tramway in Glasgow at the end of September 2014, organized by Arika (http://arika.org.uk/about-us) and featuring discussions, lectures and performances. Fred Moten and Saidiya Hartman were among the participants, as were Kara Keeling, M. Lamar, Arthur Jafa, Miss Prissy, and the Legendary Pony Zion Garçon. "We take the tragedy and make the magic" was a line voiced by trombonist Craig Harris during his performance at the Carrie Mae Weems-curated event "The Shape of Things," which took place at the Park Avenue Armory on December 17, 2017.

25. In their otherwise very different book-length studies of negativity in political theory and philosophy, Diana Coole and Benjamin Noys come to a similar conclusion. Coole (2000: 6) conceives of negativity in terms of its political "*generativity*," as a "creative-destructive force that engenders as well as ruins positive forms." Likewise, Noys ([2008] 2010: 164–165) writes: "Negativity no longer lines up with a purely destructive will. . . . Instead, the persistence of the negative undermines exactly this structure by excavating a negativity that is suspensive and preservative, rather than one dreaming of a fantasmatic apocalypse." In other words, both authors point to the productive, relational, and mundane dimensions of negativity, which makes it available—however precariously and erratically—to political projects and practices.

26. Stefano Harney and Fred Moten distinguish study from officially recognized, sanctified, and institutionalized forms of knowledge production. Study, true study,

which for them is Black study, is a collective and ongoing project of the undercommons—a concrete and improvised articulation of Esposito's *communitas*—where a mutual "debt without credit" compels those without access to the conventional means of knowledge production to come together and create new modes of knowing and being in the know. As they write: "These other ones have a passion to tell you what they have found, and they are surprised you want to listen, even though they've been expecting you. Sometimes the story is not clear, or it starts in a whisper. It goes around again but listen, it is funny again, every time. This knowledge has been degraded, and the research rejected. They can't get access to books, and no one will publish them" (Harney and Moten 2013: 68).

References

Adorno, Theodor W. (1973) 2007. *Negative Dialectics*, trans. E. B. Ashton. New York: Continuum.

Agamben, Giorgio. 2000. *Means without End: Notes on Politics*. Minneapolis: University of Minnesota Press.

Agathangelou, Anna M., M. Daniel Bassichis, and Tamara L. Spira. 2008. "Intimate Investments: Homonormativity, Global Lockdown, and the Seductions of Empire." *Radical History Review* 100:120–143.

AIDS Foundation of Chicago, AVAC: Global Advocacy for HIV Prevention, Black AIDS Institute, International Rectal Microbicide Advocates, National Minority AIDS Council, Project Inform, and San Francisco AIDS Foundation. 2011. "PrEP: Roadmap to the Real World." *The Body*, August. Accessed December 4, 2015. http://www.projectinform.org/pdf/prep_roadmap.pdf.

Allen, Jafari S. 2009. "For 'the Children' Dancing the Beloved Community." *Souls* 11 (3): 311–326.

———. 2011. *¡Venceremos? The Erotics of Black Self-Making in Cuba*. Durham, NC: Duke University Press.

———. 2012. "Black/Queer/Diaspora at the Current Conjuncture." *GLQ* 18 (2–3): 211–248.

Althaus-Reid, Marcella. 2003. *The Queer God*. London: Routledge.

Anidjar, Gil. 2011. "The Meaning of Life." *Critical Inquiry* 37 (4): 697–723.

Appleseed. 2011. "Johns Hopkins Lives Here: State of Maryland." Accessed December 4, 2015. http://www.appleseedinc.com/wp-content/uploads/2013/12/Johns-Hopkins-Lives-Here-State-of-Maryland.pdf.

Arendt, Hannah. (1951) 1979. *The Origins of Totalitarianism*. Orlando, FL: Harcourt.

Arthur, Catherine R., and Cindy Kelly. 2004. *Homewood House*. Baltimore: Johns Hopkins University Press.

Bailey, Jonathan. 2016. "As Proud of Our Gayness as We Are of Our Blackness." *Black Perspectives*, February 24. Accessed December 10, 2017. http://www.aaihs.org/as-proud-of-our-gayness.

Bailey, Marlon M. 2009. "Performance as Intravention: Ballroom Culture and the Politics of HIV/AIDS in Detroit." *Souls* 11 (3): 253–274.

———. 2013. *Butch Queens Up in Pumps: Gender, Performance, and Ballroom Culture in Detroit*. Ann Arbor: University of Michigan Press.

———. 2014. "Engendering Space: Ballroom Culture and the Spatial Practice of Possibility in Detroit." *Gender, Place and Culture* 21 (4): 489–507.

Bailey, Marlon M., and Rashad Shabazz. 2014. "Editorial: Gender and Sexual Geographies of Blackness: Anti-Black Heterotopias (Part 1)." *Gender, Place and Culture* 21 (3): 316–321.

Balibar, Étienne. 2010. "Antinomies of Citizenship." *Journal of Romance Studies* 10 (2): 1–20.

Baptist, Edward E. 2014. *The Half Has Never Been Told: Slavery and the Making of American Capitalism*. New York: Basic.

Barrett, Lindon. 1999. *Blackness and Value: Seeing Double*. Cambridge: Cambridge University Press.

Bean, Joseph W. 1994. *Leathersex: A Guide for the Curious Outsider and the Serious Player*. San Francisco: Daedalus.

Bell, David, and Jon Binnie. 2000. *The Sexual Citizen: Queer Politics and Beyond*. Cambridge: Polity.

Bender, Courtney. 2010. *The New Metaphysicals: Spirituality and the American Religious Imagination*. Chicago: University of Chicago Press.

Berger, Jane. 2007. "'There Is Tragedy on Both Sides of the Layoffs:' Privatization and the Urban Crisis in Baltimore." *International Labor and Working-Class History* 71 (1): 29–49.

Berlant, Lauren G., ed. 2000. *Intimacy*. Chicago: University of Chicago Press.

———. 2007. "Slow Death (Sovereignty, Obesity, Lateral Agency)." *Critical Inquiry* 33 (4): 754–780.

———. 2009. "Neither Monstrous nor Pastoral, but Scary and Sweet: Some Thoughts on Sex and Emotional Performance in Intimacies and What Do Gay Men Want?" *Women and Performance* 19 (2): 261–273.

———. 2011a. *Cruel Optimism*. Durham, NC: Duke University Press.

———. 2011b. "A Properly Political Concept of Love: Three Approaches in Ten Pages." *Cultural Anthropology* 26 (4): 683–691.

———. 2014. "A Momentary Anesthesia of the Heart." *International Journal of Politics, Culture, and Society* 28 (3): 273–281.

Berlant, Lauren G., and Lee Edelman. 2014. *Sex, or the Unbearable*. Durham, NC: Duke University Press.

Bersani, Leo. 1995. *Homos*. Cambridge, MA: Harvard University Press.

———. 2000. "Sociality and Sexuality." *Critical Inquiry* 26 (4): 641–656.

———. 2009. *Is the Rectum a Grave? And Other Essays*. Chicago: University of Chicago Press.

Bersani, Leo, and Adam Phillips. 2008. *Intimacies*. Chicago: University of Chicago Press.

Best, Stephen M. 2004. *The Fugitive's Properties: Law and the Poetics of Possession*. Chicago: University of Chicago Press.

Bestor, Jane Fair. 2003. "Titian's Portrait of Laura Eustochia: The Decorum of Female Beauty and the Motif of the Black Page." *Renaissance Studies* 17 (4): 628–673.

Black AIDS Institute. 2011. "AIDS: 30 Years Is ENUF! The History of the AIDS Epidemic in Black America." Black AIDS Institute, Los Angeles. Accessed December 4, 2015. https://www.Blackaids.org/images/reports/enuf.pdf.

Bor, Jonathan. 2007. "An Epidemic's Unseen Cause." *Baltimore Sun*, November 4. Accessed December 4, 2015. http://articles.baltimoresun.com/2007-11-04/news/0711040035_1_living-with-hiv-hiv-or-aids-aids-diagnoses.

Bosniak, Linda. 2006. *The Citizen and the Alien: Dilemmas of Contemporary Citizenship*. Princeton, NJ: Princeton University Press.

Bost, Darius. 2015. "At the Club: Locating Early Black Gay AIDS Activism in Washington, D.C." *Occasion* 8:1–9.

Brandzel, Amy. 2016. *Against Citizenship: The Violence of the Normative*. Champaign: University of Illinois Press.

Brooks, Richard R. W. 2002. "Covenants and Conventions." Northwestern Law and Economics Research Paper no. 02-8. Accessed December 4, 2015. http://papers.ssrn.com/sol3/papers.cfm?abstract_id=353723.

Brown, Michael. 2006. "Sexual Citizenship, Political Obligation and Disease Ecology in Gay Seattle." *Political Geography* 25 (8): 874–898.

Brown, Vincent. 2009. "Social Death and Political Life in the Study of Slavery." *American Historical Review* 114 (5): 1231–1249.

Brown, Wendy. 1995. *States of Injury: Power and Freedom in Late Modernity*. Princeton, NJ: Princeton University Press.

Browne, Kath, Andrew Kam-Tuck Yip, and Sally R. Munt, eds. 2010. *Queer Spiritual Spaces: Sexuality and Sacred Places*. Farnham, UK: Ashgate.

Browne, Simone. 2015. *Dark Matters: On the Surveillance of Blackness*. Durham, NC: Duke University Press.

Butler, Judith. 2006. *Precarious Life: The Powers of Mourning and Violence*. London: Verso.

———. 2010. *Frames of War: When Is Life Grievable?* Reprint, London: Verso.

Butler, Judith, Ernesto Laclau, and Slavoj Žižek. 2000. *Contingency, Hegemony, Universality: Contemporary Dialogues on the Left*. London: Verso.

Canguilhem, Georges. 2008. "Health: Crude Concept and Philosophical Question." *Public Culture* 20 (3): 467–477.

Carrette, Jeremy R. 2000. *Foucault and Religion: Spiritual Corporality and Political Spirituality*. London: Routledge.

Centers for Disease Control and Prevention (CDC). 2011. "CDC's New High-Impact Approach to HIV Prevention Funding for Health Departments: Advancing the

National HIV/AIDS Strategy." July 21. Accessed December 4, 2015. http://www.cdc.gov/hiv/funding/announcements/ps12-1201/factsheet.html.

Cervenak, Sarah Jane, and J. Kameron Carter. 2017. "Untitled and Outdoors: Thinking with Saidiya Hartman." *Women and Performance* 27 (1): 45–55.

Chen, Mel Y. 2012. *Animacies: Biopolitics, Racial Mattering, and Queer Affect*. Durham, NC: Duke University Press.

Chen, Mel Y., and Dana Luciano, eds. 2015. "Queer Inhumanisms." *GLQ* 21 (2–3): 183–422.

Clark, Laurel A. 2007. "Beyond the Gay/Straight Split: Socialist Feminists in Baltimore." *NWSA Journal* 19 (2): 1–31.

Clayton, Ralph. 2000. "A Bitter Inner Harbor Legacy: The Slave Trade." *Baltimore Sun*, July 12. Accessed December 4, 2015. http://articles.baltimoresun.com/2000-07-12/news/0007120236_1_slave-pens-pratt-street-slave-trade.

Cobb, Michael L. 2001. "Pulpitic Publicity: James Baldwin and the Queer Uses of Religious Words." *GLQ* 7 (2): 285–312.

Cohen, Cathy J. 1999. *The Boundaries of Blackness: AIDS and the Breakdown of Black Politics*. Chicago: University of Chicago Press.

Cohen, Ed. 2009. *A Body Worth Defending: Immunity, Biopolitics, and the Apotheosis of the Modern Body*. Durham, NC: Duke University Press.

Cohen, Myron S., Ying Q. Chen, Marybeth McCauley, Theresa Gamble, Mina C. Hosseinipour, Nagalingeswaran Kumarasamy, James G. Hakim, et al. 2011. "Prevention of HIV-1 Infection with Early Antiretroviral Therapy." *New England Journal of Medicine* 365 (6): 493–505.

Cohn, Meredith. 2010. "Baltimore Names Its First Food Czar." *Baltimore Sun*, May 11. Accessed December 4, 2015. http://articles.baltimoresun.com/2010-05-11/health/bs-hs-food-policy-director-20100511_1_food-czar-healthful-ebt-machines.

Collins, Patricia Hill. 2004. *Black Sexual Politics: African Americans, Gender, and the New Racism*. New York: Routledge.

Condorelli, Céline, ed. 2014. *Support Structures*. Berlin: Sternberg.

Cone, James H. 2010. *A Black Theology of Liberation*. Fortieth anniversary ed. Maryknoll, NY: Orbis.

Coole, Diana. 2000. *Negativity and Politics: Dionysus and Dialectics from Kant to Poststructuralism*. London: Routledge.

Copeland, Huey, and Naomi Beckwith. 2014. "Black Collectivities: An Introduction." *Nka Journal of Contemporary African Art* 2014 (34): 4–7.

Copeland, M. Shawn. 2013. "Blackness Past, Blackness Future—and Theology." *South Atlantic Quarterly* 112 (4): 625–640.

Cossman, Brenda. 2007. *Sexual Citizens: The Legal and Cultural Regulation of Sex and Belonging*. Stanford, CA: Stanford University Press.

Crawley, Ashon. 2008. "Circum-religious Performance: Queer(ed) Black Bodies and the Black Church." *Theology and Sexuality* 14 (2): 201–222.

———. 2013a. "Blackqueer Aesthesis: Sexuality and the Rumor and Gossip of Black Gospel." In *Race and Displacement: Nation, Migration, and Identity in the Twenty-First Century*, ed. Maha Marouan and Merinda Simmons, 27–42. Tuscaloosa: University of Alabama Press.

———. 2013b. "Breathing Flesh and the Sound of BlackPentecostalism." *Theology and Sexuality* 19 (1): 49–60.
———. 2015. "Otherwise, Instituting." *Performance Research* 20 (4): 85–89.
———. 2017. *BlackPentecostal Breath: The Aesthetics of Possibility*. New York: Fordham University Press.
Crenson, Matthew A. 2017. *Baltimore: A Political History*. Baltimore: Johns Hopkins University Press.
Crimp, Douglas, ed. 1988. *Cultural Analysis, Cultural Activism*. Cambridge, MA: MIT Press.
Cruz, Ariane. 2015. "Beyond Black and Blue: BDSM, Internet Pornography, and Black Female Sexuality." *Feminist Studies* 41 (2): 409–436.
———. 2016a. *The Color of Kink: Black Women, BDSM, and Pornography*. New York: New York University Press.
———. 2016b. "Playing with the Politics of Perversion: Policing BDSM, Pornography, and Black Female Sexuality." *Souls* 18 (2–4): 379–407.
Das, Moupali, Priscilla Lee Chu, Glenn-Milo Santos, Susan Scheer, Eric Vittinghoff, Willi McFarland, and Grant N. Colfax. 2010. "Decreases in Community Viral Load Are Accompanied by Reductions in New HIV Infections in San Francisco." *PloS One* 5 (6): e11068.
Davies, Jonathan S., and Madeleine Pill. 2012. "Hollowing Out Neighbourhood Governance? Rescaling Revitalisation in Baltimore and Bristol." *Urban Studies* 49 (10): 2199–2217.
Davis, Mark. 2008. "The 'Loss of Community' and Other Problems for Sexual Citizenship in Recent HIV Prevention." *Sociology of Health and Illness* 30 (2): 182–196.
Dean, Tim. 2009. *Unlimited Intimacy: Reflections on the Subculture of Barebacking*. Chicago: University of Chicago Press.
de Lauretis, Teresa. 2011. "Queer Texts, Bad Habits, and the Issue of a Future." *GLQ* 17 (2–3): 243–263.
Deleuze, Gilles. 1980. "Seminar on Spinoza." Lecture delivered at the University of Vincennes, Paris, November 25. Accessed December 4, 2015. http://deleuzelectures.blogspot.nl/2007/02/on-spinoza.html.
Deutscher, Penelope. 2013. "The Membrane and the Diaphragm: Derrida and Esposito on Immunity, Community, and Birth." *Angelaki* 18 (3): 49–68.
Dillon, Stephen. 2013. "'It's Here, It's That Time': Race, Queer Futurity, and the Temporality of Violence in *Born in Flames*." *Women and Performance* 23 (1): 38–51.
Dinshaw, Carolyn, Lee Edelman, Roderick A. Ferguson, Carla Freccero, Elizabeth Freeman, Judith Halberstam, Annamarie Jagose, Christopher S. Nealon, and Tan Hoang Nguyen. 2007. "Theorizing Queer Temporalities: A Roundtable Discussion." *GLQ* 13 (2): 177–195.
Donà, Massimo. 2006. "Immunity and Negation: On Possible Developments of the Theses Outlined in Roberto Esposito's *Immunitas*." *Diacritics* 36 (2): 57–69.
Douglass, Patrice, and Frank B. Wilderson III. 2013. "The Violence of Presence: Metaphysics in a Blackened World." *Black Scholar* 43 (4): 117–123.
Drabinski, Kate. 2015. "Recording the Rainbow Revolution: As Gay Bars in Baltimore Shut Their Doors, Activists Work to Document LGBTQ History." *Baltimore City*

Paper, July 21. Accessed December 4, 2015. http://www.citypaper.com/news/features/bcp-072215-feature-preserving-lgbt-history-20150721-story.html.

Duggan, Lisa. 2003. *The Twilight of Equality? Neoliberalism, Cultural Politics, and the Attack on Democracy*. Boston: Beacon.

Edelman, Lee. 2004. *No Future: Queer Theory and the Death Drive*. Durham, NC: Duke University Press.

———. 2007. "Ever After: History, Negativity, and the Social." *South Atlantic Quarterly* 106 (3): 469–476.

———. 2011. "Against Survival: Queerness in a Time That's Out of Joint." *Shakespeare Quarterly* 62 (2): 148–169.

Elfenbein, Jessica, Thomas Hollowak, and Elizabeth Nix. 2011. *Baltimore '68: Riots and Rebirth in an American City*. Philadelphia: Temple University Press.

Eng, David L. 2010. *The Feeling of Kinship: Queer Liberalism and the Racialization of Intimacy*. Durham, NC: Duke University Press.

Esposito, Roberto. 2008. *Bíos: Biopolitics and Philosophy*. Minneapolis: University of Minnesota Press.

———. 2009. "Community and Nihilism." In *The Italian Difference: Between Nihilism and Biopolitics*, ed. Lorenzo Chiesa and Alberto Toscano, 37–54. Melbourne: Re.press.

———. 2010a. *Communitas: The Origin and Destiny of Community*. Stanford, CA: Stanford University Press.

———. 2010b. "For a Philosophy of the Impersonal." *CR: The New Centennial Review* 10 (2): 121–134.

———. 2011. *Immunitas: The Protection and Negation of Life*. Cambridge: Polity.

Evans, David T. 1993. *Sexual Citizenship: The Material Construction of Sexualities*. London: Routledge.

Fanon, Frantz. (1967) 2008. *Black Skin, White Masks*, trans. C. L. Markmann. London: Pluto.

Fassin, Didier. 2009. "Another Politics of Life Is Possible." *Theory, Culture and Society* 26 (5): 44–60.

———. 2014. "True Life, Real Lives: Revisiting the Boundaries between Ethnography and Fiction." *American Ethnologist* 41 (1): 40–55.

Fenton, Kevin A. 2007. "Changing Epidemiology of HIV/AIDS in the United States: Implications for Enhancing and Promoting HIV Testing Strategies." *Clinical Infectious Diseases* 45 (supp. 4): S213–220.

Ferguson, Roderick A. 2004. *Aberrations in Black: Toward a Queer of Color Critique*. Critical American Studies. Minneapolis: University of Minnesota Press.

Fernández-Kelly, Patricia. 2015. *The Hero's Fight: African Americans in West Baltimore and the Shadow of the State*. Princeton, NJ: Princeton University Press.

Florida, Richard L. 2002. *The Rise of the Creative Class: And How It's Transforming Work, Leisure, Community and Everyday Life*. New York: Basic.

Floyd, Kevin. 2010. "The Importance of Being Childish: Queer Utopians and Historical Contradiction." *Cultural Logic: An Electronic Journal of Marxist Theory and Practice*. Accessed December 4, 2015. http://clogic.eserver.org/2010/floyd.pdf.

Foucault, Michel. 1988. "Power and Sex." In *Politics, Philosophy, Culture: Interviews and Other Writings, 1977–1984*, ed. Lawrence D. Kritzman, 110–124. London: Routledge.

———. 1990a. *The History of Sexuality, Volume 1: An Introduction*, trans. Robert Hurley. New York: Random House.

———. 1990b. *The History of Sexuality, Volume 2: The Use of Pleasure*, trans. Robert Hurley. New York: Random House.

———. 1996. *Foucault Live: Interviews, 1966–1984*, ed. Sylvère Lotringer. New York: Semiotext(e).

———. 2003. *"Society Must Be Defended": Lectures at the Collège de France, 1975–1976*, ed. Mauro Bertani, Alessandro Fontana, and François Ewald, trans. David Macey. New York: Macmillan.

———. 2007. "What Is Critique?" In *The Politics of Truth*, ed. Sylvère Lotringer, 23–82. Los Angeles: Semiotext(e).

———. 2010. *The Government of Self and Others: Lectures at the Collège de France, 1982–1983*. New York: Macmillan.

———. 2011. *The Courage of Truth: Lectures at the Collège de France, 1983–1984*, trans. Graham Burchell. New York: Picador.

Freire, Paulo. (1970) 2000. *Pedagogy of the Oppressed*. New York: Bloomsbury.

Gallant, Zachary. 2015. "First, Do No Harm? The Johns Hopkins System's Toxic Legacy in Baltimore." *The Leveller*, August 18. Accessed December 4, 2015. http://theleveller.org/2015/08/first-do-no-harm-the-johns-hopkins-systems-toxic-legacy-in-baltimore.

Geoghegan, Bernard Dionysius. 2011. "From Information Theory to French Theory: Jakobson, Levi-Strauss, and the Cybernetic Apparatus." *Critical Inquiry* 38 (1): 96–126.

German, Danielle, and Carl A. Latkin. 2012. "Social Stability and HIV Risk Behavior: Evaluating the Role of Accumulated Vulnerability." *AIDS and Behavior* 16 (1): 168–178.

German, Danielle, Frangiscos Sifakis, Cathy Maulsby, Vivian L. Towe, Colin P. Flynn, Carl A. Latkin, David D. Celentano, Heather Hauck, and David R. Holtgrave. 2011. "Persistently High Prevalence and Unrecognized HIV Infection among Men Who Have Sex with Men in Baltimore: The BESURE Study:" *JAIDS Journal of Acquired Immune Deficiency Syndromes* 57 (1): 77–87.

Giffney, Noreen, and Myra J. Hird, eds. 2008. *Queering the Non/Human*. Aldershot, UK: Ashgate.

Gold, Thea. 2010. "Is Queer Secular? Netalie Braun's Gevald." *GLQ* 16 (4): 623–633.

Goldberg, David Theo. 2009. *The Threat of Race: Reflections on Racial Neoliberalism*. Malden, MA: Wiley-Blackwell.

Goltz, Dustin Bradley. 2013. "It Gets Better: Queer Futures, Critical Frustrations, and Radical Potentials." *Critical Studies in Media Communication* 30 (2): 135–151.

Gomez, Marisela B. 2012. *Race, Class, Power, and Organizing in East Baltimore: Rebuilding Abandoned Communities in America*. Lanham, MD: Rowman and Littlefield.

Granich, Reuben M., Charles F. Gilks, Christopher Dye, Kevin M. De Cock, and Brian G. Williams. 2009. "Universal Voluntary HIV Testing with Immediate Antiretroviral Therapy as a Strategy for Elimination of HIV Transmission: A Mathematical Model." *The Lancet* 373 (9657): 48–57.

Hägglund, Martin. 2008. *Radical Atheism: Derrida and the Time of Life*. Stanford, CA: Stanford University Press.

———. 2009. "Chronolibidinal Reading: Deconstruction and Psychoanalysis." *CR: The New Centennial Review* 9 (1): 1–43.

Hall, H. Irene, Lorena Espinoza, Nanette Benbow, and Yunyin W. Hu. 2010. "Epidemiology of HIV Infection in Large Urban Areas in the United States." *PloS One* 5 (9): e12756.

Halperin, David M. 2007. *What Do Gay Men Want? An Essay on Sex, Risk, and Subjectivity*. Ann Arbor: University of Michigan Press.

Hanhardt, Christina B. 2013. *Safe Space: Gay Neighborhood History and the Politics of Violence*. Durham, NC: Duke University Press.

Hanson, Ellis. 2011. "The Future's Eve: Reparative Reading after Sedgwick." *South Atlantic Quarterly* 110 (1): 101–119.

Haraway, Donna J. 1991. *Simians, Cyborgs, and Women: The Reinvention of Nature*. New York: Routledge.

Harney, Stefano, and Fred Moten. 2013. *The Undercommons: Fugitive Planning and Black Studies*. New York: Minor Composition.

Hartman, Saidiya V. 1997. *Scenes of Subjection: Terror, Slavery and Self-Making in Nineteenth Century America*. Oxford: Oxford University Press.

———. 2007. *Lose Your Mother: A Journey along the Atlantic Slave Route*. New York: Farrar, Straus and Giroux.

Hartman, Saidiya V, and Frank B. Wilderson III. 2003. "The Position of the Unthought." *Qui Parle* 13 (2): 183–201.

Harvey, David. 1989. "From Managerialism to Entrepreneurialism: The Transformation in Urban Governance in Late Capitalism." *Geografiska Annaler: Series B, Human Geography* 71 (1): 3–17.

———. 2001. *Spaces of Capital: Towards a Critical Geography*. New York: Routledge.

HIV Stops with Me. 2011. "HIV Stops with Me: National HIV Prevention Campaign." Accessed December 4, 2015. http://www.hivstopswithme.org/about.

Hofmann, Regan. 2011. "R.I.P. HIV." *POZ Magazine*. October–November, 30–39. Accessed November 24, 2018. https://issuu.com/smartandstrong/docs/poz_hiv_aids_0175.

Holbraad, Martin, Morten Axel Pedersen, and Eduardo Viveiros de Castro. 2014. "The Politics of Ontology: Anthropological Positions." *Cultural Anthropology Online*. Accessed December 4, 2015. http://culanth.org/fieldsights/462-the-politics-of-ontology-anthropological-positions.

Holmes, Kwame. 2015. "What's the Tea: Gossip and the Production of Black Gay Social History." *Radical History Review* 122:55–69.

Honig, Bonnie. 2009. *Emergency Politics: Paradox, Law, Democracy*. Reprint, Princeton, NJ: Princeton University Press.

Hunt, Stephen, ed. 2009. *Contemporary Christianity and LGBT Sexualities*. Farnham, UK: Ashgate.

Hyra, Derek S. 2006. "Racial Uplift? Intra-racial Class Conflict and the Economic Revitalization of Harlem and Bronzeville." *City and Community* 5 (1): 71–92.

Infectious Disease and Environmental Health Administration. 2011. "The Enhanced Comprehensive HIV Prevention Plan for the Baltimore-Towson Metropolitan Statistical Area: Executive Summary." Infectious Disease and Environmental Health Administration, Baltimore. Accessed December 4, 2015. http://www.cdc.gov/hiv/pdf/prevention_demonstrations_echpp_baltimore.pdf.

Isin, Engin F. 2002. *Being Political: Genealogies of Citizenship*. Minneapolis: University of Minnesota Press.

Jacobson, Joan. 2013. "Book on Hopkins Redevelopment by a Leader of the Opposition." *BaltimoreBrew*, February 19. Accessed December 4, 2015. https://www.baltimorebrew.com/2013/02/19/book-on-hopkins-redevelopment-by-a-leader-of-the-opposition.

Jakobsen, Janet R., and Ann Pellegrini. 2003. *Love the Sin: Sexual Regulation and the Limits of Religious Tolerance*. New York: New York University Press.

James, William. 1996. *A Pluralistic Universe: Hilbert Lectures at Manchester College on the Present Situation in Philosophy*. Lincoln: University of Nebraska Press.

———. 2004. *The Varieties of Religious Experience: A Study in Human Nature*. New York: Barnes and Noble Classics.

Jeffries, Judson L. 2010. *On the Ground: The Black Panther Party in Communities across America*. Jackson: University Press of Mississippi.

Jensen, Brennen. 1996. "Forget Me Not: Anti-AIDS Effort Focuses on Men of Color." *Baltimore City Paper*, January 31. Accessed December 14, 2017. http://www.damngoodman.com/art_aids_01.pdf.

Jivraj, Suhraiya, and Anisa de Jong. 2011. "The Dutch Homo-Emancipation Policy and Its Silencing Effects on Queer Muslims." *Feminist Legal Studies* 19 (2): 143–158.

Johnson, E. Patrick. 1998. "Feeling the Spirit in the Dark: Expanding Notions of the Sacred in the African-American Gay Community." *Callaloo* 21 (2): 399–416.

———. 2008. *Sweet Tea: Black Gay Men of the South*. Chapel Hill: University of North Carolina Press.

———. 2016. *No Tea, No Shade: New Writings in Black Queer Studies*. Durham, NC: Duke University Press.

Johnson, E. Patrick, and Mae G. Henderson, eds. 2005. *Black Queer Studies: A Critical Anthology*. Durham, NC: Duke University Press.

Jung, Moon-Kie, João Costa Vargas, and Eduardo Bonilla-Silva, eds. 2011. *State of White Supremacy: Racism, Governance, and the United States*. Stanford, CA: Stanford University Press.

Justice Policy Institute and Prison Policy Initiative. 2015. "The Right Investment? Corrections Spending in Baltimore City." *Prison Policy Initiative*, February. Accessed December 4, 2015. http://www.prisonpolicy.org/origin/md/report.html.

Keeling, Kara. 2007. *The Witch's Flight: The Cinematic, the Black Femme, and the Image of Common Sense*. Durham, NC: Duke University Press.

———. 2009. "Looking for M—: Queer Temporality, Black Political Possibility, and Poetry from the Future." *GLQ* 15 (4): 565–582.
Kerekes, Carrie B., and Dean Stansel. 2014. "Takings and Tax Revenue: Fiscal Impacts of Eminent Domain." Mercatus Working Paper. Mercatus Center, George Mason University, Arlington, VA. Accessed December 4, 2015. http://mercatus.org/pub lication/takings-and-tax-revenue-fiscal-impacts-eminent-domain.
Lafontaine, Céline. 2007. "The Cybernetic Matrix of 'French Theory.'" *Theory, Culture and Society* 24 (5): 27–46.
Latour, Bruno. 1993. *The Pasteurization of France*, trans. Alan Sheridan and John Law. Cambridge, MA: Harvard University Press.
———. 2001. "'Thou Shall Not Take the Lord's Name in Vain': Being a Sort of Sermon on the Hesitations of Religious Speech." *RES: Anthropology and Aesthetics* 39:215–234.
———. 2002. "Morality and Technology: The End of the Means." Translated by Couze Venn. *Theory, Culture and Society* 19 (5–6): 247–260.
———. 2010a. "An Attempt at a 'Compositionist Manifesto.'" *New Literary History* 41 (3): 471–490.
———. 2010b. *On the Modern Cult of the Factish Gods*. Durham, NC: Duke University Press.
———. 2011. "Reflections on Etienne Souriau's *Les différents modes d'existence*." In *The Speculative Turn: Continental Materialism and Realism*, ed. Levi Bryant, Nick Srnicek, and Graham Harman and translated by Stephen Muecke, 304–333. Melbourne: Re.press.
Lenius, Steve. 2010. *Life, Leather and the Pursuit of Happiness: Life, History and Culture in the Leather/BDSM/Fetish Community*. Minneapolis, MN: Nelson Borhek Press.
Lim, Jason. 2010. "Immanent Politics: Thinking Race and Ethnicity through Affect and Machinism." *Environment and Planning A* 42 (10): 2393–2409.
Lincoln, Eric C., and Lawrence H. Mamiya. 1990. *The Black Church in the African American Experience*. Durham, NC: Duke University Press.
Linton, Sabriya L., Jacky M. Jennings, Carl A. Latkin, Gregory D. Kirk, and Shruti H. Mehta. 2014. "The Association between Neighborhood Residential Rehabilitation and Injection Drug Use in Baltimore, Maryland, 2000–2011." *Health and Place* 28 (July): 142–149.
Lister, Ruth. 1997. "Citizenship: Towards a Feminist Synthesis." *Feminist Review* 57:28–48.
———. 2002. "Sexual Citizenship." In *Handbook of Citizenship Studies*, ed. Engin F. Isin and Bryan S. Turner, 191–208. London: Sage.
Liu, Lydia H. 2010. "The Cybernetic Unconscious: Rethinking Lacan, Poe, and French Theory." *Critical Inquiry* 36 (2): 288–320.
Manago, Cleo. 1996. "A Critical Thinking and Cultural Affirmation (CTCA) Approach to HIV Prevention and Risk Reduction, Consciousness, and Practice for African American Males at HIV Sexual Risk." Los Angeles: AmASSI Center.
Mandarini, Matteo. 2009. "Beyond Nihilism: Notes towards a Critique of Left-Heideggerianism in Italian Philosophy of the 1970s." *Cosmos and History: The Journal of Natural and Social Philosophy* 5 (1): 37–56.

Marks, Susan. 2011. "Law and the Production of Superfluity." *Transnational Legal Theory* 2 (1): 1–24.
Mbembe, Joseph-Achille. 2003. "Necropolitics." Translated by Libby Meintjes. *Public Culture* 15 (1): 11–40.
———. 2004. "Aesthetics of Superfluity." *Public Culture* 16 (3): 373–405.
McClintock, Anne. 1995. *Imperial Leather: Race, Gender, and Sexuality in the Colonial Contest*. New York: Routledge.
McDougall, Harold A. 1993. *Black Baltimore: A New Theory of Community*. Philadelphia: Temple University Press.
McKittrick, Katherine. 2013. "Plantation Futures." *Small Axe* 17 (3 [42]): 1–15.
McNay, Lois. 2014. *The Misguided Search for the Political*. Cambridge: Polity.
McRoberts, Omar M. 2003. *Streets of Glory: Church and Community in a Black Urban Neighborhood*. Chicago: University of Chicago Press.
Meehan, Sarah. 2015. "Baltimore Eagle, a Landmark Gay Bar, Nears Reopening despite Struggles with the City." *Baltimore Business Journal*, June 25. Accessed December 4, 2015. http://www.bizjournals.com/baltimore/blog/charm-city-flavor/2015/06/baltimore-eagle-a-landmark-gay-bar-nears-reopening.html.
Melamed, Jodi. 2011. *Represent and Destroy: Rationalizing Violence in the New Racial Capitalism*. Minneapolis: University of Minnesota Press.
Meyer, Birgit. 2008. "Religious Sensations: Why Media, Aesthetics, and Power Matter in the Study of Contemporary Religion." In *Religion: Beyond a Concept*, ed. Hent de Vries, 704–723. New York: Fordham University Press.
Mezzadra, Sandro, and Brett Neilson. 2013. *Border as Method, Or, the Multiplication of Labor*. Durham, NC: Duke University Press.
Miller, Courtney. 2015. "The Top LGBT-Friendly Cities in the U.S." *NerdWallet*, May 27. Accessed December 4, 2015. http://www.nerdwallet.com/blog/cities/lifestyle/top-lgbt-friendly-cities-2015.
Miller, Robert L., Jr. 2005. "An Appointment with God: AIDS, Place, and Spirituality." *Journal of Sex Research* 42 (1): 35–45.
Mitter, Siddhartha. 2018. "Gentrify or Die? Inside a University's Controversial Plan for Baltimore." *The Guardian*, April 18. Accessed November 24, 2018. https://www.theguardian.com/cities/2018/apr/18/gentrify-or-die-inside-a-universitys-controversial-plan-for-baltimore.
Moisse, Katie. 2011. "Baltimore Hospital Sued over Lead Study." *ABC News*, September 16. Accessed December 4, 2015. http://abcnews.go.com/Health/Wellness/baltimores-kennedy-krieger-institute-sued-lead-paint-study/story?id=14536695.
Moore, Marlon Rachquel. 2008. "Black Church, Black Patriarchy, and the 'Brilliant Queer': Competing Masculinities in Langston Hughes's 'Blessed Assurance.'" *African American Review* 42 (3–4): 493–502.
Moten, Fred. 2003. *In the Break: The Aesthetics of the Black Radical Tradition*. Minneapolis: University of Minnesota Press. Accessed December 4, 2015. http://muse.jhu.edu/books/9780816694525.
———. 2008. "The Case of Blackness." *Criticism* 50 (2): 177–218.
———. 2013a. "Blackness and Nothingness (Mysticism in the Flesh)." *South Atlantic Quarterly* 112 (4): 737–780.

———. 2013b. "The Subprime and the Beautiful." *African Identities* 11 (2): 237–245.

Muñoz, José Esteban. 2006. "Feeling Brown, Feeling Down: Latina Affect, the Performativity of Race, and the Depressive Position." *Signs* 31 (3): 675–688.

———. 2009. *Cruising Utopia: The Then and There of Queer Futurity*. New York: New York University Press.

Nancy, Jean-Luc. 1997. *The Sense of the World*, trans. Jeffrey S. Librett. Minneapolis: University of Minnesota Press.

Negri, Antonio. 1991. *The Savage Anomaly: The Power of Spinoza's Metaphysics and Politics*, trans. Michael Hardt. Minneapolis: University of Minnesota Press.

Ngai, Sianne. 2005. *Ugly Feelings: Literature, Affect, and Ideology*. Cambridge, MA: Harvard University Press.

Nguyen, Vinh-Kim. 2010. *The Republic of Therapy: Triage and Sovereignty in West Africa's Time of AIDS*. Durham, NC: Duke University Press.

Noys, Benjamin. (2008) 2010. *The Persistence of the Negative: A Critique of Contemporary Continental Philosophy*. Edinburgh: Edinburgh University Press.

Ong, Aihwa. 1999. *Flexible Citizenship: The Cultural Logics of Transnationality*. Durham, NC: Duke University Press.

Opondo, Sam Okoth. 2015. "Biocolonial and Racial Entanglements: Immunity, Community, and Superfluity in the Name of Humanity." *Alternatives: Global, Local, Political* 40 (2): 115–132.

Parker Kelley, Louise. 2015. *LGBT Baltimore*. Charleston, SC: Arcadia Publishing.

Patterson, Orlando. 1982. *Slavery and Social Death: A Comparative Study*. Cambridge, MA: Harvard University Press.

Peay, Ralph James. 1996a. "Interview with 'Renaissance Man' Dale Madison." *Baltimore Gay Paper*, February 2. Accessed December 10, 2017. http://www.damngoodman.com/art_ren_01.pdf.

———. 1996b. "The Rich and Vibrant History of Black Gay Bars and Clubs in Baltimore." *Baltimore Gay Paper* 17, no. 11 (March 1).

Pellegrini, Ann. 2005. "Testimony and Sexuality: Or, Queer Structures of Religious Feeling: Notes Toward an Investigation." *Journal of Dramatic Theory and Criticism* 20 (1): 93–102.

Petryna, Adriana. 2002. *Biological Citizenship: Science and the Politics of Health after Chernobyl*. Princeton, NJ: Princeton University Press.

Philipsen, Klaus. 2015. "Next: A Resurgence of Community Development?" *Sustainable Cities Collective*, June 8. Accessed December 4, 2015. http://www.sustainablecitiescollective.com/klaus-philipsen/1079901/next-resurgence-community-development.

Phillips, Christopher. 1997. *Freedom's Port: The African American Community of Baltimore, 1790–1860*. Urbana: University of Illinois Press.

Pietila, Antero. 2010. *Not in My Neighborhood: How Bigotry Shaped a Great American City*. Chicago: Ivan R. Dee.

Pilkington, Ed. 2014. "Fear and Violence in Transgender Baltimore: 'It's Scary Trusting Anyone.'" *The Guardian*, August 1. Accessed December 4, 2015. http://www.theguardian.com/world/2014/aug/01/murder-transgender-women-baltimore-heighten-fears-mia-henderson.

Plummer, Ken. 2003. *Intimate Citizenship: Private Decisions and Public Dialogues.* Seattle: University of Washington Press.

Ponzini, Davide. 2009. "Urban Implications of Cultural Policy Networks: The Case of the Mount Vernon Cultural District in Baltimore." *Environment and Planning C: Government and Policy* 27 (3): 433–450.

Ponzini, Davide, and Ugo Rossi. 2010. "Becoming a Creative City: The Entrepreneurial Mayor, Network Politics and the Promise of an Urban Renaissance." *Urban Studies* 47 (5): 1037–1057.

Povinelli, Elizabeth A. 2006. *The Empire of Love: Toward a Theory of Intimacy, Genealogy, and Carnality.* Durham, NC: Duke University Press.

———. 2011a. *Economies of Abandonment: Social Belonging and Endurance in Late Liberalism.* Durham, NC: Duke University Press.

———. 2011b. "Routes/Worlds." *E-flux* 27 (September): 1–12. Accessed December 4, 2015. http://www.e-flux.com/journal/routesworlds.

———. 2012. "The Will to Be Otherwise/The Effort of Endurance." *South Atlantic Quarterly* 111 (3): 453–475.

Powell, Michael. 2009. "Bank Accused of Pushing Mortgage Deals on Blacks." *New York Times,* June 6. Accessed December 4, 2015. http://www.nytimes.com/2009/06/07/us/07baltimore.html.

Power, Garrett. 1983. "Apartheid Baltimore Style: The Residential Segregation Ordinances of 1910–1913." *Maryland Law Review* 42 (2): 289–328.

Project Inform. 2010. "TLC+: Testing and Linkage to Care Plus." Washington, DC: Project Inform.

Puar, Jasbir K. 2007. *Terrorist Assemblages: Homonationalism in Queer Times.* Durham, NC: Duke University Press.

———. 2009. "Prognosis Time: Towards a Geopolitics of Affect, Debility and Capacity." *Women and Performance: A Journal of Feminist Theory* 19 (2): 161–172.

———. 2010. "In the Wake of It Gets Better." *The Guardian,* November 16. Accessed December 4, 2015. http://www.theguardian.com/commentisfree/cifamerica/2010/nov/16/wake-it-gets-better-campaign.

———. 2012. "Coda: The Cost of Getting Better Suicide, Sensation, Switchpoints." *GLQ* 18 (1): 149–158.

Puhak, Shelley. 2015. "A Ghost Tour of Baltimore's Riots." *The Weeklings,* May 12. Accessed December 4, 2015. http://www.theweeklings.com/spuhak/2015/05/12/a-ghost-tour-of-baltimores-riots.

Race, Kane. 2001. "The Undetectable Crisis: Changing Technologies of Risk." *Sexualities* 4 (2): 167–189.

Rector, Kevin. 2014. "In Shift from Tradition, Pride Events to Be Held in Artscape Location." *Baltimore Sun,* May 7. Accessed December 4, 2015. http://articles.baltimoresun.com/2014-05-07/features/bs-gm-all-gay-pride-events-to-be-held-in-artscape-location-20140507_1_block-party-baltimore-pride-gino-cardinale.

———. 2015. "Looking Out: After Cleaning House, GLCCB to Host 'Grand Reopening.'" *Baltimore Sun,* April 3. Accessed January 2016. http://www.baltimoresun.com/features/gay-in-maryland/gay-matters/bs-gm-looking-out-glccb-cleans-house-announces-reopening-20150403-story.html.

Reddy, Chandan. 2011. *Freedom with Violence: Race, Sexuality, and the US State*. Perverse Modernities. Durham, NC: Duke University Press.

Reid, Julian. 2011. "The Vulnerable Subject of Liberal War." *South Atlantic Quarterly* 110 (3): 770–779.

Relman, John P. 2010. "Third Amended Complaint for Declaratory and Injunctive Relief and Damages." U.S. District Court for the District of Maryland, Baltimore Division. Accessed December 4, 2015. http://www.relmanlaw.com/docs/Baltimore-Complaint.pdf.

Rivera, John. 2002. "Not All Praise New Focus in Black Churches." *Los Angeles Times*, August 31. Accessed December 4, 2015. http://articles.latimes.com/2002/aug/31/local/me-pentecostal31.

Rivera Colón, Edgar. 2009. "Getting Life in Two Worlds: Power and Prevention in the New York City House Ball Community." Ph.D. diss., Rutgers University.

Rodríguez, Juana María. 2011. "Queer Sociality and Other Sexual Fantasies." *GLQ* 17 (2–3): 331–348.

Ross, Dax-Devlon. 2013. "The Great East Baltimore Raze-and-Rebuild." *Next City*, July 29. Accessed December 4, 2015. https://nextcity.org/features/view/the-great-east-baltimore-raze-and-rebuild.

Rossing, Jonathan P. 2014. "Critical Race Humor in a Postracial Moment: Richard Pryor's Contemporary *Parrhesia*." *Howard Journal of Communications* 25 (1): 16–33.

Ruti, Mari. 2008. "The Fall of Fantasies: A Lacanian Reading of Lack." *Journal of the American Psychoanalytic Association* 56 (2): 483–508.

Sahlins, Marshall. 2013. *What Kinship Is—and Is Not*. Chicago: University of Chicago Press.

Schindler, Sarah. 2015. "Architectural Exclusion: Discrimination and Segregation through Physical Design of the Built Environment." *Yale Law Journal* 124 (6): 1934–2189.

Schmitt, Carl. 2005. *Political Theology: Four Chapters on the Concept of Sovereignty*. Chicago: University of Chicago Press.

Scott, Darieck. 2010. *Extravagant Abjection: Blackness, Power, and Sexuality in the African American Literary Imagination*. New York: New York University Press.

Sedgwick, Eve Kosofsky. 2003. *Touching Feeling: Affect, Pedagogy, Performativity*. Durham, NC: Duke University Press.

Selby, Holly. 1994. "John Stuban, AIDS Activist, Dies." *Baltimore Sun*, August 16. Accessed December 4, 2015. http://articles.baltimoresun.com/1994-08-16/news/1994228007_1_aids-activism-aids-care-people-with-aids.

Sexton, Jared. 2008. *Amalgamation Schemes: Antiblackness and the Critique of Multiracialism*. Minneapolis: University of Minnesota Press.

———. 2010. "People-of-Color-Blindness: Notes on the Afterlife of Slavery." *Social Text* 28 (2 [103]): 31–56.

———. 2011. "The Social Life of Social Death: On Afro-pessimism and Black Optimism." *InTensions* 5:1–47.

———. 2012. "Ante-anti-Blackness: Afterthoughts." *Lateral* 1. Accessed November 25, 2018. http://csalateral.org/section/theory/ante-anti-blackness-afterthoughts-sexton.

Sexton, Jared, and Huey Copeland. 2003. "Raw Life: An Introduction." *Qui Parle* 13 (2): 53–62.

Shabazz, Rashad. 2015. *Spatializing Blackness: Architectures of Confinement and Black Masculinity in Chicago*. Champaign: University of Illinois Press.

Sharp, Hasana. 2009. "The Impersonal Is Political: Spinoza and a Feminist Politics of Imperceptibility." *Hypatia* 24 (4): 84–103.

Sharpe, Christina. 2010. *Monstrous Intimacies: Making Post-slavery Subjects*. Durham, NC: Duke University Press.

———. 2012. "Blackness, Sexuality, and Entertainment." *American Literary History* 24 (4): 827–841.

———. 2016. *In the Wake: On Blackness and Being*. Durham, NC: Duke University Press.

Shen, Fern. 2010. "Highway to Nowhere Coming Down? Not Really." *BaltimoreBrew*, September 24. Accessed December 4, 2015. https://www.baltimorebrew.com/2010/09/24/highway-to-nowhere-coming-down-not-really.

———. 2014. "Johns Hopkins Hospital Workers Protest 'Poverty Wage' Pay Scale." *BaltimoreBrew*, April 1. Accessed December 4, 2015. https://www.baltimorebrew.com/2014/04/01/johns-hopkins-hospital-workers-protest-poverty-wage-pay-scale.

Silk, Michael L. 2010. "Postcards from Pigtown." *Cultural Studies—Critical Methodologies* 10 (2): 143–156.

Silk, Michael L., and David L. Andrews. 2011. "(Re) Presenting Baltimore: Place, Policy, Politics, and Cultural Pedagogy." *Review of Education, Pedagogy, and Cultural Studies* 33 (5): 433–464.

Skloot, Rebecca. 2010. *The Immortal Life of Henrietta Lacks*. New York: Crown.

Smith, Neil. 1996. *The New Urban Frontier: Gentrification and the Revanchist City*. London: Routledge.

Smith, Van. 2015. "The Most Imprisoned Communities in Maryland Are Right next to Baltimore's Johns Hopkins Medical Campus." *Baltimore City Paper*, February 25. Accessed December 4, 2015. http://www.citypaper.com/blogs/the-news-hole/bcp-the-most-imprisoned-communities-in-maryland-are-right-next-to-baltimores-johns-hopkins-medical-campu-20150225-story.html.

Sneed, Roger. 2008. "Like Fire Shut Up in Our Bones: Religion and Spirituality in Black Gay Men's Literature." *Black Theology* 6 (2): 241–261.

Snorton, C. Riley. 2014. "'An Ambiguous Heterotopia' on the Past of Black Studies' Future." *Black Scholar* 44 (2): 29–36.

Spence, Lester K. 2012. "The Neoliberal Turn in Black Politics." *Souls* 14 (3–4): 139–159.

Spillers, Hortense J. 1987. "Mama's Baby, Papa's Maybe: An American Grammar Book." *diacritics* 17 (2): 65–81.

———. 2003. *Black, White, and in Color: Essays on American Literature and Culture*. Chicago: University of Chicago Press.

Stacey, Jackie. 2014. "Wishing Away Ambivalence." *Feminist Theory* 15 (1): 39–49.

Stack, Carol B. 1974. *All Our Kin: Strategies for Survival in a Black Community*. New York: Basic.

Stephenson, Joan. 2010. "Scientists Explore Use of Anti-HIV Drugs as a Means to Slow HIV Transmission." *JAMA* 303 (18): 1798–1799.

Stockton, Kathryn Bond. 2006. *Beautiful Bottom, Beautiful Shame: Where "Black" Meets "Queer."* Durham, NC: Duke University Press.

Stoler, Ann Laura. 2001. "Tense and Tender Ties: The Politics of Comparison in North American History and (Post) Colonial Studies." *Journal of American History* 88 (3): 829–865.

Stychin, Carl F. 2009. "Faith in the Future: Sexuality, Religion and the Public Sphere." *Oxford Journal of Legal Studies* 29 (4): 729–755.

Sullivan, Andrew. 2005. "The End of Gay Culture." *New Republic*, October 24. Accessed December 4, 2015. https://newrepublic.com/article/61118/the-end-gay-culture.

Sunder Rajan, Kaushik. 2006. *Biocapital: The Constitution of Postgenomic Life*. Durham, NC: Duke University Press.

Thacker, Eugene. 2010. *After Life*. Chicago: University of Chicago Press.

Thompson, Mark. 2004. *Leatherfolk: Radical Sex, People, Politics, and Practice*, rev. ed. Novato, CA: Daedalus.

Urban Land Institute. 2010. "The Westside, Baltimore Maryland: A Vision for the Westside Neighborhood." An Advisory Services Program Report. Washington, DC: Urban Land Institute. Accessed December 4, 2015. http://uli.org/wp-content/uploads/ULI-Documents/BaltimoreReport.pdf.

Van Doorn, Niels. 2013a. "Architectures of 'The Good Life': Queer Assemblages and the Composition of Intimate Citizenship." *Environment and Planning D: Society and Space* 31 (1): 157–173.

———. 2013b. "Assembling the Affective Field: How Smartphone Technology Impacts Ethnographic Research Practice." *Qualitative Inquiry* 19 (5): 385–396.

———. 2016. "The Fabric of Our Memories: Leather, Kinship, and Queer Material History." *Memory Studies* 9 (1): 85–98.

Villarejo, Amy. 2005. "Tarrying with the Normative: Queer Theory and Black History." *Social Text* 23 (3–4 [84–85]): 69–84.

Vogler, Candace A., and Patchen Markell. 2003. "Introduction: Violence, Redemption, and the Liberal Imagination." *Public Culture* 15 (1): 1–10.

Wachter-Grene, Kirin. 2016. "A Conversation with Ariane Cruz, by Kirin Wachter-Grene." *The Black Scholar* (website), November 7. Accessed May 11, 2017. http://www.theBlackscholar.org/conversation-ariane-cruz-kirin-wachter-grene.

Wagner, Bryan. 2009. *Disturbing the Peace: Black Culture and the Police Power after Slavery*. Cambridge, MA: Harvard University Press.

Walsh, Nastassia. 2010. "Baltimore behind Bars: How to Reduce the Jail Population, Save Money and Improve Public Safety." Washington, DC: Justice Policy Institute. Accessed December 4, 2015. http://www.justicepolicy.org/research/1917.

Warren, Calvin L. 2015. "Black Nihilism and the Politics of Hope." *CR: The New Centennial Review* 15 (1): 215–248.

Watson, Janell. 2012. "Butler's Biopolitics: Precarious Community." *Theory and Event* 15 (2). Accessed December 4, 2015. http://muse.jhu.edu/journals/theory_and_event/v015/15.2.watson.html.

Weber, Rachel. 2002. "Extracting Value from the City: Neoliberalism and Urban Redevelopment." *Antipode* 34 (3): 519–540.

Weeks, Jeffrey. 1998. "The Sexual Citizen." *Theory, Culture and Society* 15 (3): 35–52.

Weheliye, Alexander G. 2014. *Habeas Viscus: Racializing Assemblages, Biopolitics, and Black Feminist Theories of the Human*. Durham, NC: Duke University Press.

Weiss, Margot. 2011. *Techniques of Pleasure: BDSM and the Circuits of Sexuality*. Durham, NC: Duke University Press.

Wenger, Yvonne. 2015. "New Baltimore Slogan Nods to City's Star-Spangled History." *Baltimore Sun*, January 12. Accessed December 4, 2015. http://www.baltimoresun.com/news/maryland/baltimore-city/bs-md-ci-slogan-20150112-story.html.

Wiegman, Robyn. 2014. "The Times We're In: Queer Feminist Criticism and the Reparative 'Turn.'" *Feminist Theory* 15 (1): 4–25.

Wilcox, Melissa M. 2009. *Queer Women and Religious Individualism*. Bloomington: Indiana University Press.

———. 2012. "'Spiritual Sluts': Uncovering Gender, Ethnicity, and Sexuality in the Post-secular." *Women's Studies* 41 (6): 639–659.

Wilderson, Frank B., III. 2003. "The Prison Slave as Hegemony's (Silent) Scandal." *Social Justice* 30 (2 [92]): 18–27.

———. 2010. *Red, White and Black: Cinema and the Structure of US Antagonisms*. Durham, NC: Duke University Press.

Williams, J. K., H. C. Ramamurthi, C. Manago, and N. T. Harawa. 2009. "Learning from Successful Interventions: A Culturally Congruent HIV Risk-Reduction Intervention for African American Men Who Have Sex with Men and Women." *American Journal of Public Health* 99 (6): 1008–1012.

Winner, Langdon. 1980. "Do Artifacts Have Politics?" *Daedalus* 109 (1): 121-136.

Woods, Tryon P. 2013. "The Flesh of Amalgamation: Reconsidering the Position (and the Labors) of Blackness." *American Quarterly* 65 (2): 437–446.

Wyly, Elvin. 2010. "Things Pictures Don't Tell Us: In Search of Baltimore." *City* 14 (5): 497–528.

Wynter, Sylvia. 1994. "No Humans Involved: An Open Letter to My Colleagues." *Forum N.H.I.—Knowledge for the 21st Century: Knowledge on Trial* 1 (1): 42–73.

Yehia, Baligh, and Ian Frank. 2011. "Battling AIDS in America: An Evaluation of the National HIV/AIDS Strategy." *American Journal of Public Health* 101 (9): e4–8.

Zaleski, Andrew. 2014. "Can a Baltimore Neighborhood Avoid the Pitfalls of Gentrification?" Next City, August 4. Accessed December 4, 2015. https://nextcity.org/daily/entry/gentrification-baltimore-station-north-arts-greenmount-west.

Index

ACT UP, 50, 193n17
affective labor, 19, 20, 71, 79, 94
affirmation, 6–7, 9, 63, 78, 90, 92, 111, 123, 147–148, 153, 157; negativity and, 164–168, 171, 178
Afro-pessimism, 8, 24, 153–154, 162–164, 167, 169, 192n11, 214n1
AIDS Action Baltimore, 18, 60, 74
AIDS crisis, 18, 50, 56, 60, 64, 67, 125; post-crisis, 74, 152. *See also* HIV/AIDS: crisis
Allen, Jafari, 137–138, 170, 185, 193n15, 204n2, 205n5, 211nn15–16
alterity, 160, 214n6; citizenship and, 4–5; racial, 24, 150
ambiguity: Baltimore and, 29–30, 35, 41, 64; intimacy and, 84, 148, 152; superfluity, immunity, and, 64, 85, 87; support structures and, 178–179, 181; survival and, 158–159, 164
Anidjar, Gil, 88, 120
Anne E. Casey Foundation, 33
antiretroviral treatments, 65, 71, 84, 86. *See also* HIV prevention: PrEP
Arendt, Hannah, 88, 92, 203n13

Bailey, Marlon, 52, 78, 91, 170, 201nn2–3, 203n16, 204n18
Balibar, Étienne, 3

Ballroom community, 20, 22, 24, 68–71, 75–79, 82–83, 85–88, 91–93, 123, 163, 176, 201n6, 204n1; Balls, 68–69, 75, 77, 90–91, 93, 95, 151–152, 162–163; Baltimore Ballroom Coalition, 76, 79; church and the, 96; Commentators for, 89–90; and HIV prevention, 24, 69–71, 76, 81–83, 85–88, 91–93, 201n3, 217n19; Icon (status), 68; Legend (status), 68, 89; Star (status), 68; Statement (status), 89
Baltimore: ambiguity and, 23, 28–29, 41, 179; Ambiguity City, 29–30, 35, 64; Black Church and, 14, 23, 30, 43–46, 96, 100, 136, 217n19; Charles Village, 37, 50, 55, 194n3, 199n26; City Hall, 28, 38, 44; East Baltimore, 30–34, 36–39, 41, 194n1, 197n19; Johns Hopkins University and, 16, 23, 30–36, 38, 50, 73–74 (*see also* Johns Hopkins University); Middle East neighborhood, 19, 31–34, 36, 196n16; Mount Vernon, 16, 31, 37, 40, 42, 49–55, 57, 59, 103, 194n3, 197n20, 199n26, 210n7 (*see also* gayborhood); public transit system, 23, 30, 36–39, 42, 193n19, 195n8; revanchist urbanism, 50; urban revitalization, 27, 28, 32, 43–44, 47, 50–51, 89; West Baltimore, 31, 38, 46, 58, 80, 196n13, 196n16

Baltimore Black Coalition, 56
Baltimore Black Pride (BBP), 62, 63, 74
Baltimore City Health Department (BCHD), 18, 52, 55, 67–70, 74–77, 79, 81, 82, 89, 93, 167; AIDS Education/Outreach Program, 61. *See also* Testing and Linkage to Care Plus
Baltimore Eagle, 53, 210n7
Baltimore Gay Alliance (BGA), 50, 55–57, 199n26
Baucom, Ian, 162
BDSM (bondage and discipline/dominance and submission/sadism and masochism), 21, 123–151, 208n1, 210n6; education, 125, 129–133, 179; fantasy, 134, 143, 145–147, 149–150, 210n10, 211n13; history of slavery and, 131; leather clubs, 53, 58, 125–127, 142; Master/slave dynamic, 131, 134; spirituality and, 24, 28, 136–140, 149, 173; trauma, method of dealing with, 124, 134, 141, 164; violence and, 124, 141–142
BDSM community, 19, 24, 123–151, 163–164, 174, 179, 209n3, 213n19; Black Church and, 20, 136, 149; Black involvement in, 125, 127, 133, 136; Black queer futurity and, 163–164; history of, 24, 126, 128–129, 132, 146; predominant whiteness of, 14, 20, 24, 127, 131–132, 137; race play and, 134–135, 142, 211n13; race relations within, 24, 131–133, 142, 146, 148, 210n8; in San Francisco, 123–124, 143, 212n18
Bean, Carl, 97, 103
Behavioral Surveillance Research (BESURE), 202n8
belonging, 51, 119, 147, 160, 184, 204n20, 216n16; in the Ballroom community, 68, 90, 136; in the BDSM Community, 173–174; collectivity and, 1, 2, 10, 12; modes of, 65, 85, 153; support structures and, 17, 21; in the UFCB, 96, 136
Berlant, Lauren, 2, 82–83, 119, 140, 148–149, 171–174, 176, 206n12, 216n14
Bersani, Leo, 190n2, 203n17
biocapital, 36, 87
biopolitics, 3, 23, 29, 72, 85, 87, 88, 123, 149, 165, 169, 192n9, 193n18, 197n17
Black AIDS Institute, 71–72
Black BEAT (Black Expression Alternative Tastes), 125, 132, 209n4
Black Church, 14, 23, 30, 42–46, 96, 98, 100, 110–112, 118, 121; and the Ballroom scene, 96, 123; and the BDSM community, 20, 136, 149; and neoliberalism, 45–46, 99–100; and queerness, 136; SGL clergy, 24, 41, 96–98; SGL congregants, 101, 111; tradition, 118
Black Educational AIDS Project (BEAP), 61, 103
Black life, 5, 10, 45, 85, 142, 156, 165–166, 168–170, 196n13, 197n17, 207n14, 214n21
Black Men's Xchange (BMX), 6–7, 63, 74
Blackness: affirmative notions of, 10, 25, 62, 167–168; Afro-pessimism and, 164, 168; anti-Blackness, 18, 143, 166, 190n5, 192n10; in the BDSM community, 127, 135–136, 149, 173, 210n6; pathologization of, 6, 165–167; as a problem, 48–49; religion and, 96, 136, 149; as a structural position, 9–10, 148, 152–156, 168
Black Pentecostalism, 10–11, 20, 24, 41, 97, 116, 118, 192n14, 205n9, 207n14, 207n18
Black Pride, 6, 61–64
Black queerness, 10, 25, 96, 119, 173, 181, 186, 205n6. *See* Black queers
Black queers: activists, 60, 64; Baltimoreans, 1–3, 6, 10, 13, 15, 22, 61, 66, 76, 167, 174, 184, 200n31; and collectivities, 119, 164, 176–177, 180, 183, 185; and community, 61, 63, 70, 87, 96; empowerment of, 63; futurity of, 121, 163; groups of, 48; history of, 23, 30; life of, various forms of, 13–14, 23, 65, 88, 92, 94, 96, 151, 170, 175, 177, 180, 186, 205n5, 212n17, 216n14; men, 6, 9, 17, 65, 95, 120; personhood, 169; support structures of, 13; survival of, 170–171, 180, 218n23; women, 24, 123–124, 142, 146–147, 150, 210n6, 213n20; and world making, 4, 20, 24, 96, 151–153, 163, 170, 182, 194n20, 211n15; youth, 19–20, 23–24, 52, 64, 66, 78, 84–87, 89–90, 92–93, 95, 127, 165, 198n23, 201n1, 214n1. *See also* Black queerness
Blacks Together in Pride, 62
Blacks United for Gay and Lesbian Equality (BUGLE), 60, 200n30
body politic, 5, 119, 138, 154, 160
bondage, 134, 138; bondage and discipline/dominance and submission/sadism and masochism (*see* BDSM; BDSM community)
Bosniak, Linda, 3, 181
breath, 10–11, 16, 121, 207n14; *pneuma*, 116, 207n18. *See also* Crawley, Ashon
Brother Help Thyself (BHT), 125
Brown, Wendy, 11–12

Burger World (bar), 58, 60. *See also* Club Bunns
Bush, George Walker, 43–44
Butler, Judith, 174–175, 183

Canguilhem, Georges, 94
care, 12–15, 48, 88, 103, 105, 109; alternative modes of, 3, 10, 84–86; and the Black Church, 45, 207n14; clinical, 23, 32, 35, 52, 70, 72, 73, 76, 80, 195n5, 201n6; eroticism and, 126, 137; ethics of, 110; mutual, 96, 119; for the self, 105, 110, 119, 137, 141 (*see also* Foucault, Michel); spaces of, 78, 95, 126; support structures and, 17, 179–180
Carter/Johnson Leather Library, 125
Center for Black Equity (CBE), 63
Centers for Disease Control and Prevention (CDC), 67, 72, 74, 81, 83, 86, 95; High Impact Prevention approach, 72, 74
Chase-Brexton Health Services, 55, 61, 199n27
Children's Place, 58
citizenship: composition as a practice of, 2, 65, 92, 148, 181–183; immunity and, 4–5, 11, 13, 23, 34, 48, 64–65, 84, 87–88, 92–93, 119, 138, 142, 151, 153, 160, 177, 181, 187; language of, 3, 21–22, 153, 181, 184, 187; regimes of, 23, 151, 187; sexual, 1, 16, 51, 64, 70, 84, 92–93, 138, 142, 144, 183, 197n18
civil society, 13, 15, 53, 87, 90, 154–155, 161–162, 164, 179, 181, 187, 191n5, 213n21
clergy, 44, 46, 91, 110–111, 113; SGL, 20, 24, 41, 97; UFCB, 42, 100, 102, 116, 118, 178, 207n16
clinical trials, 31, 35
Club Bunns, 60–61. *See also* Burger World
Cohen, Cathy, 200n28
Command MC, 125
communitas, 159–160, 175, 202n11, 215n12
community-based organizations, 15, 18–19, 43–44, 46, 48, 60, 69, 74, 103, 125, 129, 180, 199n26
community development corporations (CDCs), 43–44, 46
Condorelli, Céline, 177–178, 180, 216n17
Connect to Protect (C2P), 18
consent: in the BDSM community, 130, 134, 143–144, 210n10; civic, 13; medical, 36; racialized sexuality and, 124, 144–145, 212n19; research participants and, 191n6
Crawley, Ashon, 10–11, 116, 118, 192n13, 205n9, 206n14

Critical Thinking and Cultural Affirmation (CTCA), 191n7
Cruz, Ariane, 124, 144, 146, 210n9, 211n13, 212n19

DC-Baltimore Coalition of Black Gays, 55–56
Deleuze, Gilles, 95, 167, 203n17
Derrida, Jacques, 14, 157–159, 161
Dillon, Stephen, 162–163
displacement: Black population in Baltimore, 23, 32, 34, 42, 44; Black queer youth, 90
Dixon, Sheila, 48
drag: drag performance, 52, 57, 198n21; drag queens, 130

East Baltimore Development Inc. (EBDI), 33–34
economic crisis, 104. *See also* mortgage crisis
Edelman, Lee, 24, 143, 148, 154–156, 158–160, 162–164, 170, 173–174, 176, 186, 190n2, 214n4, 216n14, 217n22
Eng, David, 142, 190n5. *See also* queer liberalism
Enhanced Comprehensive HIV Prevention Plan (ECHPP), 73–74. *See also* Infectious Disease and Environmental Health Administration (IDEHA)
entrepreneurialism, Baltimore and, 27–29, 34, 39, 43, 46–47, 50, 52, 100, 196n13, 199n27
Equality Maryland, 51, 74
eroticism: BDSM community and, 124, 134–135, 137; intimacy and, 92, 126; politics and, 135, 137–138, 170, 193n15, 211nn15–16; race and, 137; self-shattering and, 141
Esposito, Roberto, 4–5, 13, 31–32, 84–85, 88, 91–92, 159–160, 169, 175, 178, 190n4, 202n10, 203n17, 204n19, 214n5, 215n6, 219n26. *See also communitas*; immunity; immunization
ethically otherwise, 105, 106, 119
ethnography, 1, 21, 24–25, 144, 153, 186, 191n6; fieldwork 19–20. *See also* fieldwork

faith, 106, 143, 208n20; BDSM and, 20; belonging and, 119; Black queer folks and, 96, 98, 120, 164, 204n3, 205n5; care and, 22; faith-based organizations and initiatives, 19, 43–44; flourishing and, 180; self-formation and, 24; UFCB and, 99, 107, 114–115, 121

Fanon, Frantz, 154, 165–166, 169, 213n20
Fassin, Didier, 21, 194n20, 203n13
Females Investigating Sexual Terrain (FIST), 125
Ferguson, Roderick, 170
fieldwork, 6, 16–17, 19–20, 23, 28–30, 36, 41, 46, 63–65, 73, 125, 173, 180, 185
Florida, Richard, 49
flourishing, 63, 65, 176, 179, 216n14; survival and, 10, 20–21, 24, 28, 65, 83, 93, 99, 116, 138, 149, 164, 166, 168–171, 173–176, 180, 182, 184; survival as distinct from, 152, 161, 175
Foucault, Michel, 104–107, 110–111, 115–118, 123, 138, 167, 191–192n9, 205–206n11, 208n19, 208n21. *See also parrhesia*
fugitivity, 13, 165, 168–170, 178, 187, 215nn12–13, 217n20
futurity: collectivity and, 143; negativity and, 159, 164; queerness and, 161, 163; and survival, 156, 161

Garner, Eric, 11
gayborhood, 42, 50, 52, 54, 127, 199n26. *See also* Baltimore: Mount Vernon
Gay Community Center of Baltimore (GCCB), 55–56. *See also* Gay, Lesbian, Bisexual and Transgender Community Center of Baltimore and Central Maryland
Gay, Lesbian, Bisexual, and Transgender Community Center of Baltimore and Central Maryland (GLCCB), 16–19, 54–55, 59–60, 62, 65–66, 74, 199n27
Gay Liberation Front, 55
Gay Paper, 55, 58
Gay Pride, 51, 54
gender: in the BDSM community, 124–126, 129–130, 173; discrimination and, 52; equality and, 51; gender-conformity, 53; intersections of sexuality, race, class, and, 18, 20, 55, 88, 90, 147, 149; performance and expression of, 15, 20, 68
gentrification, 51, 53, 127
Goldberg, David Theo, 45
Gray, Freddie, 37, 196n16

Hägglund, Martin, 157–161
Hanhardt, Christina, 51
Hanson, Ellis, 190n3, 216n14
Hartman, Saidiya, 9, 146, 152–153, 168, 210n6, 218n24
Harvey, David, 27–28

health care, access to, 9, 73, 76, 86, 89, 92
Health Education Resource Organization (HERO), 18, 60–62, 74, 103, 200n30
Heidegger, Martin, 159, 165
heteronormativity, 68, 91, 119, 156, 180, 205n6
Hippo, 53, 57, 125, 127
HIV (human immunodeficiency virus): care and, 7, 60, 67, 69, 73–74, 77, 87, 163; incidence rates of, 14, 17, 65, 73; testing for, 23, 59, 64, 68–73, 76; treatment of, 23, 63 (*see also* Testing and Linkage to Care Plus). *See also* HIV/AIDS; HIV prevention; HIV Stops with Me
HIV/AIDS: activism and, 50, 51, 59, 61, 99, 101; crisis regarding, 88, 105, 207n17; education about, 61; epidemic of, 8, 30, 59, 73, 126; post-crisis and, 74, 152; support structures surrounding, 59, 61, 103; transmission of, 70–71, 83, 87, 203n14. *See also* HIV; HIV prevention; HIV Stops with Me
HIV prevention: in the Ballroom community, 76, 79, 81, 91–93; biomedical approach to, 70–74, 82, 84, 88, 93–94, 191n7; community, 20; federal policies regarding, 85; funding for, 18, 61–65, 72, 74, 88; initiatives and programs for, 17, 23, 31, 65, 67, 69–70, 76, 87; organizations and, 18–19, 60–61, 100; PrEP (pre-exposure prophylaxis), 65–66; self-monitoring, 87; strategies for, 61; system of Baltimore, 5, 7–8, 14, 24. *See also* HIV Stops with Me
HIV Stops with Me campaign (HSWM), 83–86, 100. *See also* HIV prevention
Hobbes, Thomas, 160, 202n10, 215n12
Holmes, Kwame, 200nn31–32
homelessness, 52, 73, 87, 165, 168, 197n20, 198n22
homonormativity, 6, 94
homosexuality: Black, 6; experiencing, 56, 59; liberalism and, 142; religion and, 103, 110–111; white male, 74
Honig, Bonnie, 14
Houses: House family, 68–70, 78, 93, 201n1; House fathers, 68, 77–79, 179; House kids, 78, 152; House of Latex, 69; House parents, 68; House support structure, 95, 174. *See also* Ballroom community
housing, 33, 40, 43–45, 49–50; discrimination and, 52; Johns Hopkins University and, 32–34
Hyra, Derek, 44, 196n11

immunity: citizenship and, 4–5, 11, 13, 23, 34, 48, 64–65, 84, 87–88, 92–93, 119, 138, 142, 151, 153, 160, 177, 181, 187; immunitary violence, 5, 14, 148, 164, 169, 172, 175, 213n20, 214n6; superfluity, ambiguity, and, 23, 28, 35, 64, 85, 87
immunization, 34, 175; paradigms and regimes of, 4, 13, 84–85, 88, 151, 214n5
Infectious Disease and Environmental Health Administration (IDEHA), 7–8, 67, 73–74, 191n8
Interfaith Fairness Coalition of Maryland, 20
intimacy: Ballroom community and, 87–88; belonging and, 10, 147; Black social life and, 166; care and, 126; citizenship and, 1–2, 93, 184, 189n1, 190n5; impersonal, 92; sexual, 86, 124, 126, 143–144, 146, 150, 211n13; spaces of, 126, 142, 144, 150; violence and, 177, 190n5, 212n19
Isin, Engin, 4, 12, 193n18

James, William, 105–107, 115, 203n17
Johns Hopkins University, 16–18, 23, 30–36, 38, 50, 59, 73–74, 77, 80–81, 191n6, 193n17, 194n1, 198n26, 200n30; Bloomberg School of Public Health (JHSPH), 30, 37, 74, 202n8; Center for Immunization Research, 31; Department of Health, Behavior, and Society, 30; Homewood campus, 16, 37, 41, 194n3, 198n24; IRB (Institutional Review Board), 17, 191n6; Johns Hopkins Medical Institutions (JHMI), 32, 36; Lighthouse, 30, 37; Medical Campus, 30–31, 36, 73, 194n1, 196n16; as the plantation, 32, 35, 194n3
Johnson, E. Patrick, 170, 204n2
Johnson, Viola, 126
Jones, Billy, 55–56

Keeling, Kara, 164, 170, 218n24
King, Martin Luther, Jr., 37
kink: Blackness and, 124, 127, 132, 135–136, 139, 215n11; history of, 126, 132, 136; pleasure and, 23, 130; queerness and, 127–128, 145, 179; racism and, 133, 145, 179; religion and, 137, 149; whiteness and, 126, 136, 144, 215n11. *See also* BDSM
kinship: alternative systems and forms of, 20, 22, 68, 93, 147, 201n1; belonging and, 10; community and, 70; immunity and, 94; intimacy and, 190n5; negativity and, 155; networks of, 2
Klein, Melanie, 171–172, 178, 216n16

Lacan, Jacques, 153–154, 156, 158, 214n2, 216n14
Lacks, Henrietta, 36
Laclau, Ernesto, 11, 156–157
Latex Ball, 76
Latour, Bruno, 106–107, 112, 115, 117, 204n20, 205n11, 207n15, 208n19
leathermen, 53, 126, 136. *See also* leather scene; leather sex
leather scene: Baltimore, 19–20, 24, 53, 125–128, 132, 134–135, 139, 142, 144, 146–148; San Francisco, 123–124, 143. *See also* BDSM community; leathermen; leather sex
leather sex, 20, 124–125, 129, 131, 135–136, 141, 143–145, 147, 208n1. *See also* BDSM; leathermen; leather scene
Leon's Leather Lounge, 53
LGBT (lesbian, gay, bisexual, transgender): LGBT community, 1, 6–7, 8, 14, 16–17, 19–20, 23, 30, 52, 54, 56–57, 62, 65, 94, 127, 174; LGBT organizations, 16, 18, 51, 55, 60, 104, 125
liberalism: neutralization of negativity, 148; race and, 45. *See also* queer liberalism
Lorde, Audre, 56, 137

Markell, Patchen, 123, 147, 213n20
Maryland Transit Administration (MTA), 38
Mbembe, Achille, 30, 32, 197n17
McClintock, Anne, 140, 143
McDougall, Harold A., 29, 195n10, 196n13
McKittrick, Katherine, 85
McRoberts, Omar, 44, 196n11
Men of Color against AIDS (MOCAA), 61
Men of Color AIDS Prevention Project (MOCAPP), 61, 201n34
Men of Color Health Awareness (MOCHA), 61
men who have sex with men. *See* MSM
Metropolitan Community Church (MCC), 7, 55
modernity: biotheology and, 120 (*see also* Anidjar, Gil); Christianity and, 106, 120; citizenship regimes and, 1, 4–5, 11, 13, 151, 153, 177, 181, 202n9; immunitary paradigm and, 4, 13, 31, 84–85, 88, 160, 169, 175, 214n5, 216n15 (*see also* Esposito, Roberto); logics of sacrifice and, 106, 120, 175; origins of immunitary political philosophy and, 160, 202n10 (*see also* Hobbes, Thomas)

mortgage crisis, 45, 104
Moten, Fred, 24, 164–170, 176, 178, 181, 192n12, 210n6, 215n10, 217n22, 218n24, 218n26
Mount Vernon–Belvedere Association (MVBA), 51, 197n20
Mr. Maryland Leather Contest, 125
MSM (men who have sex with men), 71; HIV infection rates among, 74, 85, 202n8; HIV-prevention initiatives targeted toward, 7, 73, 88–89. See also Black queers: men; Black queers: youth
Muñoz, José, 162–163, 216n14

Nancy, Jean-Luc, 107, 178, 182
National Coalition of Black Gays (NCBG), 56, 199n28
National Coalition of Black Lesbians and Gays (NCBLG), 56, 60, 200n31
National HIV/AIDS strategy (NHAS), 72
National Institutes of Health (NIH), 193n17
National March on Washington for Lesbian and Gay Rights, 56
National Third World Lesbian and Gay Conference, 56
negativity: abjection and, 149; Afro-pessimism and, 8, 153; Black, 5, 163, 168, 182, 185; citizenship and, 5, 142, 184; community and, 157, 160, 175–176; futurity and, 143, 156; immunity and, 84, 214n6; intimacy and, 2, 211n13; liberalism and, 148; queerness and, 154–156, 158–161, 182, 185, 213n20, 214nn3–4 (see also Edelman, Lee); racial, 63, 150; relational, 159–160; reparativity and, 24, 153, 170, 174, 212n16; survival and, 151–152, 158, 180, 184, 213n20, 218n23
Negri, Antonio, 183–184
neoliberalism: Baltimore and, 28, 48, 51, 89; Black community and, 45–47, 145, 197n17
neo-Pentecostalism, 46. See also neoliberalism
Ngai, Sianne, 206n13
nihilism, 24, 156, 214n4; community and, 159–160
Noys, Benjamin, 218n25

Odell's, 58
O'Malley, Martin, 23, 33, 47–49, 51, 100, 196n15
ONYX, 209n3
Our Place (bar), 58

outreach, 63, 68, 74, 76, 100; Ballroom community, 24; community, 100–101, 103; educational, 59; HIV, 13; outreach programs, 5, 61; outreach workers, 75, 80, 82, 85, 87, 93–94, 179

Paradox (club), 64, 193n19
parrhesia, 104–105, 117–118, 145, 147, 150, 205n11. See also truth telling
Patterson, Orlando, 192n11, 215n8
Peabody Institute, 37, 50
Peay, Ralph James, 58, 200n29
People with AIDS Coalition of Baltimore, 61
pharmaceutical industry, 64–65
Pierce, Charles S., 105
Pietila, Antero, 43
plantation: plantation futures, 85, 94; plantation logics, 87, 94. See also Johns Hopkins University: as the plantation
Playhouse (BDSM venue), 21, 127, 135, 167, 210n7
pleasure: BDSM and, 128–130, 136–137, 139, 141, 145–146, 149–150; pleasure negativity, 148; politics and, 91, 110; sexual, 24, 86, 144, 147; violence and, 24, 123–124, 142
Portal (community center), 7, 63, 74
Porthole (bar), 57
Povinelli, Elizabeth, 14, 105, 166, 205n8, 206n12
prayer, 6, 101, 108–109, 117, 183
predatory lending practices, 46. See also Wells Fargo
public health, 7, 48, 52, 60, 65, 67, 70–72, 163, 165
public-private ventures: development projects, 47; partnerships, 27–28, 33–34

queer Blackness, 96, 119, 205n6, 209n6
queer liberalism, 142–148, 190n5
queerness, 25, 156; and negativity, 25, 148, 153, 155, 161, 213n20; religion and, 96, 207n18; as a structural position, 152, 154, 156, 161; superfluity and, 119; theorizations of, 10, 18, 96, 170, 209n6; white queerness, 49–52. See also Black queerness

racism: BDSM community and, 133–134, 144; heteronormativity and, 91, 94; immunitary violence and, 5, 14; liberalism and, 45; poverty and, 18; society and, 68, 90–91; state-sanctioned, 56, 191n9; violence and, 32, 88

radical democratic theory, 11–12, 177, 183, 218n23
Rawlings-Blake, Stephanie, 48, 197n19
Reagan, Ronald, 44, 56, 196n14
real estate, 41, 43–45, 49; real estate development, 48; real estate market, 32; real estate speculation, 51
redlining, 43, 45, 195n10; Wells Fargo's lending practices (reverse-redlining), 45–46
reparativity: citizenship and, 181, 183; ethnography and, 25, 184–186; impulse toward, 170, 178, 180; love and, 172, 175, 186; negativity and, 24, 152–153, 170–174, 212n16, 216n14; reparative reading, 171 (see also Sedgwick, Eve Kosofsky); support structures and, 1, 153, 173, 176–177
reproductive futurism, 156, 158–160, 164, 214n4. See also Edelman, Lee
revanchist urbanism, 50
Rodríguez, Juana María, 146

sacrifice: immunitary practice as, 88, 150, 164; logics of, 71, 84, 88, 120, 121, 144–145; sacrificial love, 121, 164
safe sex, 89, 201n34
same-gender-loving. See SGL
Save Middle East Action Committee (SMEAC), 32–33
Schaefer, William Donald, 38–39, 44, 47
Schmitt, Carl, 120, 191n9
Schmoke, Kurt, 47
Scott, Darieck, 209n6, 213n20
Sedgwick, Eve Kosofsky, 170–174, 178, 216n14
segregation: Baltimore and, 14, 23, 30, 35, 40–43, 57, 73, 126; in the LGBT community, 52, 57, 126
self-empowerment, 99
self-formation, 24, 96, 105, 108, 120, 137
self-love, 104, 173, 201n34
self-preservation, 4, 8–9, 172
self-shattering, 140–141, 149, 154, 174
Sexton, Jared, 24, 165–168, 190n5, 212n19, 214n21, 215n10, 216n13
SGL (same-gender-loving), 6, 7, 96, 117; SGL clergy, 20, 24, 41, 97–98; SGL men, 80, 111; SGL women, 101, 113; SGL youth, 75
Shabazz, Rashad, 52, 196n16
Sharpe, Christina, 10–11, 142, 192n14, 209n6, 212n19
Sheraton Inner Harbor Hotel, 69, 89–90

slavery, 5–6, 10, 35, 42, 124, 126, 131, 134–136, 145, 192n11; afterlife of, 9, 24, 85, 140, 153, 162, 166, 186, 191n5. See also slaves
slaves: BDSM slaves, 131, 133–135, 138, 209n6, 211n12; postslavery subjects, 145, 212n19. See also slavery
social death, 10, 165–167, 182, 184, 192n11, 215n8, 216n13
social justice, 51, 63, 70, 94, 99, 101; activism, 51, 199n26
Spence, Lester, 46
Spillers, Hortense, 162, 203n15, 209n6, 217n17
Spinoza, Baruch de, 94, 95, 203n17
spirituality, 24, 96, 98, 205n4; and BDSM, 24, 28, 136–140, 149, 173; political spirituality, 115, 118, 138
STAR TRACK, 69
Status Update (campaign), 85–86
Stuban, John, 193n17
superfluity: Baltimore and, 28, 35–36, 47; Black populations and, 5, 28, 36, 40, 47; body politic and, 119; to citizenship regimes, 151, 177, 181; to civil society, 162; immunity, ambiguity, and, 23, 28, 35, 64, 85, 87; to treatment regimes, 65
support structures, 1, 13–14, 17, 21, 78, 138, 153, 170, 176–181; reparativity and, 153, 170, 177
surveillance, biomedical, 52, 71, 74, 76, 83, 87–88, 162, 165
survival: ambiguity and, 152, 156, 158, 164; flourishing and, 10, 20–21, 24, 28, 65, 83, 93, 99, 116, 138, 149, 152, 161, 164, 166, 168–171, 173–176, 180, 182, 184; futurity and, 156, 159, 161; immunity and, 92–93, 157–159, 161, 175

tax increment financing (TIF), 195n4
Testing and Linkage to Care Plus (TLC+), 71–74, 81–84, 87–88, 93, 201n5
Thacker, Eugene, 116
Tikkis (bar), 58
Torch (bar), 57
trans(gender): awareness of, 52; LGBT community and, 174; trans(gender) Black men, 9, 65, 120, 146, 155; trans(gender) Black women, 210n7; trans(gender) sex workers, 52–53; trans(gender) support, 17; violence toward trans(gender) persons, 198n22
truth telling, 104–123, 145–146, 150, 178, 204n2, 205n11. See also parrhesia

undercommons, 165, 169, 215n12, 219n26. *See also* Moten, Fred

Unity Fellowship Church of Baltimore (UFCB), 41–42, 46, 96–104, 107, 109, 112, 114–118, 120–121, 123, 136, 163–164, 174, 176, 178–179, 183, 206n13, 207nn14–16, 217n19; clergy at, 41–42, 97, 100, 102, 110–111, 116–118, 178; congregation of, 20, 41, 43, 96–98, 101–102, 173, 176, 207n16; relationship to the Black Church, 42, 96, 100, 110–112, 118, 121, 206n13, 217n19; Spiritual Development class at, 42, 97–99, 108–109, 113, 178; Youth and Young Adult Ministry of, 101

University of Maryland, 18, 69, 74, 80

urban revitalization, 27, 28, 32, 43–44, 47, 50–51, 89

violence: anti-Black, 5, 10, 32, 85, 92, 167, 185–186, 190n5, 192n10, 215n12; antiqueer, 10, 92, 185; BDSM and, 24, 123–124, 141, 145–149, 163–164, 210n6, 213n20; immaturity, 5, 14, 148; pleasure and, 24, 123–124, 129, 136, 139, 141, 145–149, 174, 213n20; structural, 3, 5–6, 32, 99, 126, 134, 145

Viveiros de Castro, Eduardo, 186

Vogler, Candace, 123, 147, 213n20

vulnerability, 2, 51, 121, 216n15; ethics of, 174–177, 183

Waters, John, 51

Weheliye, Alexander, 85

Weiss, Margot, 142–144, 147, 212n18

Wells Fargo, 45–46

white gays: middle-class, 15, 53; white gay community, 6; white gay culture, 59

whiteness, BDSM scene and, 124, 143, 146–147, 149, 215n11

white supremacy, 4, 99, 169, 191n5, 205n6

Wiegman, Robyn, 152, 163, 172

Wilderson, Frank B., 24, 153–156, 161–162, 166–168, 186, 214n1

world making, 4, 13–14, 83, 88, 166, 170, 173, 186; Ballroom community, 93, 166; Black queer, 4, 20, 24, 96, 151–153, 163, 170, 182, 194n20, 211n15; practices of, 24, 88, 184–187; in the Unity Fellowship Church of Baltimore (UFCB), 24, 96, 107–108

Wyly, Elvin, 45, 196n12

NIELS VAN DOORN, a former postdoctoral research fellow in the Department of Political Science at Johns Hopkins University, is an Assistant Professor of New Media and Digital Culture in the Department of Media Studies at the University of Amsterdam.

www.ingramcontent.com/pod-product-compliance
Lightning Source LLC
Chambersburg PA
CBHW041733300426
44116CB00019B/2972